BECOMINGS

BECOMINGS

Edited by ELIZABETH GROSZ

Explorations

in Time,

Memory,

and Futures

Cornell University Press

Ithaca and London

First published 1999 by Cornell University Press

Printed in the United States of America

Library of Congress Cataloging-in-Publication Data

Becomings: explorations in time, memory, and futures / edited by
    Elizabeth Grosz.
        p.   cm.
      Includes bibliographical references and index.
      ISBN 0-8014-3632-X (cloth). — ISBN 0-8014-8590-8 (paper)
      1. Time.   2. Becoming (Philosophy)   I. Grosz, E. A. (Elizabeth A.
    BD638.B355   1999
    115—dc21   99-35004

Cornell University Press strives to use environmentally responsible suppliers and materials to the fullest extent possible in the publishing of its books. Such materials include vegetable-based, low-VOC inks, and acid-free papers that are recycled, totally chlorine-free, or partly composed of nonwood fibers. Books that bear the logo of the FSC (Forest Stewardship Council) use paper taken from forests that have been inspected and certified as meeting the highest standards for environmental and social responsibility. For further information, visit our website at www.cornellpress.cornell.edu.

Cloth Printing   10 9 8 7 6 5 4 3 2 1
Paperback Printing   10 9 8 7 6 5 4 3 2 1

FSC FSC Trademark © 1996 Forest Stewardship Council A.C.
SW-COC-098

CONTENTS

Elizabeth Grosz

BECOMING . . .
AN INTRODUCTION

> Time . . . gives nothing to see. It is at the very least the element of invisi-
> bility itself. It withdraws whatever could be given to be seen. It itself
> withdraws from visibility. One can only be blind to time, to the essential
> *disappearance* of time even as, nevertheless, in a certain manner, nothing
> *appears* that does not require and take time.
>
> JACQUES DERRIDA, *Given Time: 1. Counterfeit Money*, 6

Time is one of the assumed yet irreducible terms of all discourse, knowledge, and social practice. Yet it is rarely analyzed or self-consciously discussed in its own terms. It tends to function as a silent accompaniment, a
shadowy implication underlying, contextualizing, and eventually undoing
all knowledges and practices without being their explicit object of analysis or speculation. Time has a quality of intangibility, a fleeting half-life,
emitting its duration-particles only in the passing or transformation of objects and events, thus erasing itself as such while it opens itself to movement and change. It has an evanescence, a fleeting or shimmering, highly
precarious "identity" that resists concretization, indication or direct representation. Time is more intangible than any other "thing," less able to be
grasped, conceptually or psychically. This is perhaps why Derrida, above,
wants to grant it the status of the invisible, the scotomized: that to which
we are blind.

Time is that which disappears as such in order to make appearance, all
appearance and disappearance, that is, events, possible. Its disappearance
is twofold: it disappears into events, processes, movements, things, as the

1

mode of their becoming. And it disappears in our representations, whether scientific or artistic, historical or contemporary, where it is tied to, bound up in, and represented by means of space and spatiality. It suffers, or produces, a double displacement: from becoming to being, and from temporal to spatial.

The apparently equally pervasive and abstract concept of space has generated a vast body of discourses, knowledges, and disciplines whose focus and specialization are the analysis, measurement, regulation, and management of space and of movements within space (one need only fleetingly think about the discourses and practices of architecture, urban studies, geography, and geology, among others, to recognize space and spatiality as privileged objects of scientific and social regulation). Only relatively few names, however, are associated with studies of time and duration and there is no corresponding discipline or specifically focused and self-contained study of time and its unique characteristics. History, arguably the discipline most closely associated with time within the humanities, is notable for its failure to address the question of the ontological, epistemic, and political status of time. Its privileged objects of reflection, historical events, and processes, those that occurred in the past and retain some traces, some residue, in the present and the future, raise serious ontological and epistemic, and thus political and ethical, questions, methodological questions that the disciple has not even tried to address. Time and becoming remain unreflected and undertheorized, except in rare and isolated cases, in the history of Western thought.

Within the natural sciences there seems to be a large investment in concepts of time and space, investments that are not entirely the same as, or completely different from, those in the humanities. Classical physics, for example, has tended, with few exceptions, to regard the "arrow of time" as irrelevant to understanding the nature of time and has tended to be committed to an idea of temporal reversibility, the physical and temporal indiscernibility of past, present, and future. The biologically oriented sciences, primarily, have insisted that time does have an irreducible directionality and that the history and temporal placement of an organism or biological process have major explanatory relevance in assessing the current and future states of that organism or process. Biological explanation requires that temporally irreversible relations are constitutive of the organism in its particularity. Yet, although physics and biology do take time as one of the relevant vectors in their respective investigations, either discussion remains highly abstract or time tends to be taken as of peripheral interest to its major preoccupations—the study of matter (in the case of physics) or the study of life (in the case of biology). Time is understood as the neutral "medium" in which matter and life are framed rather than as a dynamic force in their framing.

Although temporal concepts are rarely absent from any discourse, these concepts are not usually discussed or framed explicitly or self-consciously. *Becomings: Explorations in Time, Memory, and Futures* is an attempt to render these temporal processes and forces more explicit and to provide some intellectual tools through which further research, in both the sciences and the humanities, may be undertaken, research which highlights and takes seriously the temporal foundations of both matter and culture.

This collection does not address each and every historically significant figure who has thought about duration; rather, it explicitly focuses on and develops out of the work of a privileged few who have insisted on the fundamental openness of time to futurity, who have resisted all attempts to reduce time to the workings of causality, and who have seen in it the force of becoming—Nietzsche, Bergson, and Deleuze. These are not the only names that figure prominently here. Others could be considered philosophers of becoming, among them Heidegger, Merleau-Ponty, Derrida, Foucault, Klossowski, and Irigaray. Yet there is one who is in many ways more powerful and more pervasive in his understanding of time and becoming than all the others and who is not highlighted in this collection. This is Charles Darwin, who enabled both cosmology and biology to consider time as an open-ended, even random, becoming; who is the silent support of a new "contemporary" understanding of temporality; and whose work had a powerful, even pervasive influence not only on the sciences but also on the arts and humanities. The intricate and profound effects of this openendedness have yet to be adequately worked through.

An uncanny convergence is evident in the ways in which time is conceived in the writings of Darwin, Nietzsche, Bergson, and Deleuze, a point of resonance in otherwise disparate projects and methods. This point of resonance harmonizes or at least synchronizes a cluster of concepts: chance, randomness, openendedness, and becoming. Charles Darwin, with his account of the random temporality of individual variation and natural selection; Friedrich Nietzsche, with his understanding of eternal recurrence as the time of futurity; Henri Bergson, with his account of the paradoxical unity and multiplicity of duration; and Gilles Deleuze, with his figuring of Bergsonism as the very logic of becoming—each conceptualizes time as becoming, as an opening up which is at the same time a form of bifurcation or divergence. Each conceives of *time* as *difference*. Clearly intricate connections and relations exist between their various texts—each refers to his predecessors and provides a self-conscious development, if not a critique, of prior positions. It is clear that these four theorists do not form a cohesive philosophical position or a broad movement. Nevertheless, they share several characteristics that could be considered crucial elements, formative historical contributions, to an understanding of becoming and futurity. They share common enemies, particularly assumptions provided by everyday and scientific concepts of directionality, progress, development, accumulation, and lineage, that signal the potential significance of their work for postmodern thinkers. Each rejects the notion of time as passivity, a mode of passing, a neutral immersion of things in a temporal medium; each refuses to think of time as a modality or dimension of space. Instead, each asserts that the logic of time functions in conceptual (if not actual) separation from the logic of space. Each problematizes the central position accorded to determinism and to the virtues of a science or knowledge contained by and at the mercy of the imperative of predictability as one of the defining concepts within sciences, recognizing that determinism is the annulling of any concept of temporality other than the one structured by the terms and conditions of the past and present. Determinism annihilates any future uncontained by the past and present.

More positively, each in his own way affirms time as an open-ended and fundamentally active force—a materializing if not material—force whose movements and operations have an inherent element of surprise, unpredictability, or newness. It is significant that this future-oriented temporality brings with it the centrality of the concept of chance, of what is in principle unpredictable, in the work of each thinker; and chance, the concept of the random or the unpredictable, is of the essence of a time that is not regulated by causality and determination but unfolds with its own rhythms and logic, its own enigmas and impetus. Chance is that which signals the openness of the future, its relative connection to but also its relative freedom from the past, the possibilities of paths of development, temporal trajectories uncontained by the present. Chance here cannot be regarded as *indetermination,* as the absence of a cause (as it is represented in classical philosophy); rather, it is the *excess,* superfluity, of causes, the profusion of causes, which no longer produces singular or even complex effects but generates events, which have a temporal continuity quite separate from that of their "causes."

Darwin locates chance at the heart of natural selection, as that which indicates an organism's openness, its potentially mortal susceptibility to changing environments, environments hitherto unseen or not yet in existence. ("Fitness" designates not superiority in a given milieu or environment but rather the adaptability of the organism, in its given state, to changing environments—a notion more in keeping with Darwin's own writings than with more contemporary readings of evolutionary theory, which regard fitness as success within a *given* environment.) Thus from this time on, the random, the accidental, that which befalls an individual entity, becomes an essential ingredient in the history and development of that entity and all that follows it.

Nietzsche too claims that the random, the arbitrary throw of the dice, is the substance, the stuff of the eternal return: what eternal recurrence repeats is the random event that lives only by being willed again, by being actively chosen while passively bestowed. Chance too, the obstacle that befalls one, is the motor of Bergson's creative evolution, the openness of any living being, and the universe itself, to becoming, to external invention, which interrupts and moves along its own internal or organic processes. And in Deleuze, chance is closely associated with repetition and difference, in their modulations, in the modes by which repetition is never the generation of the same but the motor of the new.

Darwin, Nietzsche, Bergson, and Deleuze form, or perhaps should or will form, an assumed horizon for contemporary philosophical and cultural concepts of time. Among them, time is dynamized, seen as a virtual force and as that which builds, binds, contains, and transforms all relations, whether natural, cultural, or personal while also ensuring their dispersal, their development beyond current forms and parameters. Among them they make clear that something links the life of planets and universes to the life of organisms and their histories, and to the "life" of nonorganic or chemical beings, and this something is the endless unfolding of the new, restless transformation, upheaval, redirection and digression, which ensures the impossibility of the same even through the modes of repetition that each of these thinkers sees as central to the surprise and unpredictability of difference. (Difference and repetition may prove to be two linked names that stand in for the name of time itself.)

It is no surprise that the concept of time is raised as a question at this particular historical moment: while history is always at the point of junction of a fixed or given past that is irretrievable as a present, an opaque present whose interests cannot be given to itself, and a future that has the capacity not only to rewrite but also to entirely overwrite events of the past or present—that is, while history itself is at the mercy of temporality and a temporal structure that makes reconstruction / remembering and anticipation possible—it is also true that it is history (history as both the past itself and as the story of that past) that provides the conditions for and inflects the way time is conceptualized and the weight placed on it as an explanatory concept. Time's ontological structures make the epistemic structure of history possible. This moment in history—the end of the millennium, marked as a ritualized emblem of the meeting of history (the twentieth century and before) with a future full of promise and yet without form or flesh, the postmodern moment, a moment of decolonization, of resurgence of subjugated minorities, of difference—calls for an openness to the new, a willingness or desire to explore the potentialities of the future and to revel in the surprise that time brings as its legacy and gift. The marking of the millennium, no different in principle from the marking of any day or any moment, may serve to signal the openness of each day, and one's lifetime, to the next day, the next moment, which potentially can initiate the surprise of the new.

While the brief for the contributors was extremely broad—a call for an examination of all kinds of becomings, and through these becomings, an exploration of concepts of time and temporality—a remarkable confluence of texts, concepts, and interests emerged. While Deleuze's work is not entirely ubiquitous, the influence of his writings on the ways in which becomings, virtuality, and duration are theorized is clear. A resurgence of interest in Deleuze's work, in part, along with other influences, has induced a recent return to and a more careful reading of the works of Bergson and Nietzsche and, indirectly, Darwin. Deleuze is not the only point of confluence: Derrida's work on *différance* as a mode of the spatialization of time and the temporalization of space, and the powerful influence of Heidegger and the question of ontology in both Derrida and Deleuze, are also theoretical strands running through the papers in this volume.

This book raises time as a question, as the question of the promise of the new. We cannot know what the new will bring, what the promise of the future is for us: to know the future is to deny it as future, to place it as a given, as past. This book is not about predicting what will happen, nor is it an exercise in futurology (or in that speculatory field in economics known as futures), which is the extrapolation of images (whether fiscal, scientific, or cultural) of the future from trends in the present; rather, it explores the various ontological, epistemological, political, and social implications of considering time in terms of the supervalence of the future.

The essays collected here focus in detail on the forces of time and becoming. The book positions itself both within and in the interstices between the natural sciences, the social sciences, the humanities, particularly cultural and political theory. While not in any way hostile to concepts of temporality and duration developed in the natural sciences (two papers—those by De Landa and Grosz—address these concepts), this collection instead explores the ontological, epistemic, and political implications of rethinking time as a dynamic and irreversible force. It takes whatever resources are useful, whether these are provided by physics, chemistry, geology, biology—or, equally, from literature, philosophy, politics, and cultural analysis—for rethinking temporality in terms of the surprise of the new, the inherent capacity for time to link, in extraordinarily complex ways, the past and present to a future that is uncontained by them and has the capacity to rewrite and transform them. Although all the papers presented here are in some broad sense theoretical or even philosophical, they are multidisciplinary in focus and difficult to classify conventionally. They represent the interests, among other things, that literary, cultural, political, and social and cultural theory, as well as science and technological studies, postcolonial theory, feminist theory, and contemporary epistemology, have in the replacement of an ontology of being by an ontology of becoming. What they demonstrate is that both an open-ended temporality and the supervalence of the future over the past and present have implications that have rarely been considered and now need to be taken seriously.

The task of an anthology editor involves negotiating some kind of order or rationale from a body of texts that have been written by individuals with various styles, interests, and methods. The task of ordering and organizing disparate material always involves arbitrary divisions and modes of distribution, and yet to evade this imperative is to abandon an editor's responsibility to make a text as coherent and cohesive, as readable and accessible, as possible. This is rarely a task that can produce total integration and smoothness. I hope I have provided some alignments and connections that may prove fruitful without taking away from the originality and singularity of the individual contributions gathered together here.

This book has three parts. Part One, "The Becoming of the World," presents a broad introduction to the concepts of time, becoming, and the open-endedness of the future. Part Two, "Knowing and Doing Otherwise," addresses more specific modes of becoming, concrete becomings that somehow link the body, subjectivity, and desire to the time of futurity, to what is yet to come. Part Three, "Global Futures," focuses more specifically on some of the political and human implications of producing and living the time of the future—whether this proves to be the time of the techno-body, a time in which bodies and technologies meld to actively transform each other with an openness never before acknowledged; whether it proves to be the time of postcolonial and, by implication, feminist and antiracist struggles, struggles that seek a time beyond colonization or beyond current forms of oppression while nevertheless remaining in debt to them; or whether this time of the future is the noble time of the lost cause, the time of an impossible future, in which one must struggle for, and achieve, a beyond in the most apparently hopeless and oppressed of positions.

The four chapters in Part One explore the general implications of concepts of becoming in disparate realms—ontology, physics, politics, and epistemology. My paper "Thinking the New: Of Futures Yet Unthought" addresses the concepts of becoming and the new and how they problematize the assumed distinctions between the physical and biological sciences through a borderline concept of viral life. In his paper "Deleuze, Diagrams, and the Open-Ended Becoming of the World," Manuel De Landa provides a closely linked analysis of the ways in which the genesis of form, whether geological, chemical, biological, or social, can be explained in terms of the processes of a generalized though quite specific series of chemical becomings rather than in terms of the unfolding of a given essence or being. Becoming is not a process limited to the human or even to life; rather, becoming inscribes all of existence in all its molecular complexity. In his contribution to this volume, "Diagram and Diagnosis," John Rajchman explores the "time of the political," a time that is, by definition, "out of joint," a time that can no longer be contained in the model, plan, blueprint, or representation of the present, but must be seen as a positive leap into an unknown, into a time that is as yet unrepresentable but is nevertheless of this world. At its best, this may prove to be the time of subjugated positions, a time in which that which has been precluded, subordinated, can flourish. While these political interests also underlie Linda Alcoff's chapter, "Becoming an Epistemologist," her major focus here is the way in which truth and knowing, so long bound up with the static logic of propositions, of fixed identities and eternal, perspectiveless truths, can be opened up to their own kinds of becoming and futurity.

Part Two, "Knowing and Doing Otherwise" also comprises four chapters, which take as their point of departure the idea that social and subjective becomings must invoke latencies and possibilities hitherto unelaborated or undeveloped. Edward S. Casey's chapter, "The Time of the Glance: Toward Becoming Otherwise," provides a subtle and detailed analysis of the ways in which perceptual functions—in this case, the glance—unhinge and disrupt any concept of a linear, systematic time, where time is divisible into a static past, a given present, and a predictable future. The glance brings with it a peculiar, dislocating temporality, for it touches on, and in this process opens up, a future in contiguity with its comprehension of the present and the past; the glance fissures temporality modalities, making clear that the present is neither given in nor detached from the future the glance actively solicits. In her chapter "Flows of Desire and the Body-Becoming," Dorothea Olkowski returns us to the pivotal figure of Deleuze and introduces a specifically feminist strand, later elaborated in this section of the book, when she draws out the implications of Deleuze's reconceptualization of desire as an open, pre-personal series of becomings. Olkowski provides something of a systematic introduction to Deleuze's and Guattari's understanding of becoming by linking it to desiring production and to the movements of territorialization and deterritorialization that constitute both politics and subjectivity. Deleuze, Foucault, and Nietzsche also figure strongly in Claire Colebrook's essay "A Grammar of Becoming: Humanism, Subjectivism, and Style," where she asks whether becoming is a strategy of subjectivity or whether, perhaps, subjectivity can be regarded as a strategic effect of becoming. Is *becoming* that which operates through and as a subject rather than that which a subject is? Eleanor Kaufman's chapter, "Klossowski or Thought-Becoming," concludes this part. Kaufman explores the nexus of writings of Nietzsche, Foucault, and Deleuze through Klossowski's *Laws of Hospitality* and *Nietzsche and the Vicious Circle*. Klossowski, Kaufman argues, enacts through a kind of realignment and transposition of terms, the disjunction of the person and the body and the movement of becoming more and other that are generated either, in Nietzsche's case, through the ill and suffering body or, in the case of Roberte and Octave, the characters of Klossowski's hospitality trilogy, through a perverse eroticized prostitution of marriage. The joyous suffering or the extreme sexual humiliation of the subject may prove to be precisely the path for the subject's self-overcoming.

The third and final section of the book, "Global Futures," brings together three disparate representations of lived and political futures. Gail

Weiss, in "The Durée of the Techno-Body," argues that instead of regarding technology and the various technological interventions into and transformations of the body as modes of freezing the body's lived time and reality, they can be regarded more productively as both the sites and the means through which new becomings, new political schemas, and new bodily modes can be engendered and experimented with. Rather than focus on the possibilities of bodily-becoming that emerge from the invention and incorporation of technologies in and as bodies, Pheng Cheah takes the spectral becoming of the nation, especially the newly emergent postcolonial nation, as the object of investigation in his chapter "Spectral Nationality: The Living-On [*sur-vie*] of the Postcolonial Nation in Neocolonial Globalization." He explores the peculiar status of the nation straddled between organic life and the political death, a status that Derrida's work helps to explain as spectral or ghostly. He argues that the nation, as the promise of life, status, and longevity for the future of its people, must be understood in terms of nation-becomings that are distinctively its own. The becoming of nations and peoples cannot be adequately represented in terms of the becomings of nature, life, or the human, but has peculiar economic, political, and psychological inflections that mark its own historical specificities. Alphonso Lingis provides a moving conclusion to this volume in "Innocence." He outlines the remarkable struggle of the Tupac Amaru Revolutionary Movement in the Peruvian Andes. This struggle culminated in the globally reported siege of the Japanese embassy in Peru, where six hundred hostages were held by a handful of guerrillas in 1996–1997. Lingis outlines the peculiarly liberating futurity of those struggles that "defy the impossible," of those peoples whose nobility lies in a lost cause, who face death for a cause, a value: to accompany the dying, to partake in dying, need not be the obliteration or end of time but contains within it the energy and force of a future whose value is worth dying for. This is a future inscribed by the blood and struggles of one's ancestors, family, neighbors, allies. Death is not the end of time but can be the ballast of a future that requires blood and sacrifice to make it different from the past and present. The politics of the hopeless cause, the cause ennobled precisely because it is hopeless, improbable, unlikely to succeed, introduces another time, another dimension, into the concept of what politics and struggle are. To struggle not to win so much as to make a mark, to mark a time and a place as particular, is to imbue time (and space) with a hope that is beyond the hope of actual outcomes, to give it a nobility that marks it out of its time, and in the time of a future where its hopelessness has had an effect, has produced more than was ever foreseeable.

Taken together, these essays demonstrate that there is much to consider, much to rethink, about how time is conceptualized and represented in the various branches of knowledge and in representations of practice. Only if we open ourselves up to a time in which the future plays a structuring role in the value and effectivity of the past and present can we revel in the indeterminacy, the becoming, of time itself.

Such a rethinking of concepts of time involves reconceptualizing many of the most central concerns of epistemology, ontology, ethics, and politics, for each, in its own way, contains assumptions about temporality and futurity that need to be questioned and moved beyond. What, for example, would politics be like if it were not directed to the attainment of certain goals, the coming to fruition of ideals or plans, but rather required a certain abandonment of goals? What would a science or a body of knowledge be like that, instead of invoking the criteria of repeatability and the guarantee of outcomes required for industrial and technological efficiency, sought to endlessly experiment without drawing conclusions, without seeking law-like regularities? Would such a science approximate the singularity and uniqueness of art or intuition? Could experimental techniques themselves be derived experimentally, artistically, inventively, nonteleologically? What would an ethics be like that, instead of seeking a mode of equivalence, a mode of reciprocity or calculation, sought to base itself on absolute generosity, absolute gift, expenditure without return, a pure propulsion into a future that does not rebound with echoes of an exchange dictated by the past? These questions, when posed acutely and intensely enough, when posed in a *timely,* which is perhaps to say, in Nietzschean, terms, an *untimely* fashion, may provoke new modes of knowing, being, responding, and initiating.

Elizabeth Grosz
New York

PART

1

The Becoming of the World

1

THINKING THE NEW: OF FUTURES YET UNTHOUGHT

Elizabeth Grosz

Thus the living being essentially has duration; it has duration
precisely because it is continuously elaborating what is new and
because there is no elaboration without searching, no searching
without groping. Time is this very hesitation.

BERGSON, *The Creative Mind:*
An Introduction to Metaphysics

The *élan vital* creates the future before us, and it is the only thing
that does it. In life everything that has direction in time has *élan,*
pushes forward, progresses toward a future. In the same way, as
soon as I think of an orientation in time, I feel myself irresistibly
pushed forward and see the future open in front of me. And this
fact of "being pushed" has nothing passive in it. This does not
mean that exterior forces compel me to look in front of me and
to progress in that direction. . . . It means that I tend spontaneously with all my power, with all my being, toward a
future. . . .

MINKOWSKI, *Lived Time: Phenomenological*
and Psychopathological Studies

TIMES

I will explore the "nature" of time, the precedence of the future over the
present and past, and the strange vectors of becoming that a concept of the
new provokes. This chapter argues that unless we develop concepts of time
and duration that welcome and privilege the future, that openly accept the

rich virtualities and divergent resonances of the present, we will remain closed to understanding the complex processes of becoming that engender and constitute both life and matter. My goal here is to think, in a highly provisional and preliminary way, about some key terms by which to conceptualize temporality and futurity, in all their richness, as modalities of difference.

The concept of the absolutely new raises many anxieties. While it is clear that *newness, creativity, innovation,* and *progress* are all terms deemed social positives, the more disconcerting notion of unpredictable, disordered, or uncontainable change—the idea of chance, of indeterminacy, of unforeseeability—that lurks within the very concept of change or newness, seems to unsettle scientific, philosophical, political, and cultural ideals of stability and control.[1] Predictable, measured, regulated transformation, change under specifiable conditions and with determinate effects, seems a readily presumed social prerequisite; upheaval, the eruption of the event, the emergence of new alignments unpredicted within old networks, threatens to reverse all gains, to position progress on the edge of an abyss, to place chaos at the heart of regulation and orderly development. How is it possible to revel and delight in the indeterminacy of the future without raising the kind of panic and defensive counterreactions that surround the attempts of the old to contain the new, to predict, anticipate, and incorporate the new within its already existing frameworks? Michel Foucault, among others, has devoted considerable attention to the ways in which a supervising, regulating power needs to contain unpredictability, the eruption of the event, the emergence of singularities, and the consequent realignments of power. Indeed, it may be possible to understand his concept of power as that which functions, if not to dampen and suppress the impetus to invention and newness, then at least to link it as firmly and smoothly as possible to that which is already contained. Power functions to make the eruption of the event part of the fabric of the known. Foucault makes explicit the vast range of strategies available, for example, in existing knowledge and disciplines to capture, explain, organize, and categorize any eruption that may effect a transformation of such knowledge: criticism, commentary, categorization, and disciplinary conformity are all modes by which the uncontained is woven into a containing framework and the new is made recognizable and tied to the known.[2]

Ironically, the concept of the new, the absolutely new, lurks everywhere, especially where it is least able to be called by that label. This preoccupation with the new can be readily transcribed into many other terminologies, each of which has its own political lineage and its own specific maneuvers and anxieties. Instead of the language of the new, for example, the more common political concept of revolution could be substituted. Is the concept of revolution so tied to a set of weary discourses that, within their terms, it can now mean only predictable transformation, transformation that follows a predesignated path, innovation within legitimized parameters, that is, controlled and regulated progress (whether the rule of the proletariat, the equalization of relations between the sexes, or racial integration)? Or does it involve the more disconcerting idea of *un*predictable transformation—mutation, metamorphosis—upheaval in directions and arenas with implications or consequences that cannot be known in advance?

This is a most disconcerting and dangerous idea: politics seems to revel in the idea of progress, development, movement, but the very political discourses that seem to advocate it most vehemently (Marxism, feminism, postcolonial and anticolonial discourses, the discourses of antiracism) seem terrified by the idea of a transformation somehow beyond the control of the very revolutionaries who seek it, of a kind of "anarchization" of the future. If the revolution can carry no guarantee that it will improve the current situation or provide something preferable to what exists now, what makes it a sought-for ideal? What prevents it from blurring into fascism or conservatism?

Although common preoccupations of certain of the natural sciences (physics and certain branches of the life sciences), the nature of temporality or duration, the relations between past, present, and future, have remained elided within the humanities and social sciences, philosophy nonetheless has made a number of assumptions regarding time, movement, and change. Underlying these assumptions about change are various commitments to upholding the values of predictability and stability, or, more rarely, commitments that revel in the idea of the unpredictable, both of which need careful analysis and reconsideration.

Time, or more precisely duration, is an extraordinarily complex term which functions simultaneously as singular, unified, and whole, as well as in specific fragments and multiplicitous proliferation. There is one and only one time, but there are also numerous times: a duration for each thing or movement, which melds with a global or collective time. As a whole, time is braided, intertwined, a unity of stands layered over each other; unique, singular, and individual, it nevertheless partakes of a more generic and overarching time, which makes possible relations of earlier and later,

relations locating times and durations relative to each other. Such a durational—that is to say, wholistic *and* fragmentary—concept defies any simple linear model of the arrow of time, in which the time of beings and
processes is elided in favor of a measured movement whose uniform, reg-
ular beat generates an objective, measurable, clock time. What is significant about clock time is that it homogenizes and measures all other modes
of passing insensitively, with no reference to or respect for the particularity of the duration of events and processes. It imposes rather than extracts
a unity and wholeness through homogenization and reduction.

One cannot contain temporal concepts within those explicitly focused
on. Concepts of each of the three temporal modalities (past, present, and
future in all their conjugative complexities) entail presumptions regarding
the others that are often ill- or unconsidered: how we understand the past,
and our links to it through reminiscence, melancholy, or nostalgia, prefigures and contains corresponding concepts about the present and future; the
substantiality or privilege we pragmatically grant to the present has implications for the retrievability of the past and the predictability of the future;
and, depending on whether we grant to the future the supervening power
to rewrite the present and past, so too we must problematize the notions of
identity, origin, and development. The ways in which we consider the past
to be connected to and thus to live on through the present / future have direct implications for whatever concepts of futurity, the new, creativity, production, or emergence we may want to develop. If the past constitutes a
remnant, a ghost or mode of haunting of the present, this is only insofar as
we can no longer consider the present itself to be fully self-present. The
present can be seen, through this inhabitation, which is as unavoidable as
it is problematic, as a mode of differing or differentiation.

This is not to suggest that the relations between the past and present, or
between the present and future, that is, relations of progress or directionality, are bound, or given their direction, only by scientific laws, whether
relations of causality (in classical science) or relations of statistical prob-
ability (in contemporary science). The extent to which one remains committed to determinism is precisely the degree to which one refuses the
open-endedness of the future.[3] In seeking an open-ended future, one is not
required to affirm that misnomer, "free will," but to acknowledge the capacity of any future eruption, any event, any reading, to rewrite, resignify,
reframe the present, to accept the role that the accidental, chance, or the
undetermined plays in the unfolding of time. It is this open-endedness that

Derrida affirms through his understanding of the power of iteration[4] and that contemporary biology has designated by the notion of emergence, which is neither free nor determined but both constrained and undecidable. And it is precisely such a notion of open-endedness and of emergence that contemporary physics, especially in its flirtations with biochemistry, seems to have put in place of the emphasis on determinism so powerful in classical physics.[5] Finally, it is such a notion of open-endedness that leads Deleuze to seek in Bergson and Bergsonism a concept of duration that is adequate for thinking about all the temporal resonances of becoming, as we will see shortly.[6]

What kind of difference must it be to differ not only from itself and what is other (difference as divergence, as the breakdown or failure of identity) but also to differ from its own differing: in short to diverge in (at least) two directions at once? How to think of direction or trajectory without being able to anticipate a destination? It is this idea, direction without destination, movement without prediction, that is also so intriguing about current research regarding genetic algorithms, biological emergence, cellular automata, and the formulation of programs and computer simulations of animal and insect behaviors that are described as "artificial life." There seems to be a convergence between these so-called "new sciences" and the movement of difference within the humanities.[7] What these scientific discourses make clear is that the unpredictability of daily and cosmological life can be duplicated and rendered indiscernible from the ways in which the computer program exhibits emergent properties inherently unpredictable by their programmers or present users. The evolution of life itself, from the simplest organic forms to complex biological beings, seems to parallel the inherent openness of the structure of matter itself.[8]

Much of contemporary physics is impelled closer toward the interests and presumptions of biology, which itself has been transformed in the process: their mediation is to a large extent a function of the privilege granted to the random and the unpredictable in both discourses. Biologists no longer accept a simple subsumption of the principles of biology to those of physics and chemistry; instead, they have insisted on boundaries and conditions specific to the nature of biology. In doing so, physics has been forced to accept that certain of its well-known presumptions (entropy, to mention the most obvious) need reconsideration in the light of biology (which breaches the principle every minute of the day). The more closely physics comes to providing modes of mathematical modeling for biological processes, the more committed both disciplines must be to the power of the random and the event, to contingency and openness. In other words, the possibilities of convergence between these two sciences seem to depend to some extent on the translatability or interchangeability of mathematical languages of the type preferred in physics with the logical and computer languages and programs now to some extent guiding biological modeling. This convergence or prototranslatability seems possible because otherwise incommensurable disciplines share a certain core commitment to chance and randomness that may allow them to be rendered comparable.[9] Chance and randomness are no longer simply construed as hidden or complex determinants, whose causal complexity is beyond human calculation or beyond the limits of current technologies. This is at best the attribution of *provisional randomness,* to be superseded by a more sophisticated and complex determinism. Rather, randomness or indeterminacy is now regarded in some branches of science and mathematics as a principle, or as ineliminable.

Chance is both a central and an extraordinarily complex concept in Darwin's understanding of evolution. Chance erupts both at the level of random variation and at the level of natural selection and, perhaps more interestingly, in the gap or lag that exists in their interaction. At the level of individual variation, chance emerges in the processes, unknown to Darwin at the time and quite possibly unknowable in principle, of genetic reproduction and recombination, which produce multiplicitous, usually minute, and usually insignificant variations in organisms. What dictates these variations is both unknown and in some sense irrelevant, at least as far as natural selection is concerned, for natural selection works only on the viable and inherited results of such randomness. At the level of natural selection, Darwin suggests that changes in the environment, and in the various pressures facing organisms within that environment, are also unpredictable. But more significant than the randomness of either individual variation or the randomness of natural (or artificial) selection is the randomness of individual variation *relative to* natural selection. Furthermore, the randomness of individual variation, although in no sense causally connected to the randomness of natural selection, may actively transform the criteria by which natural selection functions.[10] The randomness so central to the biological notion of evolution seems to have provided the means by which biology has opened itself to futurity and thus aligned itself with certain contemporary physicists' notion of indeterminacy[11]

CONCEPTS

Is knowledge opposed to the future? Is the future inherently unknowable? Although it may be true that certain modes or forms of knowing or thinking are incapable of thinking about the new, the future, or becoming, there seems no essential opposition between them. If dominant modes of knowledge (causal, statistical) are incapable of envisioning the absolutely new, maybe other modes of knowing, other forms of thinking, need to be proposed. Only if thinking is itself part of the provenance of the new—which clearly involves a new account of what thought is—can thinking be an appropriate modality for dealing with the future, for coping with and producing the new.

This is the reservation expressed in the opposition between knowledge on the one hand and the immersion in temporality, and thus possibilities of the future, on the other, posited in some of the writings of Bergson and many of his disciples. It is for this reason that Bergson is so insistent on the distinction between intuition and the intellect. It is only intuition that has access to duration; at best, the intellect reduces duration to spatialization. In Minkowski's analysis of lived time, for example, he raises the question, "How do we live the future, independent of and before all knowledge?"[12] Where memory and perception, the past and the present, are in play, epistemological concerns can be somehow addressed. The possibility of knowledge exists, but where it is a matter of futurity, of life and the direction forward, somehow knowledge can function only as a mode of resistance to the play of vital forces, the *élan vital:* "As for memory, it always concerns recorded events or things heard. It is much closer to knowledge than to life and consequently can occupy only a secondary place in an analysis of lived time" (Minkowski, 80).

Futurity is not amenable to exact prediction (except within the most experimentally contained and limited contexts). Indeed, for Minkowski, it is the outsideness, the fundamental alienness, of futurity to knowledge that is part of the awe and mystery, part of the *hold* that the future has over us as living subjects who are inevitably propelled forward: "We look at the future and we see it in a broad and majestic perspective stretching out to lose itself in the distance. This majesty approaches the mysterious. But this mystery is as indispensable to our spiritual life as pure air is to our respiration. It makes of the future a reservoir of eternal and inexhaustible forces without which we could not continue to live" (81).

We need to affirm, along with Minkowski, the joyous open-endedness of the future, without, however, asserting that such indeterminacy functions only in the realm of consciousness, or even life itself. Vitalism is the philosophical commitment to a specific life force, a life energy, which distinguishes the organic from the inorganic. As part of an ancient tradition within philosophy, vitalism is conventionally opposed to mechanism, the belief that objects, things, are composed of externally or mechanically connected atomic elements. Vitalism is committed to the belief that the organism is greater than the sum of its parts, while mechanism claims that the unity of the organism comes from its particular ingredients in their specific configurations. Where vitalism seems unable to think adaquately of matter and its capacities for transformation, mechanism seems unable to think of the specificities and distinctive features of organic existence, the peculiar properties of life. This opposition prefigures and is to some extent undermined by the opposition and convergence between physics (the conceptual descendent of mechanism) and biology (which can be seen to be oriented more by at least certain elements of vitalism).

The opposition Bergson, Minkowski, and other vitalists[13] assume between the organic and the inorganic, between consciousness or mind and matter (or, in their terms, between duration and space), must be questioned while simultaneously being taken seriously. Bergson, Minkowski, and others have accepted, as few have, the perpetually impending precedence of the future over the past and present; they have acknowledged and delighted in the uncaptured playing out of the forces of duration, temporal continuity, and eruption or emergence and the coincidence of this movement with the surprise and openness of life itself. However, their commitment to vitalism, and their understanding of duration or becoming as the privileged domain of the lived, the experienced, remains limited in at least three respects:

1. This view refuses to see spatiality as just as susceptible to the movement of difference as duration. If time has numericized and mathematized duration, then so, too, mathematization has rendered space itself a kind of abstraction of place or locus. Just as time is amenable to both flow and discontinuity (to de- and reterritorialization), so too is space. Space is no more inherently material than duration and is no more the privileged domain of objects than memory is subjective and to be denied to spatial events: each is as amenable as the other to being disconcerted by difference, which in any case refuses such a clear-cut distinction between them. (Bergson himself seems to come close to this position in his later writings.)

2. This view refuses to accord to matter itself the indeterminacy and openness that it attributes to life. Yet it is no longer clear, following Darwinism and its implication that the evolution of life emerges from the most elementary biotic combinations of nonorganic material elements, where the boundary between life and nonlife, between the organic and the inorganic, can be drawn. What is the ontological status, for example of those strings of RNA which lie halfway between the organic and the inorganic, which we call viruses? Are viruses self-reproducing organisms, or are they more biochemical programs? Does it literally matter whether they are enacted in a carbon- or silicon-based form? A virus has been regarded as a self-replicating, evolving organism, whether it is carbon- or silicon-based, whether its content is chemical or informational. There are striking analogies between biological and computer viruses, such that the latter may well be considered forms of artificial life. At the very least, they blur the conceptual and definitional boundaries between what is regarded as inorganic and what has an organic-like life of its own. Viral infections of both biological and silicon form can be considered programs (genetic or computing) that are injected into the body of a larger "cell" or application. The cell is thereby infected and converted into a system for the production of many replicas or clones, and possibly mutations. A computer virus is a small segment of computer memory (at its most simple, from 2 to 20 KB) that is capable of copying its code onto host programs, which, when executed, spread the virus further. Biological viruses are similar in their informational length (usually around 3 to 30 KB) and in their various capacities.[14] How can any clear line be drawn in any case, such that material objects are characterized by inertia and by temporal self-containment (i.e., by being) that the organic world enlivens (through becoming)?

3. This view is unable to realize that it is not simply matter, organic or inorganic, but—more intriguingly and less straightforwardly—information, at least information insofar as it is bound up with a particular mode or organization of matter, that becomes, that expands itself as it is impelled to the future. It is significant that although there is an ostensible commitment to materialism within biology, as one would expect, nevertheless, there seems to be a stronger commitment to the independence of information from matter. Matter figures as significant only insofar as the complexity of its particular

modes of organization can support the demands / requirements for the transmission and reproduction of information. It is the peculiar transmigration of matter and information that seems to mark the "materialist" commitments of contemporary biology, and to provide a space in which the notion of "artificial life," life generated in simulated space, life generated through information alone, can gain not only a plausible but also perhaps an inevitable role in biological modeling.[15]

Becoming is what immerses both matter and information: it is for this reason that temporal modeling, though not prediction, is as possible in social and cultural activities as in ethnology, biology, physics, or genetics.[16] This is made abundantly clear in the ways in which information, in virtual space, in computing programs of various kinds, exhibits emergent properties even though it is difficult to ascertain exactly what their mode of materiality consists in.

LIFE

Clearly I can do no justice to the rich resources that make such a project feasible—Bergson, Deleuze, Minkowski, Derrida; writings on artificial life, on molecular biology, contemporary cosmology; and subatomic physics all provide necessary ingredients. There are, however, rare resources I can briefly indicate, where time, duration is conceived outside the contraints of mathematization and spatialization. Indeed, since Einstein, time is conceived as *the* mode for the mathematization of space. It is largely Deleuze's reading of Bergson that has rescued the latter from the kind of oblivion dealt to once popular figures of yesteryear, who are often treated as little more than anachronistic amusements. Deleuze's reading of Bergson[17] has taken a very long time to have any impact on the reassessment of Bergson's work, and on refiguring concepts of time in literary, cultural, filmic, and scientific contexts. For the purposes of this chapter, I will look at only a tiny fragment of Bergson's work on duration and its links to the notion of virtuality, which will be of use to reconceiving becoming and the new.[18]

The Bergson of *Matter and Memory* claims that a distinction between subjective and objective (or duration and spatiality, life and the nonorganic) can be formulated in terms of the distinction between the virtual and the actual. Bergson suggests that objects, space, and the world of inert matter exist entirely in the domain of the actual. They contain no virtuality. Matter has no hidden latency, no potentiality, no hidden becoming. Although there is more to matter than our images of it (a claim that rescues him from the unwarranted accusation of idealism with which he is continually charged), material objects are nonetheless of the same kind as our images.[19]

If everything about matter is real, if it has no virtuality, the proper "medium" or milieu of matter is spatial. While it exists in duration, while clearly it is subject to change, the object does not reveal itself over time. There is no more in it "than what it presents to us at any moment." By contrast, what duration, memory, and consciousness bring to the world is the possibility of unfolding, hesitation, uncertainty. Not everything is presented in simultaneity. This is what life (duration, memory, consciousness) brings to the world: the new, the movement of actualization of the virtual, expansiveness, opening up.

> Thus the living being essentially has duration; it has duration precisely because it is continuously elaborating what is new and because there is no elaboration without searching, no searching without groping. Time is this very hesitation.[20]

Time is a mode of stretching, protraction, which provides the very conditions of becoming, however faltering they may be. Time is the hiccoughing that expands itself, encompassing past and present into a kind of simultaneity. Both exist; they concur "at the same time."[21] But they do not exist in the same order: they function, not in terms of the possible / real relation but, as Deleuze suggests, in terms of the relations between actual and virtual. Matter and the present are to be placed on the side of the actual; and mind or duration and the past, on the side of the virtual.

In doing so, Bergson in effect displaces the dominance of the possible / real relation. The process of realization, that "movement" or vector from the possible to the real, is governed by the two principles of *resemblance* and *limitation*. The real exists in a relation of resemblance to the possible, functioning as its exact image, to which the category of existence or reality is simply added. In other words, the real and the possible are conceptually identical (since, as Kant argued, existence is not a quality or attribute). Realization also involves the process of limitation, the narrowing down of possibilities, so that some are rejected and others made real. The field of the possible is broader than the real. Implicit in the coupling of limitation and resemblance, Deleuze suggests, is preformism: the real is already preformed in the possible insofar as the real resembles the possible. The possible passes into the real by a process of culling. Deleuze suggests that this relation entails fixity: the real emerges as given (rather than produced), though the possible could just as readily be seen as the "retrospective" projection of the real.[22] The possible is both more and less than the real. It is more, insofar as the real selects from a number of coexisting possibles, limiting their ramifying effects. But it is also less, insofar as the possible is the real minus existence.[23]

Realization is a temporal process in which creativity and the new are no longer conceivable. Making the possible real is simply giving it existence without adding to or modifying its conception. The question begs to be posed: Is the possible the foundation or precondition of the real, or does the real project itself backward to produce the possible? Is the real an image of the possible, or is the possible an image of the real?[24] To reduce the possible to a preexistent phantomlike version of the real is to curtail the possibility of thinking about emergence, an open future not bound directly or strictly to the present.[25]

In *Difference and Repetition* (1994), Deleuze claims that there are at least three ways in which the virtual should be distinguished from the possible. First, existence, the acquisition of the status of reality by the possible, can be understood either as an inexplicable eruption or as a system of all-or-nothing: either it "has" existence, in which case it is real; or it "lacks" existence, it which case it remains merely possible. If this is the case, Deleuze argues, it is hard to see what the difference is between the existent and the nonexistent, if the nonexistent is a possibility that retains all the characteristics of the existent. Existence is regarded as the same as the possible: function as conceptual duplicates. Existence or reality is simply the unfolding of a predesignated possibility.[26] By contrast, the virtual cannot be opposed to the real: it is real. It is through its reality that existence is produced. Instead of an impoverished real (the possible), the virtual can be considered more a superabundant real that induces actualization.

Second, if the possible is considered in place of the virtual, difference can be understood only as restriction and containment rather than production. Where the possible "refers to the form of identity in the concept," the virtual designates a pure multiplicity that radically excludes the identical as prior condition. The self-identity of the image remains the same whether possible or real; it is precisely such an understanding of self-identity that the virtual renders unthinkable.

And third, while the possible is regarded as a mode of anticipatory resemblance of the real, the virtual never resembles the real that it actualizes. It is this sense that actualization is a process of creation that resists both a logic of identity and a logic of resemblance and substitutes differentiation, divergence, and innovation. While the concept of the possible doubles that of the real, the virtual is the real of genuine production, innovation, and creativity. It is only actualization that engenders the new.[27]

The process of actualization is one of genuine creativity and innovation, the production of singularity or individuation. Where the possible / real relation is regulated by resemblance and limitation, the virtual / actual relation is governed by the two principles of difference and creation. For the virtual to become actual, it must create the conditions for actualization: the actual in no way resembles the virtual. Rather, the actual is produced through a mode of differentiation from the virtual, a mode of divergence from it which is productive. The process of actualization involves the creation of heterogeneous terms. The lines of actualization of virtuality are divergent, creating multiplicities, the varieties that constitute creative evolution. This is a movement of the emanation of a multiplicity from a virtual unity, divergent paths of development in different series and directions.[28]

The movement from a virtual unity to an actual multiplicity requires a certain leap of innovation or creativity, the surprise that the virtual leaves within the actual. The movement of realization seems like the concretization of a preexistent plan or program; by contrast, the movement of actualization is the opening up of the virtual to what befalls it. In the terms of another discourse, actualization is individuation, the creation of singularity (whether physical, psychical, or social), insofar as the processes of individuation predate the individual yet the individual is a somehow open-ended consequence of these processes. Individuation contains the "ingredients" of individuality without in any way planning or preparing for it.[29] Individuation is the alignment of virtualities, which make both being and becoming possible. Individuation is in no sense tied to the human: it is what characterizes cloud formations, the formation of crystals, and ocean currents, as well as the development of cells and the creation of individuals. Individuation is a series of processes of radical excentering and self-exceeding, whether psychically, organically, or at the level of the nonorganic. This is what becoming is of necessity—a movement of differentiation, divergence, and self-surpassing or actualization of virtualities in the light of the contingencies that befall them.

Insofar as time, history, change, and the future need to be reviewed in the light of this Bergsonian disordering, perhaps the concept of the virtual may prove central in reinvigorating the concept of the future insofar as it refuses to tie it to the realization of possibilities (the following of a plan), linking it instead to the unpredictable, uncertain actualization of virtualities. This point is not simply semantic: it is a question not of dumping the word "possible" and replacing it with "virtual," but of understanding the concept in an entirely different way, understanding the processes of production and creation in terms of openness to the new instead of preformism of the expected.

Bergson's concept of virtuality provides us with a way of seeing the future as bound up with the continual elaboration of the new, the openness of things (including life—here I must depart from Bergson to attribute the possibilities of becoming to the nonorganic or the quasi-organic as well as to life in its more traditional sense). This is what time *is* if it is anything at all: not simply mechanical repetition, the causal ripple of objects on others, but the indeterminate, the unfolding, and the continual eruption of the new.

Time is intrication and elaboration. The model that Bergson himself develops, with great prescience in view of the current transformations and upheavals going on in biology and biological modeling, is more akin to the randomness of evolution, the unfolding of lineage and mutation. Elaboration is time's mode of acting, but an elaboration that frees up, undetermines, interrupts, and deflects rather than causes.[30]

Duration proceeds not by continuous growth, smooth unfolding, or accretion, but through division, bifurcation, dissociation—by difference—through sudden and unexpected change or eruption. Duration is a mode of infecting self-differentiation: difference is internal to its function, its modes of elaboration and production, and is also its ramifying effect on those objects located "within" its milieu. This means that not only must concepts of time (in physics, biology, philosophy, cultural studies, and social theory) be opened up to their modes of differentiation, but also that our very concept of objects, matter, being—well beyond the concept of life itself—needs to be open to the differentiations that constitute and continually transform it.

2

DELEUZE, DIAGRAMS, AND THE OPEN-ENDED BECOMING OF THE WORLD

Manuel De Landa

With the final mathematization of classical physics in the nineteenth century, a certain dominant picture of the world emerged, in which clockwork determinism reigned supreme and time played no creative role, so that the future was effectively closed, completely given in the past. Although the set of equations with which Hamilton was able to unify all the different fields of classical physics (mechanics, optics, and the elementary theory of electromagnetism) did contain a variable for time, this variable played only an extrinsic role: once the equations were defined for a specific instant, both the past and the future were completely determined and could be obtained mechanically by simply integrating the equations. To be sure, this static, timeless picture of reality did not go unchallenged within science, because thermodynamics had already introduced an arrow of time that conflicted with the symmetric concept of classical mechanics, where the past and the future were interchangeable. Nevertheless, as the history of statistical mechanics makes clear, much scientific effort has been spent in our century to reconcile time asymmetry at the level of large aggregates with the still accepted time symmetry at the level of individual interactions.

Thus it would become the task of philosophers and social scientists to attempt to reconceptualize the world in order to give time and history a creative role, with the vision of an open future that this implies. Although a variety of strategies have been used to achieve this open future, here I would like to concentrate on two contrasting approaches. The first is perhaps best illustrated by the intellectual movement that is today known as "social constructivism," but whose roots lie in linguistic and anthropological theories that go back to the turn of the century. At the risk of oversimplifying, we may say that the core of this approach is a neo-Kantian theory of perception, in which individual experience is completely structured by the interplay of concepts and representations, but one in which Kant's transcendental concepts (of space and time) have been replaced by the conventional concepts of a given culture. The guiding image of this strategy may be said to be, "Each culture lives in its own world," an image central to many theoretical approaches in this century, from the cultural relativism of Margaret Mead and Franz Boas to the linguistic relativism of Edward Sapir and Benjamin Whorf to the epistemological relativism of Thomas Kuhn's theory of scientific paradigms. Again, oversimplifying somewhat, the key idea in all these theories is "incommensurability" across worlds, each conceptual scheme constructing its own reality so that bridges between worlds are hard, if not impossible, to build.

Although these influential schools of thought deserve a more careful characterization, these few remarks will suffice for my purpose here. If indeed every culture and subculture inhabits its own conceptually constructed reality, then the world and the future become open again. Far from being completely given in the past, the future is now unbound, the world itself becoming a text open to innumerable interpretations. The problem now is, of course, that we have made the world open at the expense of giving up its objectivity; in other words, the world becomes open only through human intervention. For some, this relativism may not seem like a problem, particularly when the only alternative is believed to be a realism based on a correspondence theory of truth, a realism deeply committed to essentialism and rationalism. Clearly, if the idea of material objects independent of human experience is based on a concept of their genesis in terms of preexisting essences, then we are back in a closed world where all possibilities have been defined in advance by those essences. Similarly, if the world is pictured as a fixed set of beings to which our theories correspond like a reflection or a snapshot, then that world would be hardly capable of an open becoming.

Yet the work of the philosopher Gilles Deleuze makes it clear that a belief in the autonomous existence of the world does not have to based on essentialist or rationalist views. It will be the task of this essay to make a case for what we may call Deleuze's "neorealist" approach, an approach involving a theory of the genesis of form that does away with essences, as well as a theory of epistemology that does not rely on a view of truth as a faithful reflection of a static world of beings. I would like to begin with a quotation from what is, in my view, Deleuze's most important work, *Difference and Repetition*. Since Kant, it has been traditional to distinguish between the world as it appears to us humans, that is, the world of phenomena or appearances, and those aspects of the world existing by themselves and referred to as "noumena." Deleuze writes:

> Difference is not diversity. Diversity is given, but difference is that by which the given is given. . . . Difference is not phenomenon but the noumenon closest to the phenomenon. . . . Every phenomenon refers to an inequality by which it is conditioned. . . . Everything which happens and everything which appears is correlated with orders of differences: differences of level, temperature, pressure, tension, potential, difference of intensity".[1]

Several things deserve notice in this passage. First of all, it is clear that for Deleuze noumena are not (as they were for Kant) beyond human knowledge. On the other hand, that which is beyond what is given to us in experience is not a being but a becoming, a difference-driven process by which the given is given. Let me illustrate this idea with a familiar example from thermodynamics. If we have a container separated into two compartments, and we fill one compartment with cold air and the other with hot air, we thereby create a system embodying a difference in intensity, the intensity in this case being temperature. If we then open a small hole in the wall dividing the compartments, the difference in intensity causes a spontaneous flow of air from one side to the other. It is in this sense that differences in intensity are morphogenetic, giving rise to the phenomena of experience, even if in this case the phenomenon that emerges is too simple. The main idea, however, is much more general: many phenomena, in geology, meteorology, biology, and even economics and sociology, emerge spontaneously from the interplay of intensity differences. Indeed, one can build an entire theory of the genesis of form (geological, biological, or cultural) on the basis of processes of becoming driven by intensity differences. Essentialism views matter as an inert receptacle for forms that come from the outside (transcendental essences); here; by contrast, matter is seen as possessing its own immanent, intensive resources for the generation of form from within. (Deleuze refers to the essentialist model of morphogenesis as the "hylomorphic schema.")

However, on the page following the passage above, Deleuze argues that, despite this important insight, nineteenth-century thermodynamics cannot provide the foundation he needs for a philosophy of form. Why? Because that branch of physics became obsessed with the final equilibrium forms, at the expense of the difference-driven morphogenetic process that gives rise to those forms. In other words, intensive differences are subordinated to the extensive structures (structures extended in space-time) they give rise to. But as Deleuze argues, most of the important philosophical insights can be grasped only during the process of morphogenesis, that is, before the final form is actualized, before the difference disappears. This shortcoming of nineteenth-century thermodynamics—to overlook the role of the intensive and stress only the extensive, to concentrate on the equilibrium form that emerges only once the original difference has been canceled—has today been repaired in the latest version of this branch of physics, appropriately labeled "far-from-equilibrium thermodynamics." Although Deleuze does not explicitly refer to this new branch of science, it is clear that far-from-equilibrium thermodynamics meets all the objections that he raises against its nineteenth-century counterpart. In particular, the systems studied in this new discipline are continuously traversed by an intense flow of energy and matter, a flow that maintains these differences and keeps them from canceling themselves, that is, a flow that does not allow the intensive process to become hidden underneath the extensive results. It is only in these far-from-equilibrium conditions, only in this singular zone of intensity, that difference-driven morphogenesis comes into its own and matter becomes an active material agent, one that does not need form to come and impose itself from the outside.[2]

Even at this early stage of my analysis, the contrast with constructivist philosophies should be clear. Although many constructivists declare themselves "antiessentialist," they share with essentialism a view of matter as inert, except that they do not view the form of material entities as coming from a Platonic heaven or from the mind of God, but from the minds of humans (or from cultural conventions expressed linguistically). The world is amorphous, and we cut it out into forms using language. Nothing could be further from Deleuzian thought than this linguistic relativism, which does not break with the hylomorphic schema. For Deleuze, the extensive boundaries of individual entities do not exist only in human experience, drawn by the interplay of concepts; rather, they are real, the product of definite, objective processes of individuation. Thus, the extensive boundaries that define living creatures (their skin, but also the folds that define their internal tissues and organs) are the result of complex processes of individuation (or actualization) during embryogenesis. As Deleuze writes:

> How does actualization occur in things themselves? . . . Beneath the actual qualities and extensities [of things themselves] there are spatiotemporal dynamisms. They must be surveyed in every domain, even though they are ordinarily hidden by the constituted qualities and extensities. Embryology shows that the division of the egg is secondary in relation to more significant morphogenetic movements: the augmentation of free surfaces, stretching of cellular layers, invagination by folding, regional displacement of groups. A whole kinematics of the egg appears which implies a dynamic.[3]

So far I have made a case for a nonessentialist realism, but this by itself does not address the question of an open future. Deleuze used at least two lines of argument to defend the idea that the future is not given in the past. The first one is directly related to his theory of individuation or actualization just mentioned, that is, a theory of intensive processes of becoming involving spontaneous spatiotemporal dynamisms or, as I refer to them, processes of self-organization. The simplest self-organizing processes seems to be those involving "endogenously-generated stable states," such as states of minimal energy acting as "attractors" for a process. The spherical form of a soap bubble, for instance, emerges out of the interactions among its constituent molecules as these are constrained energetically to "seek" the point at which surface tension is minimized. In this case, there is no question of an essence of "soap-bubbleness" somehow imposing itself from the outside (hylomorphic schema), an ideal geometric form (a sphere) shaping an inert collection of molecules. Rather, an endogenous topological form (a point in the space of energetic possibilities for this molecular assemblage) governs the collective behavior of the individual soap molecules, and results in the emergence of a spherical shape.

Moreover, one and the same topological form, the same minimal point, can guide the processes that generate many other geometrical forms. For example, if instead of molecules of soap we have the atomic components of an ordinary salt crystal, the form that emerges from minimizing energy (bonding energy in this case) is a cube. In other words, one and the same topological form can guide the morphogenesis of a variety of geometrical forms. A similar point applies to other topological forms that inhabit these spaces of energetic possibilities. For example, these spaces may contain closed loops (technically called "limit cycles" or "periodic attractors"). In this case the several possible physical instantiations of this space will all display isomorphic behavior: an endogenously generated tendency to oscillate in a stable way. Whether one is dealing with a sociotechnological structure (such as a radio transmitter or a radar machine), a biological structure (a cyclic metabolism), or a physical structure (a convection cell in the atmosphere), one and the same immanent resource is involved in their different oscillating behavior.

Deleuze calls this ability of topological forms to give rise to many different physical instantiations a process of "divergent actualization," taking the idea from the French philosopher Henri Bergson, who, at the turn of the century, wrote a series of texts in which he criticized the inability of the science of his time to think of the new, the truly novel. According to Bergson, the first obstacle was a mechanical and linear view of causality and the rigid determinism that it implied. Clearly, if all the future is already given in the past, if the future is merely that modality of time where previously determined possibilities become realized, then true innovation is impossible. To avoid this mistake, he thought, we must struggle to model the future as truly open-ended and the past and the present as pregnant not only with possibilities which become real, but also with virtualities which become actual.

The distinction between the possible and the real assumes a set of predefined forms (or essences) which acquire physical reality as material forms that resemble them. From the morphogenetic point of view, realizing a possibility does not add anything to a predefined form, except reality. The distinction between the virtual and the actual, on the other hand, does not involve resemblance of any kind (e.g., our example above, in which a topological point becomes a geometrical sphere); and far from constituting the essential identity of a form, intensive processes subvert identity, because now forms as different as spheres and cubes emerge from the same topological point. As Deleuze writes, "Actualization breaks with resemblance as a process no less than it does with identity as a principle. In this sense, actualization or differentiation is always a genuine creation."[4]

Deleuze's criticism of nineteenth-century thermodynamics should be understood in this context. By concentrating on the final, extensive form achieved once the intensive process is finished, thermodynamics failed to see that, before the differences in intensity are canceled, the final form (or more exactly, its topological counterpart) is already there, guiding (or acting as an attractor for) the morphogenetic process. In other words, topological attractors have a perfectly real existence, as virtual entities, even before a given geometrical form becomes actual. And this simply emphasizes Deleuze's ontological attitude toward the world: he is a realist not only regarding the actual, but also regarding the virtual.

This realm of virtual entities capable of divergent actualization is only one of the several immanent resources that ensure the openness of the future. I will discuss in a moment other forms of material creativity behind the open-ended evolution of the world, but before doing that I would like to address one aspect of virtual forms of the attractor type that may seem paradoxical in the context of this discussion. One would think that open-endedness is a concept intrinsically opposed to determinism and, hence, that the creative potential of matter derives from a connection with chance. And yet the processes involved in spatiotemporal dynamism governed by attractors are completely deterministic. Hence, we may have to go beyond the simple dichotomy between complete determinism and complete indeterminism and introduce (in Deleuze and Guattari's words) "reverse causalities or advanced determinisms" between these two extremes.[5]

These intermediate forms of determinism, lying between two extremes—complete fatalism based on simple and linear causal relations, and a complete indeterminism in which causality plays no role—arise in physical interactions involving nonlinear causal relations. The most familiar examples of nonlinear causality are causal loops known as "feedback loops," which may involve mutually stabilizing causes, as in the negative feedback process exemplified by the thermostat, or mutually intensifying causes, as in the positive feedback process illustrated by an explosion or a spiraling arms race. These forms of circular causality, in which the effects react back on their causes, in turn, are one condition for the existence of forms of determinism (attractors) that are local and multiple instead of global and unique. (The other condition is a flow of matter-energy moving in and out of the physical process in question.) "Advanced" determinism of this kind may be static (yet multiple and hence local, since a system can switch between alternative destinies) but also dynamic, allowing for simple stable cycles or for complex forms of quasi-periodic behavior, as in deterministic chaos.[6] Thus the fact that attractors come in several types, that they occur in groups, and that each group is capable of divergent actualization, explains away the apparent paradox between some degree of determinism and an essentially open future. On the other hand, it is important to emphasize that these deterministic processes are only one resource that matter and energy have at their disposal.

There is another, less deterministic process that is even more intimately connected with the emergence of novelty keeping the world from closing: the spontaneous formation of "machinic assemblages" of diverse elements. Deleuze and Guattari introduce the notion of "consistency" (or "self-consistency") to designate this morphogenetic process, which generates new structures without homogenizing the components and without submitting them to hierarchical control or, in other words, without imposing on them a hylomorphic model: "Consistency necessarily occurs between heterogeneities, not because it is the birth of a differentiation, but because heterogeneities that were formerly content to coexist or succeed one another become bound up with one another through the "consolidation" of their coexistence or succession. . . . What we term machinic is precisely this synthesis of heterogeneities as such."[7]

Although this remark occurs as part of a discussion of the self-assembly of animal territories, it would be a mistake to think that machinic assemblages (or "meshworks" as I call them) occur only in animals whose behavior is highly "decoded," that is, not rigidly programmed by their genes. To be sure, a flexible behavioral repertoire does increase the ability of particular creatures to enter into complex combinations with heterogeneous elements in their environment (life does involve a gain in consistency, or a "surplus value of destratification"[8]), but meshworks can be formed at all levels of reality, including in inorganic materials, as the following passage illustrates:

> [W]hat metal and metallurgy bring to light is a life proper to matter, a vital state of matter as such, a material vitalism that doubtless exists everywhere but is ordinarily hidden or covered, rendered unrecognizable, dissociated by the hylomorphic model. Metallurgy is the consciousness or thought of the matter-flow, and metal the correlate of this consciousness. As expressed in panmetallism, metal is coextensive to the whole of matter, and the whole of matter to metallurgy. Even the waters, the grasses and varieties of wood, the animals are populated by salts or mineral elements. Not everything is metal, but metal is everywhere. . . . The machinic phylum is metallurgical, or at least has a metallic head, as its itinerant probehead or guidance device.[9]

Deleuze and Guattari argue that the hylomorphic model is totally alien to the history of technology up to the nineteenth-century, particularly to that ancient branch known as metallurgy. For the blacksmith, "it is not a question of imposing a form upon matter but of elaborating an increasingly rich and consistent material, the better to tap increasingly intense forces."[10] In other words, the blacksmith treats metals as active materials, pregnant with morphogenetic capabilities, and his role is that of teasing a form out of them, of guiding, through a series of processes (heating, annealing, quenching, hammering), the emergence of a form, a form in which the materials themselves have a say. His task is less realizing previously defined possibilities than actualizing virtualities along divergent lines. But, again, it would be a mistake to think that the relevance of metals for the question of innovation is solely due to human intervention.

To see this we need to explain an obscure phrase in the passage above. What does it mean to say that "the machinic phylum has a metallic probehead"? The key idea here is to think of metals as being the most powerful catalysts on the planet. (The only exception is organic enzymes, but these have been evolved to achieve that potency.) A catalyst is a substance capable of accelerating or decelerating a chemical reaction, without itself being changed in the process. That is, a catalyst intervenes in reality, recognizes specific targets, triggers effects, causes encounters that would not have taken place without it, and yet it is not consumed or permanently changed in these interactions, so that it can go on triggering effects elsewhere. We can imagine our planet, before living creatures appeared on its surface, as populated by metallic particles which catalyzed reactions as they flowed through the Earth, in a sense allowing the planet to "explore" a space of possible chemical combinations, that is, allowing the planet to blindly grope its way around this space, eventually stumbling upon proto–living creatures, which, as many scientists now agree, were probably autocatalytic loops of materials, that is, proto-metabolisms.[11]

A crucial question regarding open-ended evolution is the nature of these "spaces of chemical (or biological, or social) combinations." It is becoming increasingly clear that a crucial ingredient for the emergence of innovation at any level of reality is the "combinatorial productivity" of the elements at the respective sublevel, that is, at the level of the components of the structures in question. Not all components have the same "productivity." For example, elementary particles have a relatively low productivity, yielding only ninety-two possible atoms on this planet, although we can artificially stabilize a few more transuranic elements, beginning with plutonium in World War II. However, when we move to the next higher level, the assembly of molecules from atoms, the number of combinations becomes immense, essentially unsurveyable. Similarly, the number of cell types on Earth (e.g., nerve, muscle, bone) is relatively small—a couple of hundred—but the number of organisms that may be built combinatorially from these elements is, again, immense. As the physicist George Kampis has remarked, "The notion of immensity translates as irreducible variety of the component-types. . . . This kind of immensity is an immediately complexity-related property, for it is about variety and heterogeneity, and not simply numerousness."[12]

The point here is that a key ingredient for combinatorial richness, and hence for an essentially open future, is heterogeneity of components. Another key element is processes that allow heterogeneous elements to come together, that is, processes that allow the articulation of the diverse as such. Here we can take a clue from another passage in Deleuze and Guattari's *A Thousand Plateaus*:

> It is no longer a question of imposing a form upon matter but of elaborating an increasingly rich and consistent material, the better to tap increasingly intense forces. What makes a material increasingly rich is the same as what holds heterogeneities together without their ceasing to be heterogeneous. What holds them together in this way [is] intercalary oscillations, synthesizers with at least two heads.[13]

Meshworks combine heterogeneous elements by using their functional complementarities. For example, an ecosystem brings together a large variety of distinct species, interlocking them into food webs through alimentary complementarities: parasite-host, predator-prey, and others. But often these heterogeneities do not mesh well, and special intercalary elements are needed to effect the link, such as symbiotic microorganisms lining the gut of animals, allowing them to digest their food. Or, to take a different example, precapitalist marketplaces were meshworks that interconnected buyers and sellers through complementary demands. Barter could indeed effect this meshing, but a chance encounter between two people with exactly matching demands was very rare. In this circumstance money (even primitive money such as cowrie shells or salt blocks) could act as an intercalary element allowing complementary demands to find each other at a distance, so to speak.

Thus there are two questions that connect the theory of meshworks or machinic assemblages to the theme of an open-ended future. One question is the existence of special combinatorial spaces that are more open than others (for example, the space defined by carbon, an element that, thanks to its ability to bond in several ways with itself, has a much higher combinatorial productivity than any other element). The other question is the existence of special intercalary entities that open up possibilities by allowing heterogeneities to mesh with each other (for example, metallic catalysts which insert themselves between two poorly meshing chemical substances, recognizing them with a lock-and-key mechanism, to facilitate their interaction). Philosophically, these two questions boil down to one, the singular nature of either carbon or metallic catalysts (to stick to examples from chemistry). Deleuze tackles this issue in a way that parallels his approach to attractors. As I said above, he proposes to get rid of the distinction between the possible and the real, keeping only the latter but distinguishing in the real between the virtual and the actual. Similarly, he suggests that we get rid of the dichotomy between the essential and the accidental, affirming that everything is accidental, but distinguishing in the latter between the ordinary and the singular (or the special, the remarkable, the important). As he writes:

> It will be said that the essence is by nature the most "important" thing. This, however, is precisely what is at issue: whether notions of importance and non-importance are not precisely notions which concern events or accidents, and are much more "important" within accidents than the crude opposition between essence and accident itself. The problem of thought is tied not to essences but to the evaluation of what is important and what is not, to the distribution of the singular and regular, distinctive and ordinary points, which takes place entirely within the unessential or within the description of a multiplicity, in relation to the ideal events that constitute the conditions of a problem.[14]

It hardly needs to be added that, as a realist philosopher, Deleuze sees the distributions of the singular and the ordinary as perfectly objective, the world itself exhibiting traits that are more or less important or remarkable regardless of whether there is a human being to carry on these evaluations. Carbon and metallic catalysts are objectively unique in this sense, and so are the topological forms we discussed above, which Deleuze refers to as "singularities." Attractors are indeed remarkable (states that minimize free energy, for instance, are rare and unique), as are the bifurcations that change one set of attractors into another, such as the special points in intensity (temperature) at which water changes from liquid to solid or from liquid to gas. Yet, as the passage quoted above illustrates, there is a close relation between these objective distributions and the nature of human knowledge (the "problem of thought"). I would like to conclude this essay with a few remarks on Deleuze's special approach to epistemology (an epistemology of problems), an approach that further distinguishes his thought from older forms of realism that are too closely linked to rationalism.

Instead of rejecting the dichotomy between true and false, thus plunging into a form of relativism, Deleuze extends it so that it applies not only to answers to questions but also to the questions themselves. That is, he makes "truth" a predicate that applies primarily to problems and only derivatively to their solutions. Yet problems for him are not a human creation (and problem solving a human activity) but possess their own objective reality. As he puts it, the concept of the "problematic" does not mean only a particularly important species of subjective acts, but "a dimension of objectivity as such that is occupied by these acts."[15] Problems exist in reality defined by singularities; hence problem solving is an activity in which all kinds of material assemblages may engage. To illustrate with examples we have already used, a population of interacting physical entities, such as the molecules in a thin layer of soap, may be constrained energetically to adopt a form that minimizes free energy. Here the "problem" (for the population of molecules) is to find this minimal point of energy, and this problem is solved differently by the molecules in soap bubbles (which collectively minimize surface tension) and by the molecules in crystalline structures (which collectively minimize bonding energy).

Given this objectivity of problems and their conditions, what may be peculiarly human is not solving problems but posing problems, an activity that involves distinguishing in reality the distributions of the special and the ordinary, and grasping the objective problems that these distributions condition. Chapter 4 of *Difference and Repetition* is a philosophical meditation on differential and integral calculus (a mathematical tool at the heart of all modern physics) viewed precisely as a "technology" for framing true problems. But as the above remarks on metallurgy suggest, Deleuze does not think of representations (even mathematical ones) as the only, or even the most important, means of posing problems. Any kind of learning, even physical, sensual learning, involves an engagement with material assemblages that embody problems and their defining singularities. As he writes:

> For learning evolves entirely in the comprehension of problems as such, in the apprehension and condensation of singularities, and in the composition of ideal events and bodies. Learning to swim or learning a foreign language means composing the singular points of one's own body or one's own language with those of another shape or element which tears us apart but also propels us into a hitherto unknown and unheard-of world of problems.[16]

Clearly, these few remarks cannot do justice to Deleuze's complex theory of the problematic. I introduce them here simply to draw one connection between human knowledge and the open-ended evolution of the world. The latter depends, as I said, on divergent actualization, combinatorial productivity, and the synthesis of novel structures out of heterogeneous components. These define the essentially problematic structure of the world. It follows that truth cannot be a correspondence relation between representations and a static, fixed set of beings; truth is rather an open-ended relation of isomorphism between problems as actualized in reality and problems as actualized in our bodies and minds.

To conclude, unlike social constructivism, which achieves openness by making the world depend on human interpretation, Deleuze's approach achieves it by making the world into a creative, complexifying, problematizing cauldron of becoming. Because of their anthropocentrism, constructivist philosophies remain prisoners of what Foucault called the "episteme of man," while Deleuze plunges ahead into a posthumanist future, in which the world has been enriched by a multiplicity of nonhuman agencies, of which metallic catalysts, and their acts of recognition and intervention, are only one example. And, in contrast with other realist or materialist philosophies of the past (such as Engels's dialectics of nature), the key nonhuman agency in Deleuzian philosophy has nothing to do with the negative, with oppositions or contradictions; it has to do with pure, productive, positive difference. Ultimately, this positive difference, and its affirmation in thought, ensures the openness of the world.

3

DIAGRAM AND DIAGNOSIS

John Rajchman

THE TIME OF THE QUESTION

I suspect that Elizabeth Grosz's theme of "becomings" or "futures unthought" is itself a timely one—which is to say, for already settled minds,
an untimely one. I'd like to examine one reason why. It concerns politics,
or what may be called the "time of politics" and the relations politics has
had and may yet have with critical philosophy. As with all genuine questions, there is a problem of formulation. What in fact is politics or "the political"? What is the place in politics of "other futures" or of "becomings,"
and the kind of philosophy that thinks in terms of them? And do we all
have the same answers to these questions today as twenty-years ago—or
fifty years ago? I am not sure. But what makes the question puzzling also
makes it timely or untimely—a question posed to us about us today.

I'll proceed, then, in a tentative, schematic way, as if jotting down notes
toward a formulation of the problem of the "time of the political"—and
hence of the invention and reinvention of politics. One way the question is
raised today is in terms of the invention and reinvention of democracy, and
the dramatic processes of democratization of the last ten or fifteen years.
What is the "time" of democracy? What is its relation with its "frontiers"

or "borders," its geographies and points of fragility or transformation?[1] For democracy is perhaps not a single completed thing, for which the great European or American nation-states supply the model. It may itself be more strange than we suppose, capable of "becomings" in fresh circumstances in relation to new questions. I'd therefore like to approach it from an unaccustomed angle, starting from the two words of my title—*diagram* and *diagnosis*—as they figure in the work of perhaps the most radical philosopher of "becomings" in our time, the late Gilles Deleuze. My two words match with two terms in a collection of short late essays by Deleuze—*critique* and *clinique*—in which the theme of "becomings" is taken up again; but these terms are in fact found throughout his work. *Diagram,* for example, is used in one way in relation to Foucault, but in another way for Francis Bacon.

But what exactly does "diagram and diagnosis" have to do with politics—or with the time of, the reinvention of, the political? There may be as much disagreement over that as over the nature of the political in the first place. Nevertheless I think it touches on a powerful line that runs through Deleuze's work, which may yet contain secrets for us today, captured in this phrase from the 1970s: "another politics, another time, another individuation."[2]

Let me begin with some conjectures, put in a somewhat stark or brutal way, which might serve to frame the question. We might contrast the notion of "diagram-diagnosis" with other views of time in politics or in critical politics—as when, for example, the future is understood as something we might program or project, something we might know or foresee by prediction or prophesy. To diagram the future is thus not to program it or project it. It belongs to a "critical moment" of another and original kind. It is not seen or involved with taking action in the same way as with prophesy or prediction—it supposes another art of seeing and acting, which Deleuze would explore in one way in his study of how, with the emergence of time-images rather than movement-images in cinema, starting in neorealism there would arise the problem of making visible something unseen and intolerable.[3]

This brings me to my first stark conjecture. For us, the problem of the "reinvention of politics" or "time of politics" arises *after Marxism*, even if it is already posed by Marx and in Marx. With this "after" has been associated a kind of desolidarization and depoliticization, seen in many ways, now rather familiar, even overfamiliar—the sad, stale "ironies" of the postmodern, the lament for avant-gardes and the utopias that motivated them, the various "deaths" of art, and so forth. It is striking that Deleuze was never attracted to such melancholy themes, as though he saw in them only a failure of the imagination translated into nostalgia or cynicism. Repentance, bad conscience, autocritique were quite foreign to his thought; it was, rather, always a matter of inventing new styles of thinking, according to a new image of what it is to think and see critically. This new image is formulated early on his work, and then, running through his studies of Spinoza and Nietzsche, is followed up after 1968, with his actual political activities—for example, his participation with Foucault in G.I.P.

This leads to a second, more controversial conjecture: The problem of the "time of the political" in postwar French philosophy, or among Deleuze's contemporaries, is tied up with the complex destiny of Marxism, in which we see an erosion of the relationship between programs and ideology or theory and organization. Thus there would be Sartre's "project," Althusser's "conjuncture," and the complicated case of Foucault's "nominalist history." Indeed, when Deleuze called Foucault first a "new archivist" and then a "new cartographer" in the city, it was in part this problem of the "time of the political" that he had in mind: Foucault, as it were, was a man with a diagram and a diagnosis rather than a program and an ideology or critique, someone who tried to see history as the "negative conditions" of active, untimely experimentation. We might think of Deleuze's own attitude to Marx in this light, as somewhat different from the increasingly negative view of Marxism Foucault would develop. How, Deleuze asked, might we start up again in new ways the political analysis of capitalism that Marx began, in relation to new conditions Marx could not foresee, given by our globalizing information societies. How, with respect to them, might we introduce this other sense of the time of critical diagnosis or diagram which Foucault had earlier helped to introduce as archivist and cartographer?[4]

This brings me to a third point. If Deleuze was the most radical contemporary philosopher of "becomings" or "other futures," it is perhaps for two connected reasons. First, he was among those philosophers who introduced the problem into our very idea of what it is to think or think philosophically. It is by reference to the peculiar time "to come" of other futures or becomings that philosophy becomes the peculiar sort of activity that it is—different from science, art, or religion, and hence from political science, art, or religion. In all his writings he tried to work out the nature of this "time that takes thought," its differences from the time of wisdom or knowledge, its peculiar relations with time in the arts, or in the artwork.

Perhaps he was not alone in this; and indeed the problem owed something to others whom it was not intended to preclude. Yet—and this is the second point—he managed to pose the problem of the time to come, the time of becomings and other futures, in a pragmatic, even empiricist way. In this there is something quite original, something he shared with Foucault, who, starting with his thesis, was concerned with what Kant had called the "pragmatic point of view." Thus in Deleuze's concept of the "time that takes thought," we find nothing like a patience in the Black Forest, awaiting a God to save us from technology; and we find nothing like a "mystical authority of the Law"—not even in his discussion of Kafka and Kafka's "minority."

One of the most sustained discussions of the theme comes in the chapter on repetition in *Difference and Repetition*, where the problem is put in terms of three different kinds of "syntheses of time." Deleuze tries to sketch a synthesis, different from the unities of habit or memory, from causal succession or conscious memory, in which the past becomes indeterminate, the present untimely and experimental, and the future unknown, unforeseen, unthought. He finds a poetic formula for this synthesis in Hamlet's phrase "the time is out of joint"; and he asks what it would mean to introduce this out-of-joint time into very idea of revolution formulated by Marx. In these pages, written thirty years ago, just before 1968, Deleuze sees Hamlet not as the hero of doubt or skeptic, but rather as the first one to move in this other time, which divides him from himself and exposes him to other possibilities. Unlike Walter Benjamin's view of the *Trauerspiel* and its relation to ancient tragedy, Hamlet is a hero who moves in time—which is no longer that of Oedipus, whose destiny is tied to the law of the city, and not being able to know it. Hamlet is thus not a messianic mystic or protomystic; rather, the time "to come" has become a "pragmatic" matter, a matter of acting and seeing in the city, freed from any need for mysticism or spiritualism. On the contrary, with respect to religious thinkers like Kierkegaard and Pascal, it becomes a matter of shifting the whole question of "belief in the future, of the future" into belief in this world, through an original operation which Deleuze calls an "empiricist conversion." In this respect, in posing the question of a time "to come," I think Deleuze is in fact closer to Althusser's sense of the time of "conjuncture" and the "religious" (if not Catholic) structure of ideology than to the sort of "messianicity" Scholem helped introduce into the hopes and disappointments of Benjamin or Adorno. The problem of the time "to come," then, becomes a "pragmatic" problem of how to act to make repetition a feature of the future—a worldly matter of action and friendship requiring no "mystical authorization." Rather as with William James's sense not of things but of "things in the making," it is a matter of freeing our sense of time or the future from any salvationism—from judgment or judgment day—and making it a matter of trust in the world.[5] Thus it fits with a philosophical lineage that takes off from Kant and goes on to Bergson and Nietzsche—a "pragmatic" rather than a "mystical" lineage where the question of becomings or other futures becomes a question of novelty and singularity, of what we can't yet see or think in what is happening to us, of new forces which we must nevertheless diagram and diagnose.[6]

This leads me to one more remark before I proceed. *Pragmatism* is now the name given to thought that eschews the *ideology-program* characteristic of Marxism (among other philosophies), and sees the future more as piecemeal and experimental. And yet in one sense that is a strange fate for the whole side of James and Peirce, elaborated in Whitehead, concerned precisely with the problem of novelty—a side we might rather read today in terms of the question of "other futures" or "becomings," or of the time to come. The result would be something rather different from the nostalgic "neopragmatism" of Richard Rorty. In particular, it suggests a "time of the political" which, while pragmatist and nonsalvationist, is not, and cannot be, a time of consensus or communication any more than it is the time of a party or a state. I'll return to this point later.

With all this in mind, let me then turn to the problem of "diagram and diagnosis" and its relation to politics, or the time of the political. I'd like to focus on questions that arise from Deleuze's actual participation in politics following 1968. The first question is how to understand what Foucault was doing when he offered his diagram and diagnosis of the "disciplinary society"; the second concerns the problem of "minority" Deleuze formulated in his work with Felix Guattari. In both cases we find a departure from the "national state"—or what Foucault called the "welfare-warfare" state.

FOUCAULT

Foucault's book *Discipline and Punish* may be read in relation to my hypothesis about the "time of the political" in the Marxist climate of postwar French philosophy—the way it is tied up with undoing the relationship between philosophy and the party or the state, leading to the "reinvention of the political." For Foucault conceived of his work as a "history of the present" that exposed workings of "power" irreducible to any party or state, requiring another kind of philosophical activity: posing questions *to* politics, or *to* governments, which were not yet part *of* them. That was part of the whole idea of G.I.P., and its publication *The Intolerable*.

A "history of the present" is a history of the portion of the past that we don't see is still with us. Thus it involves a concept of historical time that is not linear and is not completely given to consciousness, memory, commemoration. But Deleuze thought it involved something more—a relation to the future. He would put in this way: "Not to predict, but to be attentive to the unknown that is knocking at the door." It was this relation to the future that made the "present," whose history Foucault proposed, something untimely, creative, experimental. That is what made Foucault a new cartographer, a new archivist in the city, a man with a diagram rather than a program or a project—this belief in other futures, virtual futures, at once real and to be invented.

Deleuze thus draws attention to the passage in *Discipline and Punish* where Foucault speaks of the panopticon as a "diagram of power brought to its ideal form." By *diagram*, Deleuze thought Foucault had something rather original in mind—something Deleuze would call an "abstract machine." It was a diagram of something at work in many different institutions and situations, spread out in several countries, working in a manner not given in the map of social policies and prescriptions, planned as such by no one. Basic to it was a problem deriving from demography: what to do about the "accumulation of men." In effect, discipline was a diffuse set of techniques—a "machine"—enabling one to "individualize a population" by dividing up the space and time of its activities, as with prison cells and uniforms. This was shown in a remarkable variety of situations—in the differentiation of domestic space and or the emergence of "worker cities," for example.

What was Foucault doing in proposing such a "diagram" of this "machine"? What relation does it have to the "history of the present"? Deleuze stresses that the "disciplinary society" of which Foucault was offering a diagram was not completely disciplined—rather, unlike other societies, it had this abstract machine at work within it. To point was to establish it, to see it by means of painstaking archival research. The question might then be put in this form: What does it mean to establish an "archive" through which we come to see that it is natural that "prisons resemble factories, schools, barracks, hospitals, which all resemble prisons"? How was a "discursive field" thus created in which it came to be taken for granted that prisons are supposed to rehabilitate rather than specify a criminal population? In answer to this question, Deleuze turns to some passages about the nature of the "archive" from Foucault's earlier methodological work, *The Archeology of Knowledge*, where, in the terminology of the day, Foucault says this:

> To describe the archive is to set out its possibilities . . . on the basis of discourses which have just recently ceased to be our own. . . . In this sense it becomes valid as a diagnostic for us. This is not because it makes it possible for us to paint a picture of our distinctive traits and to sketch in advance what we will look like in the future. But it deprives us of our continuities; it dissolves this temporal identity in which we like to look at ourselves. . . . Understood in this way, the diagnostic does not establish the fact of our identity by means of the interplay of distinctions. It establishes that we are difference. . . .[7]

We thus have the idea of diagnosis. It comes at those times when we are in the process of becoming something other, we know not yet what. Applied to the "diagram" of discipline in *Discipline and Punish*, what this means is that discipline is a formation that has "just recently ceased to be our own," which thus "separates us from what we can no longer see." In other words, ours is a time characterized by an inability of disciplines to deal with the formation and deformations of society. We start to see that the great "abstract machine" of discipline no longer seems to be working well; and yet since it is so much a part of the way we see and think of things, we don't yet know what to do. In Deleuze's own work, this diagnosis is connected to another.

The "forces of the future," which help bring about this state of affairs belong to what, in "global information societies"—or "societies of control"—has served to displace, for example, the centrality of the question of factories and factory discipline. The question becomes how to see what is being brought by these new forces.

In setting down his diagram of the "disciplinary society," Foucault was thus offering a kind of shock and stimulant to the imagination, and the kind of thinking concerned with what is as yet unthought; he was pointing to the question of what comes "after" disciplines; such was his "diagnosis." Not everyone saw it that way, of course. And Foucault himself? It is true that in some writings at the time of the publication of his book, Foucault also was talking about the "crisis" in disciplines, and the new questions it opened up. But I think that shortly after this Foucault underwent a sort of crisis of his own, which led him to raise the question of the "reinvention of the political" in relation to another formation, another "diagram." One might call it the crisis of the "biopolitical" state, or what Foucault would call the "welfare-warfare" state. He came to think that the "failure of political theories nowadays," the depoliticizing effects of these theories, came from not understanding the nature and role of that state "in the present."

Foucault became interested in another kind of "political" problem: population regarded as a statistical entity, linked to territory and resources, that would become the object of a new kind of knowledge— the administration of states. This was a new kind of entity, different from a people or a public, linked to modern racism, leading to the "biopolitical state," the welfare-warfare state, the state of mass social security and insurance and mass mobilization. It would lead to what might be called a "national-social" form of the state. Our problem, in effect, was a crisis in that form, that kind of "political rationality"; we are departing from it, without yet knowing what else we might invent. And it is in this context that we might see the problem Deleuze formulated of *minority*—minor literature, minor politics.

In it we may see Deleuze's own approach to the question of the reinvention of the "time" of the political; for a minority is never a given identity; it is always a becoming, a becoming-other.

In particular, we may read Deleuze's basic "diagnosis" at this time, some twenty years ago. "What characterizes our situation," he declared in 1976, "is a crisis in that great invention of nineteenth-century imperial Europe—the nation-state form—as can be seen not only in relation to the formation of integrated markets, cities, and the flow of financial capital, but also in relation to demography, domestic populations and new patterns of immigration."[8]

One of the basic question it raises is thus the question of minority.

MINORITY

A basic "danger" we face, a basic problem with which we are confronted, comes from a crisis in the nation-state form, whose "borders" would be "overdetermined" first by colonialism, then by the cold war. So thought

Deleuze. The danger was not so much national-state control, but rather the new conditions under it was no longer able to operate, leading to questions that don't fit on its map of political options and legitimizations. Today this may seem a rather familiar idea. We are told that the old left-right divisions have now been replaced by concerns about how much of the welfare state we should preserve while best allowing for competition in global markets. Foucault's idea that there was a crisis in the "biopolitical" state might find one application here—we see problems of poverty and racism that are no longer "rationalized" or "politicized" in relation to that form, giving rise to new kinds of violence within and without. They already match up with the depoliticization or desolidarization of the enthusiasms of the 1960s, captured in youth culture by the punk cry in Thatcherite Britain: "There is no future and we are living in it."

It is in this context that we may see Deleuze's formulation of the question of minority and minor politics. Minor politics is not the same thing as minority politics—which is often a politics of recognition, relying on or assuming the model of the national state. Minor politics has another sense of time, of the future, of the vitality of the future. That is why it belongs to Deleuze's search for a new "nonprogrammatic" role of philosophy that is yet "resistant to the present" or "critical." If we look at the theme of "minority" in Deleuze from this angle, we may discern three interrelated problems.

1. The problem of minority is the problem of a concept of "people" outside the nation-state form, and therefore, for example, outside what in Kant's idea of the "cosmopolitan" still presupposes it. We need a view of the "peoples" we are, not modeled in a fictive ethnicity, supplied with a language and a land. And that is what Deleuze saw in Kafka's appeal to a "people to come," a missing people. It is what kept Kafka from being a Zionist or a socialist, what made him prefer instead to try to diagnose the diabolic forces knocking at the door. The impossibility of finding such a people anywhere formed the paradoxical necessity of his writing, and the problems it raised: inventing a foreign or "minor" language within the languages supposed to secure the identities of national peoples; exposing other geographies not discernible within the borders, internal or external, of the "imagined communities" that nations were supposed to be—another time, another geography, another politics. This "people" presupposed another concept of territory, and what it is to be a "native" of a territory, which has a philosophical side that Deleuze tried to develop. It says that in some sense we are all potentially from a strange 'nowhere' prior to "ter-

ritorial" definitions, for which "utopia" has been a somewhat misleading name, since in some sense we all have our "minorities," our "becomings" that take us from the "lands" of our determinations.

Nevertheless, the question often arises in relation to problems that come from population or demography. It comes from circumstances that place people in situations where, in relation to themselves and one another, they are no longer able to tell straight narratives about their "origins." Then they become "originals" without origins; their narratives become "out of joint," constructed through superposition or juxtaposition rather than through development or progress, in the manner of the "third worlds" which Deleuze thinks came to interrupt the political assumptions of more progressive narratives in cinema. It is this other kind of "synthesis of time," complicating our sense of "time," that shows a minority to be a "future people," a "virtual people," a "people to come." In particular, Deleuze thought that this should complicate the idea of "class." It poses another kind of problem—the undefined "multiple peoples" we already are, which can't be fitted into any recognizable or nameable class or stratum, rather as with the role of the proletariat in Marx. That is why it requires another kind of intelligence or thinking, which works to complicate what are given as official classes or strata. Instead of a party through which class contradictions are seen and overcome, we have the problem of "other spaces, other times," and the ways they serve to "diagram" other ways of being and being together, posing questions, in turn, to politics. That is the second problem.

2. A minority is always somewhere a "people to come"—our minorities are those "future peoples" we might yet become. But we are thus "peoples" in a very different sense from what modern political thought calls "*the* people." A minority is rather *a* people, an indefinite people, a people not completely defined or determined. It thus has a very different relation to the whole question of representation, and in particular political representation, from what is known as "the people." It can't be found in the public-private distinctions built up on the concept of political representation. In this way "a people" or a "people to come" serves to expose what Foucault came to think of as a basic difficulty or limitation in modern political thought—the distinction between state and society, the attempt to base the first in the proper arrangements of the second. It raises another kind of question: the relation of the "undoing" of civil society or its determinations, and what is yet possible to think and to see politically. And it is just in this sense that its "to come" acquires the political sense of

an original kind, which can be seen in the formula Deleuze comes up with in a dialogue with Foucault: the "indignity of speaking for others." This might be a motto for the kind of politics concerned with what can't yet be "represented" politically—questions posed to politics which are not yet of politics, or which are raised at its borders, at the limits of what counts or is acceptable as political, in particular the borders of modern democratic politics. And that brings me to a third point.

3. De jure and de facto, modern democracy is in most cases "national-state democracy," some form of "welfare-warfare" state. The crisis of the "nation-state" form thus leads to new questions about the very idea of democracy, seen, for example, in attempts to develop notions of "citizenship" that extend beyond it.

Thus it departs from the model descended from Kant, which matches a *Rechstaat* with an enlightened public sphere kept "rational" by philosophy professors. In this regard, one may read Deleuze's remarks about a "becoming democratic" that no longer conforms to this model, or complicates it, taking it in new directions.[9] In particular, he seems to have in mind the question of what it would mean to introduce into the concept of democracy the as yet unrepresentable "time" of minority, and so oblige it to experiment with its own concept. What would it mean to introduce this "city to come," which is that of our singularities, our "originalities" without origins, into our idea of what a democracy can yet be? Such, at any rate, is the problem Deleuze formulates in relation to Herman Melville as the problem of democratic "dignity."[10] In at least these three ways the problem of minority Deleuze tried to formulate, together with Guattari, may be seen as part of an attempt to "reinvent the political," to construct a new role for theory no longer based on project or program, yet resistant to the present, stimulating the imagination of other futures. But how might one practice such a political art of "becomings" today, at a time of consensus and communication which some are fond of calling "post political" or "posthistorical"? I'll end with some remarks about that.

COMMUNICATION

Let me come back to the "time" of the question of politics, or of reinventing politics. What is its relation to themes or "consensus" or "communication" in contemporary philosophy? It is here that I think we see Deleuze's "pragmatism," his "empiricism." It leads him to an original diagnosis of the problem, which he inserts in a discussion about politics with

Toni Negri, when he declares that what we have lost, what we need most, is "belief in the world"—belief not in another world, but in other futures in this one—in other words, the futures we diagram and diagnose. Or, as he puts it elsewhere, in relation to our newfound "pieties" in politics, we need a good "empiricist conversion."[11] I have three short remarks about what Deleuze may be thought to have meant by this.

1. First, what is meant by "pragmatism" in this instance—as when, for example, Deleuze calls Foucault a "pragmatist of the multiple"? I think we can point out some contrasts with two other contemporary pragmatists: Deng Xiaoping and Richard Rorty.

We know that, against Mao, Deng urged that "practice is the only criterion of truth"—this is thought to be his great virtue. And yet this pronouncement retains the status of a party directive, like, "It is glorious to get rich." Thus it has translated into what some have diagnosed (in parallel to "socialist realism") as "market realism." Deleuze's pragmatism is very different. It has to do instead with a "diagrammatic" or "cartographic" intelligence that supposes a "time of thought" incompatible with the wisdom of any such party directive—one that, on the contrary, might be directed to what is new or troubling about the conditions of the "market realism" that has come from it.

Such an intelligence also contrasts with Rorty's ironic embrace of, his peculiar patriotic solidarity with, the New Deal welfare state. Deleuze finds another lineage in the classical pragmatist authors, tied up with the literary theme of "being without qualities," for Melville of "democratic dignity," found in other writers, like Kafka or Beckett or Musil. It involves a "time" and "geography" quite different from nationalism or cosmopolitanism, connected politically to what Thoreau called "civil disobedience," later to be taken up by Gandhi and Martin Luther King. We might then diagnose in Rorty's "neopragmatism" a certain nostalgia, which matches a failure of the imagination. Everything is thrown back into "consensus" or "solidarity" with an earlier time, an earlier state. Rorty is a Dewey-nostalgia that follows upon a loss of solidarity that came from the political enthusiasms of the 1960s—back to the New Deal and its "theory of justice," no more questions deriving from the crisis in its form, no more disobedience, even such as happened with, and following, King. Thus it is no accident that when Rorty asks about the relation of philosophy to the future, he longs for a "horizon," which he finds back in the 1930s.[12] What is involved in the "pragmatism of new forces" which Deleuze saw in Foucault is of course quite different, less easy than agreeing with some existing program—it supposes a link between the untimely and the experimental rather than between a horizon and the agreements or assent it allows.

2. This brings me to my second remark. Rorty's nostalgia seems to me to translate into a larger nostalgia, a larger failure to imagine other possibilities in the face of the new questions about information, globalization, and demography—as, for example, in the movement back to civil society. We need a critical history to save us from such nostalgia, while yet refusing the progressivism through which it has been promoted. What I have been trying to develop with the theme of diagram and diagnosis, then, may be seen as requiring us to pay closer attention to the precise nature of the conditions with which it confronts us. I think we need to set aside the familiar picture of a "global village," everywhere the same, and open our eyes to the strange worlds of "becomings" that are in fact emerging today, in different ways from what might be expected from the forms nineteenth-century imperial Europe devised to describe its own modernization or formulate its own "discourse on modernity." More than ever we thus need the kind of "cartography" that is "clinical" in Deleuze's sense—that is, diagnostic of other possibilities. In other words, we need again to "believe in the world" and the "time" of the reinvention of the political.

3. This brings me to my last remark. Deleuze spoke of "philosophical negotiations," using the words more in a military-diplomatic than a commercial sense. He came to think of his philosophy as akin to carrying on a sort of conceptual guerrilla war with powers at once within and without, leading to negotiations that go on so long one is no longer sure whether they belong to war or peace. Among such powers, for example, he counted television, analyzed by Serge Daney in relation to cinema, and new kind of debility it brings with it, the new geographies it creates. But of course conditions of war and peace have themselves altered since the time when it was thought they might be contained in the European nation-state form, or matching international bodies, in the erosion of which Deleuze diagnosed new dangers that now confront us. Is it a matter of creating a kind of global "public sphere" or instituting a sort of global "police"? Or do we need to attack the problem from the standpoint of global "minorities"—that is, in terms of those multiple peoples yet lacking or missing, yet existing virtually in and among us, those peoples tied up with the "time that takes thought," or with a belief in the future, of the future, who let us experiment with ourselves, and so see ourselves as an experiment—and *not* a contract, *not* a consensus?

That, I think, remains a timely, and so untimely, political question today.

4

BECOMING AN
EPISTEMOLOGIST

Linda Martín Alcoff

Is an epistemology based on becoming rather than being a conceptual impossibility? For some philosophers, resistance to "becoming an epistemologist" depends on the answer to this question. Epistemology as an enterprise is generally founded on the belief that one can establish clear criteria and reliable procedures for the justification of knowledge, or true belief. Moreover, truth itself is grounded in an ontological picture of "man's" relationship to the world as a thing over and apart, separated from human practices of knowing and interpretation as if across an abyss or a chasm. Claims of knowledge are conceptualized as linguistic items positioned on one side of the divide, and as successful to the extent that they correspond with a bit of reality or a discrete event on the other side. This picture is presupposed in currently dominant concepts of objectivity, truth, and what can count as a valid justificatory practice. Catherine Elgin has recently argued that this package of presuppositions constitutes a "bipolar disorder [that] incapacitates philosophy."[1] It presents impossibly stark alternatives: "Unless answers to philosophical questions are absolute, they are arbitrary. Unless a position is grounded in agent-neutral, determinate facts, it is right only relative to a perspective that cannot in the end be justified."[2] In other words, epistemic justification can only be absolute if the reasons given for a claim are not absolute, and if one were to hold that *no* reasons for *any* claim can be, then those reasons are not epistemic reasons and there is no basis for the epistemological project. Philosophers as diverse as Rorty and Chisholm take this view, from which, however, they draw opposite conclusions.

There are two aspects of this picture that might be said to involve being rather than becoming: (1) The ontological relation between knower and known is impermeable, stable, and clearly delineated. That is, we can know with clarity and distinctness that which is given or contributed by the knower and that which is, simply, given. (2) The matter of truth itself is clear-cut; that is, truth is not a matter of degree—there are no qualitative dimensions or degrees of truth—rather, truth is a matter of precise correspondence, admitting of technical procedures of verification such as those described in the following definition given by Michael Devitt: "Sentences of type x are true or false in virtue of: (1) their structure; (2) the referential relations between their parts and reality; (3) the objective and mind-independent nature of that reality."[3]

Many problems have been noted with such correspondence formulations: they both invite and even entail a devolution to skepticism by specifying an operation of correspondence which cannot, by definition, be procedurally verified or even performed, since one cannot step outside, as it were, to "check" the correspondence between a proposition and a bit of objective reality; the concept of correspondence is itself notoriously elusive of explication; they presuppose a theory of language such that a simple reference relation as might obtain with "cats" and "mats" is attributed universally across the domain of knowledge; they mistakenly reduce all forms of knowing to "knowing that," thus ignoring or repudiating the multitude of other forms human knowledge takes, such as "knowing how," "knowing what is to be done," understanding, and so on, none of which can be adequately formulated on a correspondence model.

But what is principally or most fundamentally wrong with the above formulation of verification is its ontology of truth: its representation of the structure and referential relations between the world and the known. There is no hint of mutually constitutive relations, of the immanence of truth to a lived space inflected by power, and certainly no recognition of the constitutive relations between truth and power. Thus, for many of us, the primary problem with analytic epistemology is not its slide into skepticism but its mistaken ontology. It is not a true characterization of truth.

I believe that this characterization of *truth* operates as the main obstacle for the development of an epistemology of becoming, which would have to accommodate the dynamism of the "real," its active dependence on interaction and interpretation, and the partiality and temporality of all knowing. (These points will be explained more further on.) Many contemporary accounts of *justification,* in contrast with truth, might accommodate the ontological shift from timeless stability to open-ended temporal flux, since they admit that justification is an open concept, a matter of degree, and subject to contextual conditions. Contextualists with regard to justification, such as Keith DeRose, generally understand contexts as spatial or discursive or both (as when the context of a dialogical encounter sets out the relevant standards of justification in a given situation). But this attentiveness to context could easily incorporate the temporal dimension that an ontology of becoming would require. By contrast, the dominant understanding of truth as correspondence to an "objective and mind-independent reality," as in Devitt's formulation above, would resist the implications that an ontology of becoming would surely entail.

My project in this paper, however, is not to persuade analytic epistemologists to reinvent their ontological premises, but to convince others who are inclined toward ontologies of becoming that this inclination need not entail a repudiation of either epistemology or of truth.[4] The latter *has* been assumed by a number of feminist theorists and continental philosophers who are especially concerned with the politics of truth. For those who reject the metaphysics of pure presence, there has been a mostly confused understanding of where that leads (or more correctly, leaves) epistemology. Specifically, the repudiation of the correspondence theory's ontology of truth has led many to hold some combination of the following claims:

(1) Truth is antiontological, or without ontological (or metaphysical) content or implications (a position shared between many Derrideans and Tarskian-influenced deflationary theorists of truth in analytic epistemology).
(2) Truth is collapsible to power;
(3) There is no distinction between "true" and "passing for true."
(4) Thus there is no evaluative distinction that is uniquely *epistemological* to be made between claims.

As a contribution toward defeating these four claims, this paper has two parts. In the first part, I will offer a critique of, especially, claims (2) and

(3) by criticizing two recent proponents of these views, Wendy Brown and Barry Allen, respectively. However, the status of claims (2) and (3) will be seen to bear heavily on claims (1) and (4), and thus I hope to dislodge the plausibility of those claims as well. In the second part of the paper, I will offer a more positive contribution toward reconstructing an account of truth based on an ontology of becoming, primarily through the use of Hilary Putnam's concept of internal realism, although I also take issue with this account in some central respects. Although I cannot offer an adequate answer here, the larger question I am interested in is: What sort of epistemology might work with Deleuzian metaphysics? As we move from a metaphysics of being to one of becoming, what becomes of epistemology? As a contribution toward this larger project, in this paper I hope, at least, to dislodge the conventional understanding that the shift from being to becoming requires us to forgo epistemological questions.

In the analytic tradition, epistemology's engagement with skepticism—its very demand, in fact, that in order for a theory of knowledge to even count as an epistemology it must offer a response to skepticism—situates it within modernism.[5] This is precisely because in order to generate the problem of skepticism one must assume an ontology of the abyss, of a gap between knower and known which must be bridged if we can claim knowledge at all. "Being" is thought to lie beyond that abyss, as we grope toward it with imperfect technique. But clearly there are numerous traditions of serious reflection about human knowledge, and its criteria, limits, and scope, both before and after Hegel, that are not committed to any such metaphors of "abyss," "gap," or the ever popular "veil." To employ a troubled but useful term, then, we need a "postmodern" epistemology: a transvaluation of epistemic norms and values.

But first, we must combat nihilism.

NIHILISM

What I would call epistemological nihilism is the rejection of any determinate account of knowledge, or any normative epistemology at all. One might repudiate a *general* account of knowledge, which rests on the assumption that all the diverse forms of knowledge and contexts of knowing can be effectively reduced and characterized in a single analysis. But this in itself does not constitute epistemological nihilism, which is fundamentally based on a cynicism about the possibility of improving on the *epis-*

temic status of what passes for knowledge. We can see this sort of view manifest in two recent accounts of the politics of truth, Barry Allen's and Wendy Brown's. Allen and Brown both hold that what gets called truth is constituted by discursive practices; from this they both conclude that truth is both a political issue and incapable of sustaining traditional realism. I agree with these conclusions, but I disagree that either spells the death of epistemology or of all versions of realism.

Barry Allen's very interesting *Truth in Philosophy* provides useful summations of the critique of realist metaphysics in Nietzsche, James, Heidegger, Derrida, Wittgenstein, and Foucault. But he concludes from these critiques that the position we ought to adopt in regard to truth is captured in the following, which he (mistakenly, in my view) attributes to Foucault:

> The occasional truth and the identity or existence of beings stand or fall with the practice in which truth-values circulate and difference first acquires determinability. Apart from this, there exist no two things in any respect similar or different. Order is nowhere original. Nature does not exist.

Thus far, I don't necessarily disagree; this is a repudiation of metaphysical realism, or belief in a transcendental and substantive ontology. What he is saying is that "similarity" and "difference" are attributes that can be assigned only within a given discursive regime or set of practices. Order is not original but derivative, as are the demarcating bounds of "nature." But here is the account of truth that he takes to follow:

> This conclusion may seem to abolish truth, but it does not do so. It is one thing to deny a prior and autonomous order of self-identical beings to make truths true. It is something else to deny, absurdly, that nothing passes for true. And even though what passes for true is conditioned by nothing but the historically contingent normativity that prevails in practice, there is no impressive difference between what passes for true and the truth itself.[6]

Allen goes on to reiterate (rather remarkably) that "much of what in this way passes for true really is true, the very truth itself."[7] And later he says, "There is nothing more to the 'being true' of the occasional truth than this currency, this dialogical passing for true. This is all the truth there is, the only truth to concern us, whether we are philosophers, or citizens, or subjects who want the truth."[8]

The first point that might strike one about this view is that even while Allen problematizes the difference between truth and what passes for true, he makes use of this very distinction in order to allay our worries that what passes for true may be false. He thus makes use of the conceptual distinction between truth and what passes for true to epistemically legitimate what passes for true. The fact that all we have is what passes for true does not mean that all we have is falsehoods. What he wants to say, then, is that what passes for true is in fact true. But the very concept of "what passes for true" gains intelligibility only in contrast to a notion of "what is in fact true" or some such. By defining truth as what passes for true, as "conditioned by nothing but the historically contingent normativity that prevails in practice," and as "all the truth there is," Allen is collapsing the distinction and undermining the intelligibility of the concept of "passing for true."

Without the distinction between what passes for true and what is in fact true, what can it mean to say that what passes for true is in fact true, or without any "impressive" difference from the truth? What sense of true is operating here to epistemically authorize what passes for true? If he is saying that most of the time we "get it right," and our historically contingent norms actually yield truth, then truth in this usage must have metaphysical meaning. It must mean that what passes for true generally succeeds at correctly describing reality.

However, this last option is foreclosed by Allen himself. The collapse between truth and passing for true is motivated by Allen's self-professed antiontological take on truth. "Passing for true," he explains, "is a dialogical interaction among speakers; there is an exchange, a passing of statements from one to another or others."[9] Allen takes the meaning of "real" truth to be such that a "discrepancy cannot prevail in the relationship between opinion, or what passes for true, and reality, or being, or the very truth itself."[10] This amounts to an absolute consensus theory of truth, where consensus is taken not as the *criterion* of or *route* to the truth, but as the definition of what truth means. It would hold that truth is coextensive with current cultural norms, that we can make no distinction between that which is justified here and now and that which is true.

If truth is stipulated to be the result of dialogic processes that gain consensus, then Allen is right that truth is coextensive with what passes for true. But this conclusion is hardly plausible: large groups of people achieve consensus on falsehoods all the time. Moreover, total consensus across a really large and diverse group is rarely if ever achieved, and thus we would have to say on his view that truth is rarely if ever achieved. There are some, of course, who would have no trouble with that result, preferring to define truth so strenuously as to make it an ever-elusive, unattainable good. Such a position, however, flies in the face of my sense that epistemology should generally seek to explain common epistemic practices, in which valid truth claims are everyday events, rather than impose some hypertheoretical account that invalidates most existing epistemic norms and claims. I will say more about this topic in the next section.

A further and final problem with consensus theories of truth concerns their political implications. Ideological criticism requires that we be able to maintain a distinction between what all people in a society are justified in believing by the best available methods of justification that they have at their disposal and what is, in fact, true. Justification—or the criteria for "passing" as true—*is* historically conditioned, and for that reason subject to ideological and functionalist determinations. To equate passing for true with truth leaves us no wedge for inserting a political critique.[11]

Allen's account of truth takes itself to be repudiating metaphysics by its repudiation of any metaphysical excess, any gesture toward exteriority. By collapsing truth to truth-talk, it can avoid having to explicate the referentiality of truth. But I would argue that such a view retains an implicit, untheorized commitment to neo-Kantian metaphysics which understands truth as what happens only on *this* side of the phenomena-noumena divide. On *this* side, truth is naturally understood to be dialogic and the same as passing for true; it is only about what knowers do, and it has no determinate relation with reality *on the other side*. To say, as Allen does, that *nothing* conditions truth other than a historically contingent normativity implicit in human practices is to segregate truth to one side of a bipolar metaphysic. And this suggests that Allen's rejection of realism is more apparent than real: the ontological picture that metaphysical realism conjures is left intact: we are on one side, reality is on the other, and the distinctions and categories and modes of ordering that human beings produce are not discoveries that can connect or not connect with reality but are free to play their own games on our side, unencumbered by determinate relations, however oblique and nonveridical, with the other side. It is therefore symptomatic of the bipolar disorder rather than an attempt to move beyond it.

Allen believes his account makes metaphysical sense of Foucault's claim that "Truth is a thing of this world." Habermas makes the same mistake. Habermas has argued that, for Foucault, "Not only are truth claims confined to the discourses within which they arise; they exhaust their entire significance in the functional contribution they make to the self-maintenance of a given totality of discourse. That is to say, the meaning of validity consists in the power effects they have."[12] Habermas reads Foucault as substituting power for knowledge by draining the epistemic content from truth claims. Thus, even though Allen is sympathetic to Foucault, he unites with Habermas, Putnam, Peter Dews, and others of Foucault's critics (and, as we will see, Brown as well) in reading Foucault's concept of power-knowledge as one which collapses to power, ignoring Foucault's own insistence on the dyadic character of the relation, on a relation itself rather than a reduction.

I have developed extensive arguments elsewhere against this reading of Foucault.[13] Briefly, I have tried to take seriously Foucault's own characterization of his dyadic concept "power-knowledge," which he insists collapses neither to one side or the other. The point of the dyadic concept is precisely to avoid a reduction and emphasize instead the ever-present mutually constitutive relations between power and knowledge. The force of this concept is to show not that power is the only operable criterion in constructing fields of knowledge, but that knowledge has no autonomous existence apart from power. The inability to imagine how such a position does not collapse knowledge to power reveals an implicit commitment to neo-Kantian ontologies, in which the reality that alone determines truth is imagined to be extrahuman and *therefore* transcendent of the political.

It is true that Foucault repudiated the distinction between "science" and "ideology," and he famously argued, "It's not a matter of a battle 'on behalf' of the truth, but of a battle about the status of truth and the economic and political role it plays."[14] However, Foucault's view was never that power operates "behind" knowledge, but that it is "power-knowledge, the processes and struggles that traverse it and of which it is made up, that determines the forms and possible domains of knowledge."[15] This is not power speaking as if it were knowledge, but a circular relation of partial mutual constitution, a relationship in which each part is necessary but never sufficient for the other.

Moreover, there is another important reason to read Foucault "as an epistemologist": he offered an epistemic defense of his celebrated subjugated knowledge alongside a political defense. Foucault argues that "global theories" are useful only at the price of curtailing, dividing, overthrowing, and caricaturing nonglobal discourses, and thus have proved a "hindrance to research."[16] The problem with global theories lies not only in their political effects, but also in their dismissive approach toward concrete, particular events that cannot be reduced or adequately included in their terms. Hegemonic knowledge always works through distortions and omissions at the local level in order to enable the reductionist move of containment. Subjugated knowledges that do not seek hegemony do not require the amount of violence, distortion, and omission that hegemonic knowledges require. But Foucault's suggestion is not that only hegemonic knowledges have a constitutive relation to power, but that hegemonic and subjugated knowledges each have a *different* relation to power. The generation, motivation, and distribution of subjugated knowledges still occurs only in relationship to relevant constellations of dominance, whether they are discursive or institutional.

Foucault characterizes his own genealogical strategy toward knowledge as an:

attempt to emancipate historical knowledges from that subjection, to render them, that is, capable of opposition and of struggle against the coercion of a theoretical, unitary, formal, and scientific discourse. It is based on a reactivation of local knowledges . . . in opposition to the scientific hierarchization of knowledges.[17]

This is a strategy not of the political against the epistemic, but of one set of power-knowledges against another. The oppositional status of local knowledges, and the problems Foucault has with the hierarchies of science, are at once political and epistemic, in ways that cannot be disentangled. Foucault privileges subjugated knowledges because they resist the universal pretensions of global theories which would forcibly subsume particulars under a generalized rubric. Because Foucault's arguments include independently operating epistemic criteria (independent conceptually even if never pragmatically), I take Foucault to have believed in truth as having metaphysical content. In a late interview, Foucault stressed this point: "All those who say that, for me, truth doesn't exist are being simplistic."[18] He never called for a universal retreat from truth-claims; he called for "detaching the power of truth from the forms of hegemony, social, economic, and cultural, within which it operates at the present time."[19] I would argue that, although Foucault was unquestionably concerned with what passes for true, this concern does not exhaust his concern for the "power of truth."

My main purpose here is not to revisit this debate over Foucault's account of knowledge but to challenge the belief that an assessment of power's ubiquitous role in constituting knowledge, which is Foucault's claim, entails or at least supports a move toward deontologizing truth or moving from claim (3) listed above to claim (1) (that is, moving from the claim that there is no distinction between true and passing for true and the claim that truth-claims have no ontological basis or content). The result of an antiontologic approach such as Allen's is that traditional realist ontologies are left unchallenged and unreconstructed and "truth" is collapsed to power.

Perhaps this mistake is motivated by the concern that if we get into the business of challenging traditional ontology we will be playing "its" language game, when what we want to be doing is moving to another terrain. My argument is certainly not that we should challenge traditional ontology because that is where the serious money is, or because we must work within the discourse to some extent in order to be heard, or any such foolishness. Rather, my reasons are, first, that our own arguments have ontological and epistemological implications that need to be made perspicuous; and, second, that truth retains an inherent otherness, an "aboutness," that it always exceeds the text and even the dialogic encounter. Deleuze, for one, seems unembarrassed by the aboutness of language, which is probably because he avoids collapsing the entirety of metaphysics to representational thought or what he sometimes calls state philosophy. As Massumi puts it, for Deleuze "the diagram is drawable . . . if the fissuring is arbitrarily stopped at a certain level."[20] Deleuze, like Foucault, does not shrink from description but recharacterizes what descriptive processes are doing. This does not negate truth so much as it rearticulates the scope of truth.

What is most telling, however, is Allen's motivation for being antiontologic. Allen wants to move away from an ontological and epistemological account of truth to a political account, which he sees as requiring the transcendence of ontology, and his political motivation is one that I believe is widely shared. Let me reconstruct these implicit premises.

A. If truth is ontological, it is incoherent to understand it as constituted by power.
B. If truth is not ontological, we can shift the problematic of truth to a consideration of its relation to power.

This argument is implicitly accepted by numerous theorists of power, and I want to turn next to Wendy Brown, who develops the political implications of the argument more fully than Allen.

Wendy Brown's fascinating series of essays, *States of Injury,* comprise an extended argument about how many "contemporary political formations ostensibly concerned with emancipation" retain an "ungrounded persistence in ontological essentialism and epistemological foundationalism" which results in undercutting any liberating effects they might hope to have.[21] Thus, in this book she is critiquing, not epistemology for its politics, but political theories broadly on the left for their epistemology and their metaphysics, ultimately because this ensures, in her view, their political disutility.

Within feminism, Brown's target is the familiar critique of postmodernist feminism that charges it with undercutting the center of feminism—i.e., woman as subject—as well as disabling the political effectivity of feminism by undermining its ability to claim truth. Brown offers both a psychoanalysis of these worries and also a political argument against what the worries presuppose. At times taking the tone of a dispassionate analyst, Brown argues that these worries are symptomatic of the disorientation of our postmodern times, that they are a reaction to the "postmodern assaults" on identity, subjectivity, the authority of experience, and the cohesion of community. Like Jameson and Aronowitz, Brown locates the origin of these assaults not in academic or highly theoretical circles, but simply in the everyday features of contemporary social and economic existence. But although theory has not produced this disorientation, postmodern theory itself signals "flux, contest, instability," which only increase anxiety and thus drive the flight to "reactionary foundationalism."[22]

She finds such symptoms expressed by Nancy Hartsock, Seyla Benhabib, Catherine MacKinnon, and Patricia Hill Collins. Feminist foundationalism is expressed in these authors by an "epistemological privileging [of] women's accounts of social life."[23] According to Brown, such privileging reveals that the concern over the postmodern assaults on subjectivity are motivated ultimately by what this will do to the (female) subject's assertions of truth. She claims that the "feminist attachment to the subject" is based on a desire to retain "women's experiences, feelings and voices as sources and certifications of postfoundational political truth."[24]

Brown offers a political counter based largely on the writings of Nietzsche and Foucault. From Foucault's analysis of the confessional, she suggests that "this truth" some feminists think we need "has been established as the secret to our souls not by us but by those who would discipline us through that truth."[25] Thus we are naive if we think truth will be on our side, on the side of the powerless. From Nietzsche, Brown develops the suggestion that feminism, like the Christian slave revolts, has become attached to morality as a compensation for powerlessness. Morality enacts resentment, complains against strength, and seeks to shame and discredit power while "securing the ground of the true *and* the good."[26] The principal problem with this strategy, besides its obvious Manichaean overtones, is that morality is not honest about its own ambitions regarding power; indeed, it cannot be honest about this without entailing its own self-dissolution.

Set up in this way, Brown's alternative can come as no surprise: like Nietzsche, Brown chastises those without sufficient honesty or the strength to refrain from cloaking our desires with narratives about truth and moral rightness. The need and impulse to cloak our desires in this way also comes from the nature of what we desire, which is not defensible once seen, in the light of day, as a desire to punish the strong and retain the comfort, familiarity, and righteousness of victimization. We need, then, a reorientation of what we desire. In particular, we need to forgo resentment and the desire for vengeance, and if we can forgo these we will "give up substituting Truth and Morality for politics."[27] We will move to a "politics unarmed with Truth," we will stop making "*moral* claims against domination" and move instead to the "sheerly political: 'wars of position' and amoral contests about the just and the good in which truth is always grasped as coterminous with power, as always already power, as the voice of power."[28] Such a politics, she says, can be found in Machiavelli, Gramsci, and Emma Goldman.

Brown's metapolitics is very open-ended, and thus it might be the case that some of the substantive demands that she criticizes in the book, such as those of MacKinnon or of current "identity politics," could be rearticulated as wars of position without assuming a "reactionary foundationalism," and then may escape the problems that Brown diagnoses in the current forms. However, I cannot endorse her metapolitics unreservedly. In contending that we should forgo truth claims in favor of the "sheerly political," Brown puts forward a concept of truth that once again collapses to power. If truth is merely the "voice of power," a construction that Foucault explicitly renounced, then power operates behind the scenes as the principal force determining the shape and texture of specific truth claims, such as claims about who is oppressed and who is responsible. Politics itself is denuded of epistemic investments and an epistemically informed strategic direction.

Moreover, Brown's metapolitics suggests anxieties of its own, for instance in its very counsel against any move or rhetoric which might indicate a desire for (what she calls) the arrogation of power. This seems contradictory at first, since she has argued that we should move away from morality and truth toward (mere) politics, and her alliance with Nietzsche might suggest that we should unashamedly embrace a will to power (which can be simply the will to grow and flourish). But Brown characterizes the arrogation of power as always presuming that its normative goals have a transcendental, nonnegotiable status.

Those who repudiate these presumptions have developed a politics which resists power without attempting to replace it. In a way, the distinction between these two political stances replays the debate between a Marxism that seeks state power, and an anarchism (or a version of Marxism that emphasizes Marx's own anarchist tendencies) whose aim would be to resist and subvert all centralized structures.

Brown is herself unsatisfied with a mere politics of resistance, suggesting that "the contemporary vogue of resistance is more a symptom of postmodernity's crisis of political space than a coherent response to it" and that it does not meet "the normativity challenge."[29] Therefore, against both "mere resistance" and "reactionary foundationalism" she tries to develop a third alternative, which argues that what we need is to cultivate "political *spaces* for posing and questioning feminist political norms, for discussing the nature of 'the good' for women."[30] We need to develop "postmoral and antirelativist political spaces, practices of deliberation, and modes of adjudication."[31] In essence, hers is a call for an antifoundationalist procedural political rationality, but it is difficult to call it rationality, since Brown wants no epistemic privileging of any sort.

I agree wholeheartedly with Brown's critique of the politics of mere resistance. There is a kind of quest for purity in the attempt to maintain only a resistance which is itself defined as a reaction to power rather than a fight for power. Resistance so circumscribed suggests a desire to inhabit a space free from criticism, responsibility, and accountability, to be always the critic and never the advocate. I also share many metaphilosophical positions with Brown, such as the critique of foundationalism and all forms of transcendentalism. However, I find the alternative that Brown puts forward both inadequate and unnecessary. Unless we can make substantive declarations of truth or value, there is not really much at stake in political spaces of deliberation. Brown's call to create political spaces in which norms can be questioned does not take into account the fact that challenging norms requires making truth claims. Defending any set of norms, which she acknowledges we must do, is tantamount to positing morality, and it seems disingenuous and unhelpful to avoid the word. Thus my argument here is that the retreat from truth and morality that Brown advocates is inadequate, given her own often persuasive call for the cultivation of new political spaces for political deliberation. These spaces cannot be made intelligible or meaningful without understanding them as the site of contestation over and production of truth and morality.

Brown fleshes out her position by distinguishing between identity-based political arguments, which are oriented around metaphysical accounts of subjectivity and identity and are thus focused on "who I am," and world-based political arguments that are not so focused on the self and move toward "what I want for us" in a common future space. I find it puzzling that she calls for a political conversation oriented toward "the world" (as opposed to the self), as if this can happen in the absence of truth claims. Whether one is talking about the world or the self, one is implicated in metaphysical and epistemic investments; the contrast between "world" or "self" as topics of deliberation is a distinction between the particular investments believed to be the most politically productive. Brown's arguments against MacKinnon, Barbara Ehrenreich, and others, though they often operate at a level of depth psychology and political metaphilosophy, are contestations over the nature of the real, over how meanings are produced and circulated, and over what are the most critical moral goods to fight for in this era. Her arguments against overreliance on the state even develop countermetaphysical positions on the self as a regulatory fiction rather than the source of authenticity. To deny that the liberal, modernist concept of the self is an accurate portrait is to deny certain metaphysical beliefs about the self *in favor of other such beliefs.*

The contrast Brown is trying to draw is one between foundational political claims and a nonfoundational politics, between claims about morality and truth on the one hand and claims about what we want on the other, which she characterizes as a "politics unarmed with Truth."[32] But we must still engage on the terrain of morality and truth in order to articulate, defend, and indeed even understand what we want, for any given "we." Political argument, which is what she calls for, occurs precisely over the domain of the real and the good, over whether and how power is operating in a given context, over whose description of an event or a history is most accurate, and over which vision of community and of the future is most morally defensible. Transcendental commitments to a depoliticized justificatory process or a positivist concept of the truth are not necessary to such arguments, *nor, in any case, do they usually enter in*. What does enter in, and what cannot be avoided, is the more ordinary kind of questions about truth and morality, where morality is simply the normative assessment of what follows from the truest account of a shared reality. Antifoundationalism does not require eschewing all epistemic or metaphysical commitments; it requires eschewing transcendentalism and most forms of naturalism that seek to erase the knower from the known or objectify and essentialize human characteristics. Thus, Brown's call for a politics unarmed with (all forms of) truth is unnecessary as well.

Like Rorty, Brown operates on the assumption that epistemology equals foundationalism, metaphysics entails essentialism, and all forms of truth are based on a metaphysics of presence. These assumptions are contradicted by the real heterogeneity that exists in these areas of philosophical debate, as I will show in the next section.

Like Allen, Brown uses Foucault as authoritative support for her abdication of epistemology and understands this abdication as linked to his inquiry into the politics of truth. I won't repeat here the arguments I made in relation to Allen's use of Foucault, but there is one more relevant point that reveals the contrast between Foucault's approach and Brown's. In response to questions about whether his own practice of genealogy might reify into another essentialist methodology or global theory, Foucault explained that he was not concerned about this yet because "the moment at which we risk colonization has not yet arrived."[33] This indicates a historicist self-awareness, what the hermeneuticists call effective historical consciousness, rather than trying to impose an airtight metatheoretical articulation that will ensure unrecuperable purity.

It is just such a desire to solve the problem of recuperation at the metatheoretical level that motivates the abdication of epistemology. Brown seeks a feminist politics that makes no claim to be epistemically or morally better than its adversaries. My argument against Brown is not, *qua* Hartsock et al., that we "need" epistemic foundations to do political work. If there was ever a socially constructed need, the need for epistemic foundations is a constructed need. Rather, my argument with Brown is that politics cannot be disassociated from epistemology and metaphysics, or from truth and morality, or from making claims about reality, claims to represent the real better than traditional realism represents it. Traditional realism does not exhaust the possibilities for a metaphysical account of truth claims, no more than the theory of the forms exhausts the possibilities of ontology.

IMMANENCE

Allen and Brown implicitly assume traditional neo-Kantian realist ontologies, which cannot render a concern with the politics of truth coherent within an ontological project. Thus they negotiate the bipolar disorder without attempting a cure. In place of this refusal to engage, my argument is that we need new epistemologies, new ontologies. Ultimately, however, we cannot look to Foucault for an attentive reformulation of the ontology of truth that might elucidate its relation to power, its extension beyond the present normativity, and thus its irreducibility to what "passes for true." This is not his project. Nor can we get such an account fully from Deleuze, though we can gain an ontology of becoming upon which to begin a new formulation of the meaning of truth.

Instead, I would argue that at least one place to go is neo-Hegelian traditions manifested in American pragmatism, the coherentism that emerged from the Vienna Circle especially in the work of Otto Neurath, Quinean-inspired developments of radical empiricism, and other such derided figures who work within and against analytic philosophy itself. For decades now, Nelson Goodman has been happily developing a constructivist philosophy of science that deconstructs the hallowed distinction between what humans find and what we make. Donald Davidson has been developing a metaphysics free of any concept of reference or representation; Michael Williams has used a Wittgensteinian-inspired contextualism essentially to jettison most of the modernist problematics in epistemology; and newer theorists like Catherine Elgin are moving epistemology from a focus on (empirical) knowledge to understanding. These philosophers are propelling epistemology and metaphysics past our dualist legacy rather than resigning to it. The result is an almost complete rejection of the traditional problems of philosophy, which has meant that their work is not accepted within the mainstream establishment. To some extent even this work must be read against itself, certainly against its own resistance to any political framing of epistemic questions. But as Lynn Hankinson Nelson has shown so persuasively in the case of Quine, in the works I have mentioned there is an opening toward more philosophically radical conclusions than the authors would themselves countenance.

My main interest here is the potential contribution some of this work might make toward rethinking an ontology of truth within an immanent rather than a transcendental metaphysics. An immanent account is necessary to an account of truth in terms of becoming rather than being as well as for an attentiveness to political effects even within the midst of a concern for truth. In this final section I will describe the contours of one such account as I developed it in *Real Knowing* using Hilary Putnam's concept of "internal realism."

"Truth talk" is not merely talk, or empty talk; it is a form of discursive practice with associated effects. It is embedded within a lived corporeal context, and not merely an ethereal linguistic realm separated from bodies, practices, and material reality. And truth claims are about that whole lived reality: they refer to it, intervene in it, help to constitute it, even sometimes represent it (in a nonveridical sense). To eliminate any analysis or articulation of the ontological dimension of truth serves only to conceal from examination these relationships between truth claims and reality. Truth claims are claims about the nature of life, about experience, about perception, memory, history, and explanations of the natural and the everyday. The ontology of truth is the explication of the meaning, contours, and limits of that "about."

The term *aboutness* signals representation, which is at the heart of any debate over the ontology of truth. Representation has also been the lightning rod for concerns about the politics of truth, with some arguing that claims of representation necessarily have adverse political effects by shutting down discussion and transforming political debate into absolutist stalemates. Against this view, Putnam argues that the complete repudiation of the possibility of representation in any sense entails that we cannot treat either others or ourselves as cognitive agents, that is, as capable of more or less accurately referring to reality. Like Wittgenstein, he suggests that where there is no representation at all, speakers become mere noisemakers, no different, in their representational capacities, from ants who may accidentally trace a likeness of Winston Churchill without ever knowing that they have done so.[34] Notice that here, Putnam critiques a metaphysical position for its political effects.

What manner of representation is possible, then? Representation itself can be conceptualized without the positivist account of a transparent event or "presence." For example, Putnam holds that truth is "primarily a matter of fit: fit to what is referred to in one way or another, or to other renderings, or to modes and manners of organization."[35] He agrees with Nelson Goodman that "The differences between fitting a version to a world, a world to a version, and a version together or to other versions fade when *the role of versions in making the worlds they fit is recognized.*"[36] This is also consistent with Foucault's claim that discourses construct the objects of which they speak, and it suggests the notion of a truth-operation with an ontology that is open, fluid, immanent rather than transcendent. Representation is not an association between a linguistic item and a bit of the world, but a kind of momentary constellation in which active human practice is involved though not unilaterally determinant over the outcome. In an immanent account, when truth claims accurately represent reality, they are reaching not the sphere of "being," devoid of human input, but a plane immanent to lived reality whose ontological contours are partially constituted through discourses and other practices that constitute perception as well as physical engagement. The terms *representation* and *reference*, used in this context, do not convey an appropriation of being; they convey a *productive,* always partial and temporally indexed, description of a virtual reality, that is, a composite of temporary constellations.

Putnam calls his view an internal realism because it holds that the question " 'what objects does the world consist of?' is a question that it only makes sense to ask *within* a theory or description."[37] This implies not that object-claims do not refer, but that observation reports are more like "small theories" than unmediated descriptions. Internal realism is thus committed to conceptual relativism. But Putnam rejects the cookie-cutter metaphor that imagines concepts as forming shapes (or cutting out cookies) from some primeval dough. Such a metaphor posits a two-layer reality, with a more fundamental layer beyond conceptualization. Against this, Putnam argues, like Nietzsche, that even concepts like "exist" and "object" have specific meanings only within a language, and thus his conceptual relativity entails ontological internalism as well. More radical than Kant, Putnam considers any talk about a noumenal realm unintelligible and even repellant, in positing objects without properties and an irreconcilable dualism between the worlds of phenomena and noumena. Conceptual relativity "does not mean that reality is hidden or noumenal; it simply means that you can't describe the world without describing it."[38] Along with Wittgenstein, Putnam urges philosophers to stop wondering what is "hidden behind" the world (as we know it), or what is intrinsic or completely independent of us. The problem with this kind of thinking is not simply epistemological—it is not simply because we can never *know* what is "back there"—but metaphysical.

On Putnam's account of internal or what he later calls pragmatic realism, there is no version-free description of the real; and given the fact that there are different versions, more than one (true) description of the real is possible. Putnam denies that this amounts to subjective idealism or that truth is a matter of arbitrary or conventional construction, since once a language game or version has been chosen, truth can be determined objectively. But the success of this denial hinges on the question of how a version is chosen. And to this Putnam's answer is basically pragmatic: versions of reality which become dominant have utility. It is this grounding in use that both leads to the open texture of reference, meaning, and reason, and also provides objectivity without ascribing intrinsic features to reality. Utility is extradiscursive—it cannot be imposed unilaterally on physical reality—but it is never transcendent of human action.

Putnam's theory of the real denies the existence of intrinsic properties that are version-independent or independent of theoretical language or description, just as mass and extension change according to the nearest planet and the current velocity. The notion of property, no less than the demarcation of "things," involves a host of contextual elements, outside of which the notion will lose its meaning. Internal realism thus entails an ontological pluralism that is compatible with (and helps to explain) the changes in science's ontological attributions.

Internal realism is related to an ontology of becoming in the following way: it does not portray truth claims as fallible approximations of the real or of "being." There is no implicit assumption of a bipolar ontology or a noumenal realm in which "being" is manifest beyond all conceptualization. All there is, for Putnam, is the lived world, the world in which ontological commitments are contextual and relative and truth claims do not require rendering human engagement invisible. Truth is always partial or from a particular angle; it is a matter of fit between changeable, though not arbitrary, ontological commitments and theoretical projects. Thus there is no unmediated or transparent "presence," and truth is both plural and relative. And because Putnam repudiates the idea of a noumenal backdrop to lived, mediated experience, we *can* actually claim truth. It is not always beyond our grasp, nor is it merely dialogic. Truth does not consist in a correspondence to a transcendent realm, nor is it merely a "dialogic process" or consensus. Truth is what works, but it works because it produces, generates, supplies, and connects, and not because "working" is an indicator of the nature of transcendent being. Thus, truth's aboutness ranges over the lived world, a living world, a world whose truths are constantly in the process of unfolding and being made.

Although Putnam's development of internal realism can be usefully pushed toward an immanent metaphysics, as just described, I would ultimately argue that immanent realism is distinct from internal realism in the following way. Putnam develops internal realism principally in reference to versions or models of reality within the domain of the empirical sciences. The "realism" of internal realism is then understood as internal to a conceptual frame and set of theoretical commitments. In contrast, immanent realism refers to contexts in a broader sense. To say that there are no properties which are version-independent is different from saying that there are no properties which are context-independent. Version-dependence involves being incapable of description outside a theoretical version of reality with its own ontological categories. Versions are understood to be human-made constructs. Context-dependence involves a relationship not just to theoretical description but to a larger setting which also includes not only theory, version, and language games, but also historical, spatiotemporal, and social location and a domain of practices and institutions. Thus "context" has an ontological dimension that "version" does not, even though ontologies are dependent on versions. Versions can too easily collapse to a neo-Kantian ontology in which they would be understood as located only on "this side" of the man-world Kantian schema; contexts, on the other hand, work more effectively than versions to break this schema down and overcome its bipolarity. Contexts are not mind-made versions of the world, but portions or locations of the world, historically and socially specific.

Thus I think the best term to capture this is *immanence*, invoking the opposition to a transcendental concept of reality as, by definition, beyond all human practice or intervention. The term *internal* may also connote subjectivity, as in the subjective perspective of theorists and scientists who impose an order on externality. By contrast, at least in the context of western philosophy, the term *immanence* does not connote a realm of the subjective. Rather, immanence has a connotation for philosophers involving materiality and the profane, the realm that gave Sartre nausea and that Beauvoir wanted to escape. Consider Aristotle, Hume, Kierkegaard, and Nietzsche: an unlikely assortment, but each offering a philosophy securely tethered to the realm of immanence. And their grounding in and valorization of immanence did not entail an implicit commitment to the existence of a corollary transcendent realm; certainly Kierkegaard maintained such a commitment, but it was not entailed by his conceptualization of immanence. For Kierkegaard, immanence is not the necessary opposite of transcendence, but precisely that site where corporeality and incorporeality meet.

On an immanent realist view, the difference between a true claim and a false claim is not always or simply that one represents and the other doesn't; the difference is in the nature, quality, and comprehensiveness of representation. The "aboutness" of truth is therefore not transcendental. And the term *context* can readily incorporate an entire ethos of political, social, historically situated praxis.

Immanent realism will thus be broader than version-dependent (or internal) realism by introducing more elements to which truth must be indexed beyond merely versions or ontologically descriptive theories. It is not just versions that produce particular truths when applied in particular locations, but also the larger context, which can include such elements as epistemes, subject-positions, and institutions of power-knowledge. This works to displace the centrality of the knower or subject. On Putnam's internal realism, truth is (partially) dependent on theory, which is created by scientists. This may explain why Putnam's view is often confused with forms of idealism: his view is too subject-centered. On an immanent realist view, truth is an emergent property of all the elements involved in the context, including but not limited to theory. Thus it can acknowledge more readily the formative effects that language, discourse, and power-knowledge have on the production of truths, rather than privileging the knowing subject as the necessary center of the knowing process.

My aim here has been not to provide an adequate defense of immanent realism, but to establish that epistemology can be based on a concept of knowledge without the bipolar disorder. The project of an epistemology of becoming, then, would be, not to secure *the* truth, but to explore the dimensions of the multiple forms of knowing and practices by which truths are ascertained. It would give an account of the epistemic content in distinctions between understanding and illusion. It would trace the circuitry of power coextensive with what passes for true, as well as explain how one might critique the current horizons within which even truth itself is circumscribed. There is much work ahead to develop realistic accounts of epistemic grounds for belief that are based on more realistic accounts of the processes through which the real emerges.

PART

2

Knowing and Doing Otherwise

5

THE TIME OF THE GLANCE: TOWARD BECOMING OTHERWISE

Edward S. Casey

> Qu'il s'agisse du dedans
> ou du dehors, de nous ou
> des choses, la réalité est
> la mobilité même.
>
> —BERGSON, *La pensée et le mouvant*

> Pour avancer avec la
> réalité mouvante, c'est
> en elle qu'il faudrait se
> replacer.
>
> —BERGSON, *L'évolution créatrice*

> Tout moment de notre
> vie . . . se scinde en même
> temps qu'il se pose. Ou
> plutôt il consiste dans
> cette scission même. . . .
>
> —BERGSON, *L'énergie spirituelle*

LEAPING INTO THE GLANCE

We spend most of our lives glancing—just glancing about, glancing around. You are glancing at my text as you begin to read it; at the same time, you are probably also glancing about the room you are in, perhaps out a window onto the larger world. We glance at tiny things that catch our momentary attention, a fugitive fleck or a sudden speck, but we also glance at colossal things: whole regions of landscape, the World Trade Center, the Montana sky. Thus the glance is able to take in entities of the most varied scale. Despite its seemingly limited means—it issues from two meager eyes set in our own paltry head, and is subject to quite particular atmospheric and environmental conditions such as adequate luminosity (though we often still manage to glance in the dark)—it can take note of entire worlds. "The world at a glance": there is even something perversely collusive about the alliance between the mereness of the glance and the greatness of the world. It is as if the exiguous status of the glance, its meek slenderness, disarms in advance the spirit of gravity that attends more weighty projects, penetrating these projects and their ponderous materials. The fickleness of glancing, its easy distractability, allows it to insinuate itself all the more deeply into the very heart of the matter. The *esprit de finesse* of which Pascal spoke is realized concretely and continuously in the glance; it precedes in life and thought the *esprit géometrique* that entails steady scrutiny and the long stare, those privileged avatars of vision in western philosophy and science.

I propose, just to start with, that it is the paradoxical power of the glance to find its way into the profound as well as the superficial—to glance off the surface of everything that is perceptually as well as socially significant—that allows it to be such an effective force: to be the very medium of human transactions. (And of animal life as well: for all living organisms subsist from the glances they cast, far more than we have been willing to admit. But this is quite another story.)[1] Yet the status of the glance as mediatrix of human perception and knowledge has rarely been acknowledged. It is as if the very pervasiveness of the phenomenon, its being so familiar as not to be noticed as such, has acted to marginalize it, an act of derecognition that is only reinforced by the putative fragility of its operation: what can hang on a mere glance? *Nada—y todo.*

In the case of the glance, we have to do with something not entirely unlike nomadism as interpreted by Deleuze and Guattari, who show nomadic movement to be much more pervasive than any official account, historical or anthropological, allows; it permeates the state apparatus itself, and is capable of bringing it down from within in the form of nonroyal science or guerilla warfare, or merely by the vagrant circulation of certain signs. Similarly, the glance can topple whole kingdoms, just as it can also build them up. The display of royal power is not just taken in at a glance but depends for its continued existence on repeated looks of recognition, however cursory they may be. Not to notice the accoutrements of this power, not even to glance at the royal robes, not to bother to look at the king—to glance away from these matters of state—is to begin to undo their hold on the subjects of a given aristocracy. Revolutions have started with less than such slim means; or more exactly, they have started quite powerfully with just such means, as Sartre indicates in his analysis of the role of the "group in fusion," whose minimal three members need only to glance at each other while exchanging a few words to engender a truly revolutionary situation. It is the "series," whose members are consigned to forced frontal staring, that has lost the power—the power of the free glance.

Strangely, however, neither the nomadology of Deleuze and Guattari nor the model of revolution found in Sartre's *Critique of Dialectical Reason* acknowledges this power. Nor does Derrida in his parallel assault on the metaphysics of presence, another form of state power, this time institutionalized in the history of philosophy. Derrida's case is all the more telling for coming so close to such acknowledgment. For the decisive instance of his deconstruction of presence in his early work is precisely the *blink of the eye*. It is in this blink that any claim to the unmediated presence of forms as well as that of the "now" is exploded by a momentary cut that belies the primacy and privilege of such pure presence: "Nonpresence and nonevidence are admitted into the blink of the instant. There is a duration to the blink, and it closes the eye. This alterity is in fact the condition for presence, presentation, and thus for *Vorstellung* in general."[2]

The blink of the eye, the obverse of the glance, undermines the open-eyed attestation of the kind of sheer presence that is available in essential insight, whether this is said to occur in Platonic or Aristotelian *noesis*, Cartesian intellectual intuition, or Husserlian *Wesensanchauung*. But something not taken into account by Derrida is that if the same blink detonates the now as point in time (i.e., as "source-point" in Husserl's term), by the same token it affirms the subjectivity of the subject: an abyssal subjectivity but a subjectivity nonetheless. For when I blink, for a fleeing instant I retreat into a bottomless refuge that lies, somewhere and somehow, within myself.

Similarly, the *wink*, ostensibly a bonding gesture, also manifests a moment of disjunction: I wink at the other in my very incapacity to reach that other in a more articulate way. As in the case of the blink, intersubjectivity is at once disbanded *and* affirmed: for in winking at or to another I also collaborate with that other in some significant way. I assert the link that my lack of express verbal representation has otherwise placed in question.[3]

The blink and the wink are both closely allied with the glance; they are phases of its enactment. The blink severs presence (or more exactly shows presence to be self-severing) even as it modulates the being who blinks, and the wink contests the articulate forms of intersubjective being even as it connives with them *sub rosa*. But these are ways in which the glance operates all the time: it undoes itself in its own accomplishment. For the affirmation inherent in the glance, its penetrative force, comes paired with a recessive and self-limiting depotentiation. The glance takes us out into the world, but it also brings us back to ourselves. It brings us up long and short at once.

SHOOTING THE ARROW OF TIME

The two paradoxes of the glance so far expounded (its combination of narrowness of means with extraordinary scope; its outgoing force together with its self-recoiling tendency) point to a third and even more momentous paradox. This is the way the glance puts us both into and out of time—into an intense momentary time and out of a continuous, distended time.

Into and out of *time*? Isn't the glance the epitome of an act that takes little or virtually *no time* to enact? Isn't that the very point of the glance: to be the thing we do when there is not enough time for more assiduous or prolonged seeing? Precisely in the absence of the kind of time in which we are able to scrutinize something, whether in the laboratory or with the body of the beloved, we glance instead. We take in all we can in "a thrice." No time here for the sense of sequence that is the luxury of the laboratory or of love: first this step, then taking in its sequel, then leading into the next move, and so on, all this within the unhurried context of the workplace or love nest. Rather than any such slowly unfolding succession, in glancing there is only a sense of discontinuous darting: "Quick, said the bird, find them, find them, / Round the corner . . . human kind / Cannot bear very much reality . . . Quick now, here, now, always. Ridiculous the waste sad time / Stretching before and after."[4] A glance, much like T.S. Eliot's bird, *alights*; it does not settle down but perches precariously. It alights here and there and there, in no particular order or sequence. Just as it moves mercurially over surfaces that are not themselves contiguous, leaping over intermediate points, so the glance does not fit snugly into a gapless continuum of time. Discontinuity in place is paired with discontinuity in time.

But is such double discontinuity tantamount to taking *no time?* Indeed, can any action, however fleeting, take *no time at all?* Even the blink of the eye, which splits the present, is not nontemporal; the same is true of the wink, another split-second action. Surely the glance, despite its evanescence, does take time. Even to last a split second is still to take up time, but what kind of time is this?

It will not do to say simply that each distinctive action such as the glance *takes its own time*, for time is a field factor, a dimension or parameter which, by its very character, has to be able to situate other actions as well. "Time binds," as we say. But it binds differently in different instances, and our task is to determine how it does so in the case of the glance.

We might wonder, to start with, where the time of the glance is to be situated in relation to McTaggart's celebrated A series and B series. It would seem that, at the very least, the glance demarcates *before* and *after* in any given circumstance (that is, the B series). But this is trivially true of every discrete action, and what is notable here is that such a demarcation is considerably muted in the case of the glance, when we are more conscious of being in or at the moment of transition than of coming before or after any particular event. For an external observer, it is doubtless possible to position someone's glance between one determinate event and another; but for the glancer, the glance is often what takes him or her *out of* the before / after enchainment, being its momentary suspension. This expulsive thrust of the glance is an integral aspect of its overall liberatory power, its capacity to say "No!" to any given situation, to refuse to be causally entrapped, however modestly momentary the refusal itself may be. Indeed, much as in the instance of the first paradox, the very momentariness of the glance contributes to its disruption of the forced march of the B series.[5]

How then does the glance fit into the A series, "that series of positions which runs from the far past through the near past to the present, and then from the present through the near future to the far future, or conversely"[6]? Here the plot thickens. For we notice first of all that the glance, despite its ephemerality, implicates all three phases; it arises in the present, but only as a reflection of the immediate past of interest or desire and as foreshadowing the future of current intention. Being tritemporal, the glance constitutes a genuine *moment* of time, as distinct from an *instant* of time. The instant occurs only in the present; it is the privileged form of the present, privileged because conceived as entirely actual, and actual because occurring as a *point*, in particular a now-point. It is the pointillism of the now, its essential isolation from other now-points, that generates a celebrated version of Zeno's paradox. As Bergson expresses this version: "At each instant, [the arrow] is immobile, for it cannot have the time in which to move, that is, to occupy at least two successive positions. At a given [instant], therefore, it is at rest at a given point. Immobile in each point of its trajectory, it is, during all the time in which it moves, immobile."[7] Yet the arrow moves; we can see it moving and it reaches its target after all—in fact, all too rapidly, as I know to my chagrin if I am that target!

The analogy between the moving arrow and the human glance is significant. Each is "shot" from a human subject; each aims at something in particular; each is utterly mobile.[8] Moreover, arrow and glance alike gather all three temporal modalities in their very flight. (1) Each occurs in an extended noninstantaneous present (it is this very extension that resists analysis into "before" and "after"), a present moment that is coextensive with the trajectory of the projectile itself. (2) Each brings its own past to bear on that ongoing present, a past that is its virtual image and close décalque, for "our past remains present to us"[9] rather than becoming something separate and self-contained: (3) Each does not so much move *into* a future (for there is no already existing future into which to move) as bring that future into being by its very trajectory: the arrow, like the glance, is continually *at* its own future, which is where the tip of the arrow or the extremity of the glance is going at any given moment.

The arrow and the glance show time to be (in Deleuze's words) "a perpetual *self-distinguishing*, a distinction in the [very] process of being produced; which always resumes the distinct terms in itself, in order constantly to relaunch them."[10] In particular, they show the temporality of the A series to be diasporadic from a restless present moment that, unlike the instant-point, does not allow itself to collapse into the sheer fact that it *is* where it is and as it is: that way lies time's torpor, its ontosclerosis, its *rigor temporis*. Instead, time alters—is alter to itself—by always mutating into two simultaneous lines, the past of its own present and the future of that "present which passes."[11] The dissymmetry of the two lines arises from the fact that the past is retained as virtual, a vast virtuality that bears down on the present as its ever-augmenting other, while the future is noncumulative and open.

This much, however, we could learn from analyzing not only the moving arrow and the equally moving glance but any phenomenon of change or movement as construed in the light of Bergson's philosophy of time. Triage is needed if we are to specify what is peculiar to the glance. Notice, to begin with, that the time of the arrow's flight evaporates with the completion of its arc. But in human temporality that is more than merely the time of observation (on which we have covertly drawn in discussing the arrow) there is always a greater whole at stake, whether we wish to call this "duration" following Bergson or the "memory of the world" after Merleau-Ponty.[12] Whereas physical motion taken by itself, apart from any subjectivity with which it may be involved, exhibits time only to the extent that it gives a measurable instantiation of it—hence the temptation to reduce such time to instants plus a schema of their abstract succession—any movement of human (and other) organisms takes time only within a larger ever-expanding cosmos of time.[13] Indeed, the amalgam of present, past, and future in the A series is just that larger temporal *whole* that Bergson names *durée réelle* and Heidegger *Zeitlichkeit* and that, as Augustine argued, is held together by human consciousness generously enough construed. Unlike the B series, which supports its own linear representation (Aristotle argued that before and after in time are ultimately modeled on the front and the back of ordinary physical objects), the A series dissolves the very line with which one tries to represent it: on the one hand, the line constantly splits up into the dyadic directionality of past and future in a truly self-dispersive manner; on the other hand, the parts of time are just as continually drawn back together by consciousness, duration, or Dasein's ecstatico-horizonal temporality.[14] In other words, becoming continually *becomes*; it keeps on consolidating its own gains and losses in the Whole that is at once abyssal and comprehensive.

TWO-BEAT TEMPORALITY

In the dense self-annealing massivity of time, its continual self-aggrandizement (as seen in the pyramiding of the past over the present), the glance plays hooky by its very inflection and indirection. If it does not detonate duration as dramatically as the blink dissevers the bonds of presence, it does desediment the triple overdetermination of time found in the A series, just as it disconcerts the equally relentless before-and-aftering of time operative in the B series. For the glance upsets the assurances and reassurances offered by both series: the quasi-causal linearity of being positioned before and after in time as well as the wholism of past / present / future, where these are so many sections or slices of duration.[15]

The exiguous thread of the glance unravels the dense tissue of duration as well as the equally dense series of now-points on the time line. It takes us out into the "open" of becoming, "pure ceaseless becoming."[16] It does all this without the detachment from a human subject that is required by the analysis of the arrow, which pursues its own path as measured by time as an independent variable. The glance depends on a subject, literally "leaning away" (de-pending) *from* the subject; yet it exceeds any given subject and its internalized temporality by virtue of being directed, "shot," at an object of interest. But, unlike any arrow, this shot does not simply go forward to its target, following a one-way trajectory that, once completed, lapses into nonbeing or at least nonactivity. Instead, the glance loops back onto the subject who emitted it; it *folds back on* the subject, coils over onto this subject, falling back onto it. But in what does this refolding of time consist, and how is it enacted by the glance?

The clearest case in point is *glancing at oneself in the mirror*. Here I start by looking out from myself; taking my glance with me outward, I send it before me into the mirror, where I see myself glancing at myself, catching myself in the act, as it were. No sooner does this happen, however, than my glanced-at glance returns to me and is absorbed by the very face that sent it out in the first place: it folds back over this face, rejoining it at its own surface, as if to acknowledge this face as its own progenitor. Yet the glance returns to me not simply as to the same self but to a self augmented by its own looking.

I see myself not as I am, *simpliciter*, but as I am in glancing, a glancing self, a self that knows itself as glancing at itself.[17]

The temporality of the scene is two-beat: an outbeat gesture of (usually circumscribed) *ecstasis* as my glance is released from my bodily self, and an inbeat return of the glance to the bodily-self now modified by having just perceived its own image in the mirror. Nothing like this is captured by the classical models of the B series (there is no separable before and after here, since the two beats occur together, not at two distinctly successive times) or even the A series (the threefold temporalizing of past, present, and future is too clumsily capacious to capture the infrastructure here revealed, even if the same infrastructure must somehow reflect the larger tripartite whole, as I have indicated above).

Nor is this situation to be assimilated to the Lacanian mirror-stage. For the adult glancer (whom I have taken as paradigmatic) the issue is not identification or ego-formation. There is, however, an element of *re*identification: I am reassured that I look quite like the person who last glanced at himself in the mirror. But the glance is not the narcissistic gaze that would be the adult equivalent of the child's fascination with his or her image in the mirror, an image that triumphs (albeit fictionally and in an alienated mode) over the fragmented body heretofore regnant in the child's life.

The mirror-glance exemplifies that *dédoublement* whereby one present moment of our experience immediately and forthwith spawns a virtual image of itself. This image is the past of that present, and, instead of being deferred in its formation (as we all too often assume), is formed at the very moment of perception. This virtual image is not a diminished perception, as Hume too readily thought; although it is an image *of* a perception, it is something of a different order—the order of memory, whose status for Bergson is ineluctably virtual.[18]

It is revealing that Bergson himself has recourse to the analogy of the mirror in discussing memory. In an article on paramnesia first published in 1908, he says:

> Pure memory (*souvenir pur*) is to perception that which the image apperceived behind the mirror is to the object placed before it. The object is touched as well as seen: it can act on us as we act on it; it is pregnant with possible actions, it is *actual*. The image is *virtual* and, although similar to the object, incapable of doing what the object does. Our actual existence, insofar as it unfolds in time, is thus doubled with a virtual existence, with an image in a mirror.[19]

Perhaps, then, the example of glancing into the mirror is not so contingent or delimited as it looks—at first glance. For the double-beat temporality of this kind of glance exhibits quite perspicuously the doubling of the present and its own past that is the crux of any temporality conceived outside the *rigor temporis* of the A and B series. Further, the virtualizing of the present in its own past undoes the putative primacy, the presumed self-presence, of the present itself. In a remarkable passage from the same essay, Bergson anticipates Derrida's deconstruction of the privilege of the present:

> Every moment of our life thus offers two aspects: it is actual and virtual, perception on the one hand and memory on the other. *It splits itself at the same time it posits itself. Or rather, it consists in this very scission,* for the present instant, always moving [*en marche*, and so not the immobile instant of Zeno], a limit fleeing between the immediate past that is al-

ready no longer and the immediate future that is not yet, would be reduced to a simple abstraction if it were not precisely the mobile mirror that ceaselessly reflects perception as [or into] memory.[20]

This passage, again invoking the mirror, articulates the radical thesis of *un souvenir du présent* that splits the present more effectively than the blink of the eye.[21] Or rather, it does not so much split a preexisting present as it is the very action by which the present is always already split into an actual and a virtual dimension. Every moment of our lives, then, "consists in this very scission."

THE LEAP THAT LOOPS BACK

On this comprehensive claim, *any* human act or action would be subject to such scissioning. What, then, is so special about the time of the glance? Perhaps you will grant the specialness of the glance in the mirror—where the glance literally enacts before our eyes a *dédoublement* that is otherwise invisible, inactual, inactive, impassive, even unconscious.[22] You might also concede that the mirror-glance rejoins other phenomena that are self-duplicative such as the shadow that falls from the body in sunlight or moonlight: here, too, we witness a virtual image that is immediately spawned as accompanying a perceptual actuality. Or think of those redundancies in ordinary conversation that are immediate spin-offs from the main line of discourse: "Yeah, that's right, that's it, just as you said" (as we sometimes say in agreeing with what someone else has said). Or: "How are you?—How are you?" (each phrase mimicking the other as two people first exchange greetings). In each of these cases, and without any mirror, we observe a basic movement of direct folding-back or self-return: the shadow rejoins my body at my feet; my remarks fold back on my own discourse as if in direct echolalia.

But what of the glance that does *not* see itself seeing in the mirror— is not that visibly self-schismatic? If there is something truly special about the glance in regard to time, its exemplary status in contexts other than that of the mirror—paradigmatic as this may be for the self-scissioning at work in all temporal process—must be shown.

Consider the circumstance in which glances are, as we say, "exchanged." No mirror here, yet there is reciprocity: my glance engages yours, and you return a glance to me. Your glance may not mimic mine, but it is certainly a response: it takes into account and thus incorporates my glance. The responding glance is in effect my own glance returning to me, however transformed it may be because of now being *your* glance, reflecting your beliefs, history, prejudices, and momentary whims. My initial glance still folds back on itself, however, only now as mediated by the overdetermined layers of your glance as it replies to mine. The reply is a literal *repli*, a folding back. Still present is what Deleuze calls a "small internal circuit,"[23] whose most momentous instance is that of the peeling-off of the virtual image from the actual perception. What is true of the latter in general is still true of the sociality of exchanged glances: of these, too, we can say that "each present goes back to itself as past."[24]

But what if my glance is *not* exchanged? What then? The return glance is still at stake, still expected (whether hoped for or feared), even if it is not always actualized. When it is not, I still presume the other capable of responding to my glance, if not by a literal glance back then by other actions (including the action of thought: as when the other merely muses, "Why is this person glancing at me?"). These nonglance responses may be gesticular (e.g., my glance precipitates the other's striking me) or tacit (but no less powerful, as in the case of a sullen silence that is occasioned by my glance).

We may go further yet: nonglance responses can be altogether virtual. This is often the case with nonhuman things at which we glance. The boulder at which I glance does not move, much less glance back; but from it, at some level, I expect a response: a response whose virtuality I take for granted in this case. But this virtuality can be felt as such. When Merleau-Ponty asks why we should not think that the trees see us as much as we see them, he is appealing to a virtual response on their part: "I *feel myself* looked at by the things."[25] What matters most is not the metaphysical status of this response—that is, whether trees really do look at me—but our own expectation that our glance will be returned, if not actually, then virtually. Such virtuality as is here at play is no stranger than the virtuality characterizing the pure memories that are being continually generated from every present moment. Both are "ideal" in that neither belongs to the stream of real events; yet both also belong to becoming and to the open—to "expanding virtualities in the deep circuits."[26] And because they belong to these circuits, they can be brought, through proper contraction, back into the present from which my glance first issued. Re-pli-cation is still on the agenda, and thus the special temporality which it brings with it.

This temporality can be characterized as a leap that loops back. Just as we leap back into the virtual past when we seek to remember it (Bergson's metaphors are expressly salutory in this context)[27], so the glance leaps out from our seeing eye. Such a leap constitutes the first phase of a loop that brings what we glance at into the orbit of our glance; in a second phase the past returns in memory images and the other (human or not) comes back as reply (actual or not). The ecstasy of the leaping-out is completed in the composure of the loop established between the glancer and the glanced-at by which the glance is completed. The one-way directedness of the glance—posited by Husserl in his account of intentionality—is here replaced by a two-way circuit in which inflow is as important as outflow. This has crucial implications for understanding time: the exclusively outward-tending *Blick* so often at stake in *Ideas I* supports (even as it reflects) the hypothesis of a unidirectional time line, whereas the self-returning glance confirms the looping-back of time that is implicit in the "all-at-once" structure of absolute flux, that deep stratum of time posited by Husserl beneath the time line but never fully legitimated by his own account of time-consciousness.[28]

In contrast, Bergson brings the latency of absolute flux into the patency of temporality itself, since each mental state "is borne by the fluid mass of our whole psychical existence."[29] We see this happening in the merest glance we cast. The very first concrete example cited in *Creative Evolution* is "the visual perception of a motionless external object." Bergson remarks that the object may well remain the same, but "the vision I now have of it differs from that which I have just had, even if only because the one is [ever so slightly] older than the other."[30] This could well be a case of a glance, given its quickly changing character. But the brevity of the action belies its durational depth, for "it is with our entire past . . . that we desire, will, and act."[31] In other words, the return loop of the glance includes much more than its immediate circuit; it also includes the entire pyramid of the glancer's past, a whole heritage of previous perceptions, thoughts, desires, etc. In Bergson's own model from *Matter and Memory*, the past, virtual but massive, forms a cone of ever-increasing diameter. Yet enormous as it becomes in an individual's life, it always funnels itself into a discrete (but noninstantaneous) present, represented by the tip of the cone as it touches the plane of ongoing experience. No wonder, then, that the glance can be so paradigmatic in grasping time as duration; its exiguous structure conveys in a contracted format the paradox to which all experience of time is subject: that a maximum of accumulated content is brought to bear on a minimum of current commotion. Far from being marginal, the glance is emblematic of this quite general condition of all human temporality.

The glance is of even greater significance in regard to the other great paradox of duration—that, despite its continual and complete conversion into the past, duration is the very scene of novelty, the exact place of becoming. Viewed one way, duration is an ineluctable amassing of the same (for, as virtual and past, it stays ever the same in what Merleau-Ponty would call an "existential eternity"[32]); but as a qualitative multiplicity that is ever-growing, it is always different, always in touch with the new, always a new whole, always open to "the open." If it is true that "we are supported by this [massive] past," it is also true that "we lean over [the] future."[33] We do not just edge into the future but actively embrace it, we go out to meet it; not because it already exists (as "lean over" and "embrace" and "meet" might imply, taken literally) but because our very duration is able to grow commensurately with anything that will happen to us. "We are creating ourselves continually,"[34] says Bergson, and by this he means that our duration is sufficiently capacious to contain the most unexpected events.

Being durational is being capable of the most radical *becoming*; the classic distinction between being and becoming breaks down insofar as we are capable of the kind of movement that flows with the most unlikely changes in what is now going on, and yet this happens in terms of all that we have been. Bergson is unequivocal in his affirmation that "duration means invention; the continual elaboration of the absolutely new"[35]— where by "absolutely new" he means the strictly *unforeseeable*, "that which has never [before] been perceived, and which is at the same time simple . . . an original moment of a no less original history."[36] For no one, he insists, is able to foresee how things will turn out; no one can "foresee the simple indivisible form which gives to . . . purely abstract elements [i.e., particular causal influences] their concrete organization."[37] For this organization, though simple as an overall structure, is unique in the form it will take in a given situation—a form that will emerge only in the course of the becoming of the new event itself.

Precisely in this context, glancing takes on a very special significance, for it bears directly on the "absolutely new." Indeed, it is just because the future is so unforeseeable that the glance is so valuable. It looks out in advance of what will (probably) soon happen for what might (eventually) happen; it scans the horizon of what could be before it has become actual in the present and virtual in the past. It is the sentinel of the sentient being; the outpost of the organism in its effort, its need, to come to terms with the *imprévisible* before it has become literally *visible*. It is a vanguard act, standing out before / beyond the present with the intention of discerning in advance what may happen. Indeed, the glance is the primary way in which we are watchful for the incipient future, warily aware of its becoming to come. In this regard, the glance is like an antenna receiving the future, not wholly unlike Freud's idea of the sense organs as "feelers" that probe the external world.[38]

But the glance is not just a wary surveyor of the possible future: the glance not only goes out to the future in advance but also *awaits* its happening and actively *escorts* it into the present. Beyond the active reaching out of its initial action, the glance engages in a receptive moment of attending to what is beginning to happen, taking in the new surface of its emergence: "L'attention est une attente," says Bergson.[39] The attentiveness of the glance ushers the oncoming future into the present. The imminent event is accepted, carried, supported into the present, allowed to become part of the durational scene, permitted to become at once actual and virtual and no longer only possible.

In the three moments I have just distinguished there is evident the same folding-back structure to which I have pointed before. The watchful vanguard glance goes out from the organism / self to see what might happen, while the waitful glance prepares for the watched-for event to begin to sink into the durational whole—a whole into which the same continuing glance escorts the now discernible (even if still never fully foreseeable) event. We witness here once more the same two-beat rhythm of going out and returning—this time a going out into the not yet having happened and a returning of (and with) it into what will endure within.

LACERATING TIME

Despite all of Bergson's precautions against misunderstanding duration as a mere "block" of time, he nevertheless conceives of it as a special kind of whole. This wholeness, even as always new, is in tension with Bergson's equal emphasis on its sheer qualitative heterogeneity: a self-othering that refuses to be totalized. As a *whole*, duration is all-encompassing and seamless, and yet, as it is heterogeneous, it cannot be self-contained. In particular, there is what Merleau-Ponty calls "leakage"(*échappement*) in the system.[40] Duration is perforated from within, and it is the glance that is a primary perforator of the durational matrix.[41] How is this so?

The glance lacerates; not only does it strike, as we signify in speaking of "a glancing blow," but it also *cuts*—most conspicuously in social scenes, where demeaning or insulting glances are emitted and exchanged.

Whenever we quickly "size up" a situation as beneath our dignity, or otherwise engage in invidious estimates based on mere glances, we are tearing the social fabric, perforating it, and in any case undercutting the Bergsonian axiom that "there is [nothing but] a continuity which unfolds."[42] But we perforate in the perceptual domain as well—for example, when we glance *through* an object, refusing to stay on its surface, and instead insinuate ourselves into an interior we can glimpse only translucently or else thrust all the way through the object onto its other side or far horizon. In contrast with Husserl's reassurance that "the look abides"[43]— an assurance explicitly called into question by Derrida—the glance is restless, and often takes apart that which the social and spatial world presents to us on its insouciant sleeve.

Glance-work thus proves to be lance-work. This latter is not to be confused with the separation-work of the intellect that neatly divides space and time into punctiform points and instants—that way lies the homogeneity for whose inaugural deconstruction Bergson is justly celebrated. Instead, the glance opens tiny tears in the continuous cloth of duration as well as minuscule faults in the surfaces of things, places, and people. Like David in the den of Goliath: the glance is a slingshot that penetrates the armamentarium of duration and space, creating leakage in "the universe [that] appears to us to form a single whole."[44] The glance, then, is as insidious and disruptive as it is embracing. From mere glancing, we build up and take in whole worlds; but from the same action, we tear them down as well.

EVER NEW BECOMINGS

From a first look at the innocence, the mereness and brevity of the glance, we have traveled to a more considered view of its secret force, its concealed power, its destructive edge. I have been playing off the lightness of its being against the heaviness of durational becoming by arguing that the narrowness of its defile, its slender wake, is complicitous with its very ability to bring down giants, including such otherwise opposed philosophical giants as thick durational time and thin linear temporality. But have I not overstated my case? Let us reconsider the matter for a final time.

Bergson himself would doubtless argue that the punctuating power of the glance is in the end only a ripple on the surface of deep duration.[45] He admits that it is all too easy to suppose that there is "*one* Duration of the universe" and thus to espouse "the hypothesis of *one* material and universal Time."[46] Even if he rejects the idea that there is a single universal duration—a "duration of durations" in effect—he still insists that the durational whole of each individual is indivisible and, in his own term, "Absolute."[47] Hence the Bergsonian imperative: "It's no use trying to *approach* duration: *we must install ourselves within it straight away.*"[48] Would not Bergson say the same of the glance: that we should bury it within duration right away or, more exactly, recognize that it is always already so buried—installed there in advance, as it were? Indeed, does not my own two-beat model of the glance, valorizing as it does the glance's influx as much as its outflow, fit all too well into the wholistic (if not monolithic) durational schema of Bergsonian metaphysics? So it would seem. Does not the glance return to its own durational whole?

Yet the return movement of the glance is not simply a return to the "same," a nostalgic retreat of the sort at stake in Levinas's incisive critique of an Odyssian homecoming. Instead, the glance returns bearing the world on its slender shoulder, thereby altering the subject who initiated it, enlarging and extending the glancer in ways that are as radically new and unforeseeable as the course of duration itself. The newness of the world taken in—and it is always new, in its form as in its matter[49]—acts to renew the subject who first sends the glance into that world. The subtlety of the renovation, the fact that it is often imperceptible, makes it no less momentous in and for the ongoing history of the subject. A single glance can launch a thousand ships, only a few of which may ever return; but every glance, by its own assured return, revivifies the subject who sent it forth into the world.

The glance can be considered a leading instance of the *ritournelle*, that is, the return phrase or refrain that despite its brevity or otherwise modest aspects is essential to the operation of the overall circuit of which it is a part. Deleuze and Guattari's examples are a "territory" that is indispensable to the larger circuit of the Earth, or (following Nietzsche) the small recurrence that proves decisive to "eternal recurrence."[50] Just as the refrain in classical harmonics returns to reenter the basic melody, so the glance returns to reestablish the very duration which, in its ecstatic projectedness, it had challenged. The ritornello movement is one of the most effective ways in which movement of any kind—evolutionary as well as musical, cosmic as well as terrestrial, glancing as well as staring—can gather force by folding back on itself, coiling over onto its own back, starting again from renewed power. All this is in contrast with movement that merely goes on and on and on: *phora* or transfer of motion, in contrast with *kinésis* or qualitative change. In its ritornello movement, the glance contributes kinetically to the rich qualitative multiplicity of duration. It illustrates with exemplary clarity the truth of Bergson's second durational imperative: "In order to advance with moving reality, *you must replace yourself within it*."[51] The action of replacement—or *reimplacement*, as I prefer to call it—is accomplished more effectively by the glance than by much more ponderous human actions such as scientific scrutiny, meditative contemplation, concentrated heeding, and the like, all of which are concerned with attaining or discerning an abiding presence.

Otherwise put: the tiny circuit of the glance, in its tacit and taciturn ritornello movement, reimplaces the subject within the increasingly deeper circuits of duration, its widening gyres—widening onto the world, the "open," the "whole." But it does not make a straightforward contribution to the larger scene of duration, the "world-whole," as Kant would call it. Even if (as a single sweeping glance) it may scan the entirety of given perceptual field, its penetrative particularity and its singular return act to detotalize whatever it searches out. And within the subject it undoes the inwardly embraced whole of duration that inspires Bergson to call each such whole an "absolute." It punctures the durational subject from within just as it perforates the enduring world from without: a case of double leakage.

Similarly, the time of the glance, the moment in which it endures, detotalizes any presumptive totality of time. There is always just enough time for the glance, and the time it takes, its moment of becoming, is situated between the infinitesimal instant and the infinity of duration. In its intermediacy (and in spite of its immediacy), the time of the glance has its own duration, allowing the double beat of its operation, going out into the world and sinking back into the durational flux that is the province of each subject in time.

Despite the regularity of its diphasic temporal movement, despite its continual refrain of return, the glance is never fully integrated into the time-world of its own projective subject. Its recoil brings with it foreign times as well as places, those of others whom it has glimpsed, pieces of shrapnel from their lives that cannot be fully assimilated to one's own life.[52] In this respect, the glance is a disquieting force both in its outward course—where it first encounters the "other" (for instance, in the face-to-face relation of utter exteriority)—*and* in its inward return, where it must attempt to incorporate what may be as unincorporateable as it is unfore-seeable. At stake here is not return to the "same" but constitution of the "different."

But this is only to say constitution of ever-new becomings. It is the the-sis of differentiated duration, combined with the unforeseeability of the future, that permits Bergson to reject the notion of a single becoming in general and to embrace the idea of "infinitely varied" becomings, each with its own time and duration, each traveling its own course, each find-ing its own future, each always absolutely new. In the generation of mul-tiple becomings, the glance has a crucial role to play: it gives shape to any particular becoming by being a primary vehicle of its outgoing and ongo-ing engagement with the circumambient world, and by carrying the sur-faces of that world back into the attentive subject. When Bergson writes that "an infinite multiplicity of becomings variously colored, so to speak, passes before our eyes,"[53] he could well have been speaking of the way our glances deliver to us a diversely populated world of variegated beings in space as well as informing our own continually changing becomings in time.

The glance does all this thanks to its peculiarly indirect insertion into the social and perceptual world, its laterality, its location on the agitated edge of the restless subject. Instead of proceeding by cinematographic means—"taking snapshots of passing reality"[54] as Bergson puts it—it acts kaleidoscopically, by opening us to a qualitative disparity that it manages to arrange into more or less coherent patterns. What Bergson says of the kaleidoscopic basis of perception can be said of the glance that is its trav-eling body, its proxy in the scene of otherness:

> There is, between our body and other bodies, an arrangement like that of the pieces of glass that compose a kaleidoscopic picture. Our activity goes from an arrangement to a re-arrangement, each time no doubt giving the kaleidoscope a new shake, but not interesting itself in the shake, and seeing only the new picture. . . . *The cinematographical character of our knowledge of things is due to the kaleidoscopic character of our adapta-tion to them.*[55]

With its cutting look composed of shards of perspective, the glance, like the kaleidoscope, juxtaposes the materials from which cinematographic images are fashioned in symmetry and grace. These images, as "immobile sections," are ultimately dependent on the "mobile sections" that are the movements of the glance itself. As William James remarked in commenting on Bergson, such movements "come in drops, waves, or pulses," with the result that, as James adds, "time itself comes in drops."[56]

This should come as no surprise by now, if it is indeed true that (as we read in *Creative Evolution*) "action is discontinuous, like every pulsation of life; discontinuous, therefore, is knowledge [as well]."[57] Nor should it be surprising to know that this double discontinuity of action and knowledge is in turn made possible by the discontinuity of the glance, at once an emblem and a source of the differentiation of duration and the absolute newness of each becoming.

6

**FLOWS OF DESIRE AND
THE BODY-BECOMING**

Dorothea Olkowski

From the very beginning of his work, Gilles Deleuze has played with and upon the notion of desire. Such play almost always turns upon a concept of the body. In *Nietzsche and Philosophy*[1] Deleuze articulates a multiplicity of connections involving the body, the notion of force, and desire. He writes:

> What is the body? We do not define it by saying that it is a field of forces, a nutrient medium fought over by a plurality of forces. For, in fact, there is no medium, no field of forces or battle. There is no quantity of reality, all reality is a quantity of force. (*Nietzsche*, 39 / 44)

The body is not a medium, and body does not designate substance; but it does express the relationship between forces. It is precisely because the relationship between forces is not constituted out of some kind of preexisting medium or preexisting reality that, while forces are available for in-

This paper is a revised version of "Flows of Desire and the Body," in *Continental Philosophy VII*, ed. Hugh J. Silverman (New York: Routledge, 1999). Reference numbers before the slash are English translations. The French original follows the slash.

terpretation, they are never known. With the term *body,* then, Deleuze is referring not simply to the psychophysiological bodies of human beings but to *body* in its broadest sense. Bodies may be chemical, biological, social, or political; and the distinction between these modes is not, as Deleuze argues in *Difference and Repetition,*[2] ontological. If anything, it becomes, for Deleuze (with Félix Guattari), semiological, a function of different regimes, different organizations of life.[3] This is why *body* may be too general a concept for Deleuze and so is in need of greater pragmatic and conceptual articulation. Another attempt to delineate a concept of the body is found in *Anti-Oedipus,*[4] within a system that may be far more complicated than the one found in *Nietzsche and Philosophy* but that nonetheless, relates desire to bodies.

Anti-Oedipus has, of course, been viewed suspiciously by feminist theoreticians of the body. Alice Jardine's criticism of Deleuze and Guattari is that they have abandoned the familial-psychoanalytic and even the academic-textual point of view for a cosmic vision of the world that is more likely to address "[s]ea animals, computers, volcanoes, birds, and planets than the bourgeois family hearth and its books."[5] Of course, from a certain point of view this is precisely what is remarkable, original, and revolutionary in Deleuze and Guattari's work. If desire has been conceptualized in psychoanalysis as connected to bodies in such a way that desire is nothing but a reaction to the past that seeks images of the "impossible real," then, as Jacques Donzelot has argued, "Deleuze and Guattari moved from this . . . [to the] retort that desire is the real itself. Why, they ask, see anything other than a difference in regime between desiring activity and social, technical, artistic, or political activity?"[6]

Deleuze and Guattari's is truly a nonhumanistic point of view insofar as desire is never a desire for something but is itself material production that can be regulated just like the rest of the social field. What this means, however, is that their argument is not about some utopic projection: in fact, Deleuze and Guattari argue that "it is correct to retrospectively understand all history in the light of capitalism" (*Anti-Oedipus,* 140 / 160) but only insofar as the desiring-production of bodies cannot be differentiated from the social production of capital, which alone of all social machines "liberates flows of desire" (*Anti-Oedipus,* 139 / 163), opening up the flows that realize the body without organs and desiring production. Thus desire, bodies, the real, the social—none of this makes sense apart from an analysis of capitalism.

Anti-Oedipus may be Deleuze and Guattari's best-known work, but it has often been regarded as their most difficult. In this book Deleuze and Guattari address multiple issues and carry out many philosophical tasks at once; to name a few: the critique of psychoanalytic fantasy in the form of Oedipus, the extension of Marxist materialism to desire as well as a reconception of desire as positive, the refusal of Lévi-Strauss's concept of society as a structure of exchange, a refutation of Baudrillard's concept of a Lacanian unconscious enslaved by signs, an examination of the limits of Wilhelm Reich's explanation of fascism, a schizoanalysis of capitalism, a celebration of artistic freedom at the threshold of capitalist economy. *Anti-Oedipus* is the product of a certain era as well—an era that saw the end of the alliance between Freud and Marx, the crumbling of Lacanian orthodoxy and Hegelian dialectics, and the refusal of structuralism ushered in by Foucault's archaeology. While I cannot hope to follow all these diverging movements, I will trace out here some of the chief concepts involved in the "revolutionary" reconception of desire and the body, particularly insofar as they are conceived of as processes or becomings rather than as things.

Let me begin with one of Deleuze and Guattari's introductory images in *Anti-Oedipus*. They quote from George Büchner's *Lenz*:

> He [Lenz] thought that it must give one a sense of infinite bliss to be thus touched by the individual life of every form of creation, to have a soul that would communicate with stones, metals, water, and plants, as in a dream to absorb into oneself every being in nature, as flowers absorb air according to the waxing and waning of the moon.[7]

What attracts Lenz is being touched by the individual life of every form of creation, a soul in communication with every form of living thing: stone, metal, water, plant; to exist on a microlevel prior to the categorizations imposed by consciousness-culture. This would be, from a certain point of view, a kind of nothingness, but not the empty nothingness of negation. Lenz, Deleuze and Guattari conclude, has projected himself back to a time before the man-nature dichotomy, living nature as nothing but a process of production, so that "the self and the nonself, outside and inside, no longer have any meaning whatsoever" (*Anti-Oedipus*, 2 / 8). Yet, even if we accept the determination that Lenz has "projected himself back" to a pre-dichotomous era, it nonetheless seems that Lenz has done this in the midst of a society that clearly makes such dichotomies: human-nature, self-nonself, inside-outside. All these and more are imposing themselves upon Lenz, till he is forced to find relief in extreme actions just to "recall himself to consciousness" (*Lenz,* 60). He throws himself into an icy fountain in the middle of the night; he jumps out a window, breaking or dislocating his arm; he attempts to pray, even to preach. All these are efforts to bring himself back to his "senses," to resocialize, to redichotomize, to conform to the social regime (in this case, the despotic semiotic of God and family).

But Lenz's initial insight into the connection between the stars, the sky, the mountains—all teeming with production—and himself is the insight that guides Deleuze and Guattari in their discussion of desire and bodies. This sense is that of neither man nor nature, but of the process of production "that produces one within the other" and couples various processes together. The radicalized body, the molecular and microbody communicating with stone, metal, water, and plant, the body-becoming is what they mean by desiring machines (*Anti-Oedipus,* 2 / 8). It is precisely in these terms that Deleuze and Guattari articulate the first aspect of "process" in their explanation of "process of production." While such processes are unconscious, this does not mean that they are "the secret repository of a meaning to be deciphered, but rather the state of coexistence of man and nature" in which there is nothing to express (*An Antisociology* 30 / 838). So they must not be characterized simply in human terms, and especially not in humanistic terms. Desiring-machines are everywhere; they are actively synthesizing with respect to all chemical, biological, social, and political bodies, all of which are the expressions of the relations between forces. And though these latter are pure processes, they are not purely arbitrary—elements or particles. They undergo syntheses and are "selected" by a process that is local, partial, and perceptual in nature. For example, the first articulation, the production of production, in the geological conceptualizaiton of *A Thousand Plateaus,*[8] is conceived of by Deleuze-Guattari as, "the process of 'sedimentation,' which deposits units of cyclic sediment according to statistical order" (*Plateaus,* 41 / 55); while the second articulation, the process of recording, "sets up a stable functional structure and effects the passage from sediment to sedimentary rock" (*Plateaus,* 41 / 55). In other words, a stable, functional structure is constituted, whether we are talking about geological formations or social formations. Each process involves coding, though the first is merely the creation of a certain order, while the second is already organized, thus overcoded, centered, unified, integrated, hierarchized, and finalized.

Processes of production, recording, and consumption are modes of ordering and organization, called "syntheses." All syntheses are unconscious productions of desiring-machines, requiring the rethinking of all oppositional distinctions such as those between human-nature, industry-nature, society-nature, and their correlative spheres of production, distribution, and consumption. These dichotomies have long been taken for granted, not only in philosophy, but also in social and economic spheres. Likewise, the correlative spheres of production, distribution, and consumption are presumed to be separate. But as Marx argued, if production, distribution, and consumption are taken to be separate from one another, this is only because capitalist industry believes that it extracts raw materials from nature, that it creates industrial products opposed to natural occurrences, and that the refuse and / or environmental pollutants it dumps back into the earth are simply the price "nature" must pay, since all production emanates from the body of capital and presupposes "not only the existence of capital and the division of labor, but also the false consciousness that the capitalist being necessarily acquires, both of itself and of the supposedly fixed elements within an overall process" (*Anti-Oedipus*, 4 / 9).[9]

This means that all distinctions between production, recording, and distribution, as well as all distinctions within these three syntheses of production, are part of one and the same process of production. From the point of view of capital, the productive nature of the three syntheses is invisible, and production is mapped, studied, and understood in specialized fields of knowledge according to industrial and social utility. Yet recording processes (those processes that set up stable, functional structures) are immediately utilized and thus consumed; and consummations are immediately reproduced, so that there is nothing but process, "incorporating recording and consumption within production itself, thus making them the productions of one and the same process (*Anti-Oedipus*, 4 / 10). So, as Lenz wished (and Marx's analysis determined), no differentiation can be made between human beings and nature, and this is the second meaning of process; *humans* and *nature* are not opposite terms. They are not polar terms in relations of causation, ideation, or expression (subject and object), because all such differentiations are merely idealizations of the process of production. Instead, humans and nature are caught up in the essential reality of "the producer-product," the single process for which desire serves as an immanent principle.

This introduces the third aspect of the notion of process: it is not a goal or an end in itself, but neither can it be extended indefinitely. Rather, every force extends its power only as far as it is able, so the end of any process is simply its completion. When Deleuze and Guattari point out that productive and reproductive desiring-machines reach their completion, they are simply pointing to the fact that all desiring-machines are binary; they obey laws or sets of rules which govern their associations, whereby one machine is coupled with another. "Production of production" has been characterized as a moving series of conjunctions, which have the logical form of " 'and . . . ' 'and then . . . ,' " (*Anti-Oedipus*, 5 / 11) and are thus open wholes rather than unities that transcend their parts.[10] A flow is produced by one machine, but interrupted or diminished by another machine, for while "desire causes the current to flow," it also "flows in turn, and breaks the flows" (*Anti-Oedipus*, 5 / 11).

It becomes immediately important to realize that the unconscious does not symbolize, imagine, or represent desire. Donzelot expresses this point of view when he argues that Freud had certainly already made it possible to conceive of desire as extended to all "surfaces of contact" (polymorphous perversity), but what is different in Deleuze and Guattari's conception of desire is that, "Desire is no longer viewed as a desire for something . . . [but as] the simultaneous *desubstantialization and demystification of sexuality*, such that desire no longer has a precise substance or a meaning" (*An Antisociology*, 30 / 838). Indeed, given that the concept *body* must be taken in the broadest sense, and that productive syntheses assemble, at least, stone, metal, water, plant, and animal, we can no longer make claims about desire as private, or subjective, or irrational, directed by or toward the Imaginary, that is, images of social norms.

Desiring-production is wholly social production; nature and society are not opposites or separate in any way, but express differences in intensities and organization or coding. So, insofar as it is not substantial, desire is simply machinic (not mechanical); that is, it makes connections. Lacan would call it the impossible "Real" (the process of production which for Deleuze-Guattari is precisely not impossible). What this means, for Deleuze and Guattari, is that productive, unconscious desiring-machines are "the domain of free syntheses . . . [of] endless connections, nonexclusive disjunctions, nonspecific conjunctions, partial objects[11] and flows" (*Anti-Oedipus*, 54 / 63).

Yet, following the analysis of series which Deleuze provides in *Difference and Repetition*, unconscious desiring-production proceeds along a variety of paths unless it is "subjected to the requirements of representation," that is, the requirements of hierarchy and substantial being. Then, it must yield to the representation of something like Oedipus, the despotic signifier, where production is no longer the production of the "Real, " but production only of some imaginary thing, the "unconscious expression" (*Anti-Oedipus*, 54-55 / 63-64). When the Oedipal code converts all the flows of desiring-production into the detached signified "phallus," it provides the nonsignifying signs with a signifier, assigns sexuality to one of the sexes, and recasts the history of partial objects into that of castration (lack) (*Anti-Oedipus*, 73 / 87). The second or disjunctive syntheses—in which desiring-machines attach themselves to the "body without organs" (of the living earth in primitive society, the despot in barbaric society, and capital in capitalist society), so that all organization of forces into stable entities appears to emanate from the social formation—can also operate freely by opposing the restrictive Oedipal uses that bypass the disjunction "both / and" and that produce either "exclusive, symbolic differentiations" or "the undifferentiated Imaginary" (*Anti-Oedipus*, 110 / 131). But usually, under pressure to stabilize, to join the community, the " 'ego' takes on the co-ordinates that differentiate it at one and the same time with regard to generation, sex, and vital state" (*Anti-Oedipus*, 75 / 90). Thus this synthesis, limited by Oedipus, produces parent or child, man or woman, alive *or* dead—never both at once. As Brian Massumi points out, neither Oedipus nor capital can tolerate multiple identity; no unconscious desiring-production as transparentchild, transsexual, transalivedead affirmative use of disjunctive syntheses; no spanning between the disjuncts.[12]

The third synthesis, conjunctive synthesis, is that in which the productions of connective and disjunctive syntheses are brought together to constitute "races, cultures, and their gods" (*Anti-Oedipus,* 85 / 101) forces that compromise a social field. Here too, conjunctive syntheses can be both segregative and exclusive (where one proclaims oneself part of the superior race or culture) or / and nomadic and polyvocal (where one finds the outsider and minor becoming) (*Anti-Oedipus*, 105 / 125).

In *Anti-Oedipus* and *A Thousand Plateaus*, Deleuze and Guattari discuss what happens when these three syntheses of desiring-machines are subject to their exclusive Oedipal use and so translate into the three great strata that bind us through social repression: the organism, *signifiance*, and subjectification, that is, lack, law, and signifier. Because desire is never the sign of lack or law but of force or power (*puissance*)—what a body is able to do—it is the task of the body without organs to "disarticulate" these strata, thereby opening the body to connections (*Plateaus*, 159-160 / 197). From this we can see that desiring-production confronts both social production and the "repression that the social machine exercises on desiring-machines," effecting psychic repression through social repression. Yet the production of desire does not demand a free-flowing eros of any kind simply because it assumes the existence of the "unconscious libidinal investment of sociohistorical production" (*Anti-Oedipus*, 98 / 117). As Eugene Holland has argued, "Deleuze and Guattari insist on placing the family [Oedipalized desire] in its sociohistorical context and considering culture and society as a whole."[13] Thus, they maintain that social and cultural regimes always "override" the relatively limited Oedipus complex.[14] There are many forces that "Oedipalize" the unconscious (transgression, guilt, castration); psychoanalysis merely reinforces the segregative and exclusive use of all the syntheses of the unconscious, stopping up creative flows (*Anti-Oedipus*, 112 / 133).

In the English preface to *Anti-Oedipus*, Michel Foucault appears to make this same point when he argues that Deleuze and Guattari confront fascism as their main adversary, and not merely Oedipus. However, their argument is not only against the historical fascism of Germany and Italy; more particularly, what they challenge is "the fascism in us all, in our heads and in our everyday behavior, the fascism that causes us to love power, to desire the very thing that dominates and exploits us" (*Anti-Oedipus*, xii). Above all, this is a fascism of the body, the body of desiring-production in all its articulations. Thus, while Oedipus is clearly the signifier that stratifies and overcodes desiring-production in the capitalist social formation, nonetheless, it operates and can operate only within the context of a social system that needs it, that produces Oedipus as a fascism of the body.

In order for Oedipus to restrict desire, a "displacement" takes place first, so that some aspect of desiring-production, some machinic connection of the first synthesis of productive desire is already stopped up by social prohibition. The effect of this social displacement is that desiring subjects are persuaded that *they* were trying to trespass a law of desire's limits. Why bother? Why go to such lengths to control even the simplest and most direct connections of desire, the baby taking the breast or bottle or the hand reaching out or the eye following light? Because, Deleuze and Guattari answer, desire *is* revolutionary. Their astonishing response is worth repeating:

> If desire is repressed, it is because every position of desire, no matter how small, is capable of calling into question the established order of a society: not that desire is asocial, on the contrary. But it is explosive; there

is no desiring-machine capable of being assembled without demolishing entire social sectors. (*Anti-Oedipus*, 116 / 138)

Entire social sectors! An amusing hypothesis they call this. Desire compromises exploitation, servitude, and hierarchy (exclusive connective, disjunctive, and consumptive syntheses). Desire threatens the very being of a society when that society is identical with these structures. The conclusion is that society must repress desire in order to continue reproducing itself. The problem is often how to distinguish "real" desiring-production from the social-production that represses it, and from the family, which is nothing but the agent of psychic repression (*refoulement*) bearing down on desire in service to the social, and displacing it through a process of disfigurement (*Anti-Oedipus*, 119 / 142). Under these conditions, in the place of desiring-production an Oedipal formation is synthesized: incest, desire for the mother, narcissism, hysteria.

Even when unimpeded by the signifier, desiring-production is involved in some sort of ordering or organization. *Anti-Oedipus* articulates three types of "machinic" connections in both their nonrestrictive and their restrictive uses. The nonrestrictive connective syntheses add together and so couple desiring-machines to produce localized and partial objects as well as the flow of production. They oppose the Oedipal—thus parental and conjugal—restrictive syntheses subject to a despotic signifier that operates by "assigning lack to each position of desire" and "fusing desire to a law" (*Anti-Oedipus*, 100 / 131). Thus molar collective formations take precedence over molecular and multiple partial objects. Not Lenz's connection to stone, plant, metal, water, but consciousness and landscapes.

Too often, readings of *Anti-Oedipus* reflect only the restrictive and limiting aspects of the three syntheses. Yet it seems to me that nonrestrictive desiring-productions are operating everywhere. Deleuze and Guattari punctuate their text with references to literary, musical, and visual-arts disruptions of social production as if this were the chief arena of action in which creative flows struggle for realization. Such flows and breaks of desiring-production are found in Marcel Proust's *In Search of Lost Time*, where "the two sexes are both present and separate in the same individual: contiguous but partitioned and not communicating, in the mystery of an initial hermaphroditism."[15] Within the same entity, then, one finds heterosexual series, homosexual series, and transsexual series, which, on the molar level, indicate the existence of certain global persons who are fixed subjects and fixed bodies, complete objects with regard to their sex (*Anti-*

Oedipus, 70 / 83); but molecularly, it also "designates in the individual the coexistence of fragments of both sexes, partial objects which do not communicate. *And it will be with them as with plants*" (*Proust*, 120, emphasis added).

Molecularly (on the level Lenz longs for), elementally, we are all transsexual, flowing across all sexualities (*Anti-Oedipus*, 70 / 82). In every case, desiring-production produces the coupling and breaks the coupling. Such a process is a bricolage, indicating "the ability to rearrange fragments continually in new and different patterns or configurations; and as a consequence, an indifference toward the act of producing and toward the product, toward the set of instruments to be used and toward the over-all result to be achieved" (*Anti-Oedipus*, 7 / 13). Thus, desiring-production is indifferent toward capitalist divisions of process into production, recording, and consumption.

When couplings break and desiring machines "break down," they are actually working at their best. In such circumstances they are destabilizing, deterritorializing, releasing flows which otherwise would be channeled into a (social) organism, a stabilized, territorialized order. Deleuze and Guattari also draw our attention to artists freely creating desiring-machines that break down "within an object of social production." Ravel, they note, ends his compositions with "abrupt breaks, hesitations, tremolos, discordant notes, and unresolved chords, rather than allowing them to slowly wind down to a close or die away into silence," thereby breaking down or exploding the machines of social-production (*Anti-Oedipus*, 31-32 / 39). In doing so, Ravel converts the regime of technical (capitalist) machines or social-production into a regime of desiring-machines. Alternatively, we can look at the work of artist, Barbara Kruger, who writes: "If we experience life only through the filters of rigid categorizations, and binary oppositions, things will definitely be business as usual."[16] In Kruger's visual work, commercial slogans or popular clichés appear over the top of black-and-white images so as to multiply the possible senses of those images and put into question both those slogans and clichés and the social formation within which they have become banal. In the process Kruger deterritorializes rigid categorizations and binary oppositions to make way for sites of force that are otherwise unseen and unheard, unfelt and unknown.

In spite of the makeshift nature of the process of production, in spite of how desiring-machines continually break down, such a desire does not correspond to a negative and reactive desire, which merely fills a lack, then disappears; nor do the component pieces of desiring-machines fall apart and return us to a kind of nothingness, to "a pure fluid in a free state, flowing without interruption, streaming over the surface of a full body." Although pure fluids flowing without interruption are characteristic of the body without organs, nomadic flows of unstable matter are subject to an "important, inevitable phenomenon that is beneficial in many respects, and unfortunate in many others: stratification" (*Plateaus*, 40 / 55): "Desiring-machines make us an organism . . . [though] the body suffers from being organized in this way, from not having some other sort of organization, or organization at all (*Anti-Oedipus*, 8 / 14). The body suffers from the organization of desiring-machines in the process of production, but also from no organization at all. This statement problematizes desire in a way not indicated in Deleuze's text an Nietzsche. Thus, the entire notion of desire comes into question in *Anti-Oedipus*. Clearly, there is no emancipatory precultural eros, for desiring-machines repeating themselves in the syntheses of production are precisely what constitute our organization, what give us an order or an organism by means of their constant couplings and uncouplings, and what produce even the body without organs.[17] And the body without organs, the "*field* of forces" (chemical, biological, social, and cultural), the field over which desiring-machines extend themselves, that field is the "body without an image," which—unless it escapes production by identifying producing and product in the process of production itself, which produces the nonproductive body without organs—suffers from the division of the process of production into production, distribution, and consumption. That is, Deleuze-Guattari claim, it would be better not to have any objects at all, which is a matter not of taking vows of poverty but of affirming becoming.

In *Anti-Oedipus* Deleuze and Guattari argue that the dichotomous organization of desiring-machines is what the body without organs suffers from; as such, it resists this organization by setting up a counterflow, reproducing itself, "putting out shoots to the farthest corner of the universe" (*Anti-Oedipus*, 10 / 16). So, for example: "In order to resist using words composed of articulated phonetic units, it utters only gasps and cries that are sheer unarticulated blocks of sound . . . 'primary repression' . . . this repulsion of desiring-machines by the body without organs" (*Anti-Oedipus*, 9 / 15). Such is the case in Antonin Artaud's translation of Lewis Carroll's "Jabberwocky." In *The Logic of Sense*, Deleuze compares Carroll's nonsense verse:

Twas brillig, and the slithy toves
Did gyre and gymble in the wabe
All mimsy were the borogoves,
And the mome raths outgrabe,[18]

with the schizophrenic Artaud's unarticulated blocks of sound:

When Artaud says in his "Jabberwocky" "Until rourghe is to rouarghe
has rangmbde and rangmbde has rouargnambde," he means to activate, in-
sufflate, palatalize, and set the word aflame so that the word becomes the
action of a body without parts, instead of being the passion of a fragmented organism. (*Logic*, 89–90 / 110)

Artaud's "breath-words" or "howl-words" correspond "to an organism
without parts which operates entirely by insufflation, respiration, evapora-
tion, and fluid transmission (the superior body, the body without organs of
Antonin Artaud)" (*Logic*, 88 / 108). This *repulsion* of desiring-machines is
a repulsion by the body without organs; it actively repulses the organization of the body into organs that stratify the body in an act of capture that
operates like a "black hole," overcoding and territorializing, even while
the body without organs flees from territorialization, seeks to become
destratified and deterritorialized, and sends out shoots and rhizomes
(*Plateaus*, 40 / 54).

We saw in the case of *Lenz*, for example, that Lenz functions, or tries to
function, as an open system of desiring-production. "He" is a constant
process of connecting and making connections, but his continual becoming-other takes place within the limits and the order of a social framework
that demands conformity to socially appropriate norms: he is expected to
pray to God, to marry, to speak with and use common sense. What is at
stake is a matter not simply of a body trying to remain fluid, but of a mul-
tiple-becoming resisting the imposition of certain kinds of desiring-
machines by the social formation or social machines in the midst of a society that wants to limit this body to certain restricted parameters. Thus
Deleuze and Guattari's analysis of the operations of capitalism conceptualize this same process of bodies going to the limit of their power and bodies that are dominated by stronger forces. For, if the fluid body without organs is "captured" by the black hole of stasis and overcoding (the stable
structural formations of the body's own repetitions), it is because of the

next layer in this process: the social or cultural milieu, an even greater—that is, more powerful—force, which likewise captures the body so as to produce a surplus of consummation / consumption.

Every process of *social-production* begins with a full body (whether that of earth, tyrant, or capital): that is, a *socius*, which, according to Marx, precedes the process of production of the body without organs. In fact, for Marx, there cannot be a production process without an already existent society holding land in some form (*Grundrisse*, 88); in order for there to be becomings, there must be the body of the earth, the despot, or that of capital.[19] But the socius is more than land, for land is just another kind of body. The socius includes all types of bodies in the process of becoming, becoming-multiple, as well as a set of cultural norms with which to form them, to stop them up, law in the guise of the social. So the socius often acts as the very apparatus of capture, the black hole, referred to above, which Lenz and Artaud flee in their efforts to become, to remain fluid bodies. This is why or how the socius manifests an "unengendered nonproductive attitude, an element of antiproduction" (*Anti-Oedipus*, 10 / 16) or stasis, along with production.

Antiproduction, arresting the desiring-machine, is one mode in which the body without organ resists capture by social formations, and this explains why the body without organs is always at the limits of the social formation. This schizophrenic or absolute limit is not descriptive of schizophrenia as a pathology; rather, it is the organized and overcoded socius when its codes are scrambled or deterritorialized, that is, destabilized. However, it is not the only limit. The "genius" (and I use that term guardedly) of capitalism is, if you will, that it is the only social formation to make use of decoded flows by substituting something even more oppressive than a code—a "quantifying axiomatic"—is substituted for the codes that would otherwise organize bodies in social formations. Thus capitalism is always the "relative limit" of any social formation (*Anti-Oedipus*, 176 / 207).

It would be a mistake to overly valorize primitive social formations, given that the codes governing savage societies are both cruel and repressive. Alphonso Lingis describes the rituals of the Egret people, who brought their newborn children to the temple of Tlaloc, where the females would be bled from the ear and the males from the genitals, while adults drew blood from their own earlobes, tongues, thighs, upper arms, chests, or genitals.[20] These rituals "existed to drain ever greater multitudes of blood-sacrifices toward the pyramids of the sun the Aztecs erected on that monster whose maw swallows the setting sun, the remains of the dead, and sacrificial victims" (*Abuses*, 12). These practices, radically determinate as they are, have more to do with connecting organs to the earth and marking bodies, prior to the existence of any state. According to Lingis, these practices were altered by the arrival of the Spanish conquerors, whose "imperial-despotic order seeks to extend its administration over subject societies and economies" (*Abuses*, 12). They demanded filiation, not anymore with the earth, but with the imperial despot, a coding directly opposed to that of primitive territorial alliances (*Anti-Oedipus*, 193 / 229). While this generally forced primitive societies to give up or transform their practices, it is usually the case that the primitive code continues to haunt or inhabit certain aspects of the despotic socius (*Anti-Oedipus*, 194 / 230).

Nevertheless, it is instructive that primitive and despotic social formations do whatever they can to ward off the capitalist social formation, the free flows of money and production that demand the sacrifice of all codes to quantification. To use money to buy something that, in turn is sold for money is a process of quantification, which cannot be coded, although it usually makes use of what is already coded to carry out these transactions. As a social formation, the body of capital is without a fixed center or an established authority figure; thus it is no surprise that "exchange value and the market ruthlessly undermine and eliminate all traditional meanings and preexisting social codes" (*Schizoanalysis*, 407). And even though capital decodes every previous formation, opening desiring-production socially for the first time, still, free flows of desiring-production are not the outcome of capitalism.

The existence of capitalism is not the inexorable outcome of previous social coding; it has arisen owing to the chance *conjunction* of two of these deterritorialized flows (a chance, however, that requires numerous conditions).[21] On the one hand there are workers who have nothing and so are forced to sell their labor in order to survive; and on the other hand, there is money available to buy this labor (*Anti-Oedipus*, 225 / 266). Capitalism succeeds by appropriating for itself *all* the forces of production so that it appears as the cause of all production coming from all bodies. Here Marx's analysis holds true, for:

[T]hese productive powers and the social interrelations of labour in the direct labour-process seem transferred from labour to capital. Capital thus becomes a very mystic being since all of labour's social productive forces appear to be to capital, rather than labour as such. (*Anti-Oedipus*, 11 / 17)[22]

As freely flowing desiring-production, the schizoflows of Lenz or Artaud are one limit of capital; complete capture by despotic hierarchies is the other. This is why we cannot simply assume that capital's desiring-production actually produces becoming and opens the way for molecular becomings. For, given that capital takes over the entire field of social production, it immediately operates so as to recapture these free flows into "a world axiomatic that always opposes the revolutionary potential of decoded flows with new interior limits" (*Anti-Oedipus*, 246 / 292-293). Capital thus operates as a field of immanence of which the schizoflows are the exterior, the outside. To repeat: capital is a field of immanence, a world axiomatic that captures flows of desire and the production of becomings.

Capitalist machines decode and deterritorialize the previous machines, those of primitive or despotic societies, by transforming preexisting modes of production and consummation / consumption. Yet territorial despotic machines reemerge within the capitalist machine (in the form of Oedipus in the family and in order to reap profits on previous investments in the social sphere) to code and recode, territorialize and reterritorialize the flows of desire that capitalism decodes (*Schizoanalysis*, 408). The nuclear family is an entity cut off from the social formation. In this sense, it is reterritorialized, and the desiring-production of those caught in it is fixed on the objects "Mommy, Daddy"; this is partly what allows psychoanalysis to attend to the Oedipal desire of the nuclear family with relative success (*Schizoanalysis*, 13, 410, 416 n.). But today, as the nuclear family continues to break down, "blame" is placed on a lack of paternal authority and maternal care. Deleuze and Guattari would point instead to the social formation: "Capitalism tends toward a threshold of decoding that will destroy the socius in order to make it a body without organs . . . ," (*Anti-Oedipus*, 33 / 41) in order to make it possible to unleash flows of desire on the deterritorialized field.

Yet within the capitalist social formation:

> [A]s the nuclear family breaks down and increasingly fails to perform the oedipal reinscription of desire, . . . it is precisely psychoanalysis that steps in to finish the job. If need be, the psychoanalyst shoulders the mantle of the despot in the famous "transference." (*Schizoanalysis*, 410)

In contemporary society, however, psychoanalysis performs this role less and less. Today, it is just as often the political state or religious organizations that retain or resume the despotic role. The 1998 policy of the

American Southern Baptist Convention, proclaiming that women should be "graciously" subordinate to men, has to be seen as part of an ongoing attempt to re-Oedipalize what many take to be the loosening of patriarchal power in contemporary society. But one only has to recall the rhetoric of presidential politics and remember Senator Robert Dole's televised response to the president's State of the Union address of January 1996. Again and again, Dole urged Americans to go back, to return to the values they had abandoned: "We must . . . put parents back in charge of our schools, untie the hands of our police, restore justice to the courts, and put our faith once again in the basic goodness, wisdom, and self-reliance of our people."[23]

Unlimited parental authority, uninhibited police power, and an unrestricted punitive juridical system are all aspects of the despotic regime where the hierarchic arrangement of power remains the model for family, police, and juridical functions. That this occurred in the midst of decreased funding for environmental protection and for the impoverished is a function of the capitalist social formation itself, which sacrifices all desires to the functioning of the capitalist machine. This is obvious in the polemics of workfare: women who, as children, were completely ignored by failing schools and thus never acquired adequate employment skills, are now forced into working at degrading and dead-end jobs in order to earn their welfare benefits. These programs do nothing to reverse the failure of schools to care for and properly educate the poor and the throwaway. Nor do they provide these women with transferable employment skills. Women are encouraged, instead, to stay with abusive or equally unable males in order to approximate the nuclear family regardless of the personal cost. If there is a way to empower women and children or care for and educate the impoverished and unable (an unlikely scenario), it will not be embraced by the capitalist machine unless it guarantees that machine complete control.

Given this, one of the tasks of *Anti-Oedipus* is to question the right of the Oedipal or despotic image (what Deleuze and Guattari refer to as law) to determine the organization of production. Deleuze and Guattari comment on the problem of the Oedipal image in *Anti-Oedipus*, noting that the great discovery of psychoanalysis was the production of desire, by which they mean productions of the unconscious:

> But once Oedipus entered the picture, this discovery was soon buried beneath a new brand of idealism: a classical [Oedipal Greek] theatre was

substituted for the unconscious as a factory; representation [the image] was substituted for the units of production of the unconscious; and an unconscious that was capable of nothing but expressing itself [as subject]—in myth, tragedy, dreams—was substituted for the productive unconscious. (*Anti-Oedipus*, 24 / 31)

By this means, it is possible to begin to make sense of how a people can come to desire their own repression or how individuals can, in the midst of segregation and from out of a center of domination, proclaim themselves to be revolutionaries, as well as the multiplicity of movements between the two. That is, if unconscious desiring production is segregated and Oedipalized, as well as polyvocal and nomadic, this is because every "social form of production exercises an essential repression of desiring production" and "every position of desire, no matter how small, is capable of calling into question the established order of a society" and its *global* bodies. Desire, Deleuze and Guattari have insisted again and again, is "explosive," and every desiring-machine is completely capable of demolishing entire social sectors (*Anti-Oedipus*, 116 / 138). As I have emphasized above, the same set of syntheses is at work, producing both desire and its repression; it is only the chemical, biological, social, or political body—segregative and biunivocal or nomadic and polyvocal—that makes the difference.

The problem is that western thinkers operate with the Platonic logic of desire. Desire is taken to be only a means of satisfying a need or, as Deleuze and Guattari state it, as part of an acquisition, which makes desire into something negative, even nihilistic (*Anti-Oedipus*, 25 / 32). They credit Kant with at least conceiving of desire as a cause, even if it is the cause only of hallucinations and fantasies, of psychic realities, a definition tailor-made for psychoanalysis, which conceives of desire's fantasy object as the "double" of the "real" object of social-production (*Anti-Oedipus*, 25 / 32). Ultimately, such an interpretation of desire only reinforces the Platonic concept of desire as lack of an absolute object, for the substitution of fantasies for "Ideas" is theoretically insignificant. Deleuze and Guattari argue, however, that desiring-production does not produce hallucinations; it is a material process of production, the production of what might otherwise be called bodies but might better be called becomings. Naming desire as the cause of psychic realities only reinforces the concept of desire as "lack of a real object."

Nor is the Lacanian solution satisfactory. For Lacan, Deleuze and Guattari note, need, not desire, is what gets defined in terms of lack. But desire, even while producing both itself and the fantasy (by detaching from the object), makes the lack absolute, never fulfillable. Thus the relation of need to the object as something absolutely lacking remains the underlying support of the theory of desire, since even though desire produces the fantasy, there is always an object missing from the world, the one object that would fulfill the lack (*Anti-Oedipus*, 26 / 33).

The point, for Deleuze and Guattari, is that if desire is to be construed as productive, rather than as negative and nihilistic, needs are simply derived from desire as a "countereffect of desire," an indication of the loss of desire and the loss of passive syntheses; it is the loss of ability to produce within the realm of the real, the void which Deleuze and Guattari see ever so clearly as "the loss of the objective being of man" (*Anti-Oedipus*, 27 / 35). Such lack is not a result of human nature or essence; rather, it is a planned result of social-production that "falls back upon" and appropriates productive force; the market economy in the hands of its "dominant class" "deliberately organiz[es] wants and needs in the midst of an abundance of production" (*Anti-Oedipus*, 28 / 35). Such power is indeed great insofar as it is able to fell desiring-production, to silence productive syntheses, under the force of the great fear (a created fear) of not having one's needs satisfied. Lack, then, is an effect of the separation of the process of production and the object, placing the real object outside desiring-production (in the realm of the rational), and confining desiring-production to the production of fantasy.

Desire, however, as productive, must produce real, not just psychically real, products: thus "Desire is the set that engineers partial objects, flows, and bodies, and that functions as units of production. . . . Desire does not lack anything; it does not lack its object. It is, rather, the subject that is missing in desire" (*Anti-Oedipus*, 26 / 34). In the "autoproduction of the unconscious" the object is the real; there is no place for a "fixed subject" and thus no place for fixed bodies. And since there is no distinction between the process of production and the product, there is no distinction between desire and the objects of desire. As such, "Desire is a machine, and the object of desire is another machine connected to it" the machine of the first machine (*Anti-Oedipus*, 26 / 34). It is with this process of desire and of machinic connections, which never produce stable, finished bodies, that *Anti-Oedipus* concerns itself. And while the threat is everywhere that a destabilized body can be captured by the Oedipal forces capitalism discovers to be so useful or that decoded and deterritorialized flows may segregate, reform their own centers of domination (paranoid or fascistic), and cease producing, nonetheless Deleuze and Guattari do seem to have thought through the "explosive" and so creative power of desire.[24]

Social change and individual change are inevitable, but the form they will take is unpredictable because desire is unpredictable. The most Deleuze and Guattari can postulate is the sites of the explosions. When there is becoming, when the social-systems and the subject-systems deterritorialize into flows of desire and the body-becoming, such becoming will come from one of two directions: from within or from without. There remains, they appear to believe, the body without organs, that social body-becoming that is the "ultimate residuum of a deterritorialized socius," that is, of a socius that ceases to "codify the flows of desire" by ceasing to inscribe and regulate them, thereby destabilizing the socius and opening society from within to its own revolutionary force (*Anti-Oedipus*, 33 / 40). And finally, there are the flows of desire and the body-becoming of the revolutionary residual subject in whom desiring-production "cuts across the interest of the dominated, exploited classes, and causes flows to move that are capable of breaking apart both the segregations and their Oedipal applications" (*Anti-Oedipus*, 105 / 125). As the outsider, as deterritorialized, becoming is possible—becoming any dominated or exploited class, anything but the master nation, religion, or race, anything but the global body. In neither case, from within or from without, can we predict the form of the future. For if desire is explosive and the forces or bodies it produces are processes and not substances, then the forms of production of the flows of desire and the forms of production of molecular becomings can never be known in advance.

7

A GRAMMAR OF BECOMING: STRATEGY, SUBJECTIVISM, AND STYLE

Claire Colebrook

Nothing more can be said, and no more has ever been said: to become worthy of what happens to us, and thus to will and release the event, to become the offspring of one's own events, and thereby to be reborn, to have one more birth, and to break with one's carnal birth—to become the offspring of one's events and not of one's actions, for the action is itself produced by the offspring of the event.

GILLES DELEUZE, The Logic of Sense, 149–150.

Rather than seeking the permanence of themes, images, and opinions through time, rather than retracing the dialectic of their conflicts in order to individualize groups of statements, could one not rather mark out the dispersion of the points of choice, and define prior to any option, to any thematic preference, a field of strategic possibilities?

MICHEL FOUCAULT, The Archaeology of Knowledge, 37.

This paper seeks to explore the notion of strategy alongside the idea of a grammar of becoming. In so doing I will argue that there are two modalities of strategy. In Nietzschean terms we might define these as active and reactive. On this account the concept of the subject is not one concept among others, to be deployed for this or that strategy; rather, it bears in its very structure a certain mode of strategy. The very concept of the subject is tied to a strategy of being and essence, rather than becoming. And this

Gilles Deleuze, *The Logic of Sense,* trans. Mark Lester, ed. Constantin V. Boundas (New York: Columbia University Press, 1990).
Michel Foucault, *The Archaeology of Knowledge and the Discourse on Language,* trans. A. M. Sheridan Smith (New York: Pantheon), 1972.

is because the subject is not just a political category or representation but a movement of grammar. The very notion of a subject in the grammatical sense, as a being capable of predication, is also tied to a broader notion of grammar whereby political subjects or identities are effected through certain ways of speaking. The concept and logic of the subject as such, then, demands or provokes a movement of thought, a specific temporality and, ultimately, a strategy of reactivism, recognition, and being (rather than becoming). This paper will argue that a sustained consideration of strategy in general necessarily calls for a strategy of becoming. A strategy of the subject, on the other hand, can only *subordinate* strategy to some pre-strategic end. Whether such subordination is avoidable or desirable is a question I will pursue via a contrast between the genealogy of the self in Foucault and the geology of eternal return in Deleuze and Guattari.

WHAT SORT OF STRATEGY IS A PHILOSOPHY OF THE SUBJECT?

"Without cruelty there is no festival: thus the longest and most ancient part of human history teaches—and in punishment there is so much that is *festive!*" (67).[1]

It is perhaps in *On the Genealogy of Morals* that Nietzsche argues most forcefully for the idea of the subject as reactive. For the very idea of the subject depends upon the temporal logic of reactivism whereby an effect is grounded as a cause. According to Nietzsche's philosophy of will, there is initially the assertion of a certain force, an event of becoming or an activity. As an effect of this becoming, a site or position can be created. Reaction takes place when the effect of force—the marking out of a site or position—is taken as the cause, ground, essence, or *subject* of force (37). In explaining the inherently reactive character of morality, Nietzsche argues that there was originally a "festive cruelty"—an act of violence and force—that subsequently organized itself into a system of justified causes, such as punishment. The punishable "crime" is defined after (and as a reaction to) the active event of punishment or cruelty:

> ... To *make* suffer was in the highest degree pleasureable, to the extent that the injured party exchanged for the loss he had sustained the displeasure caused by the loss, an extraordinary counterbalancing pleasure: that of *making* suffer—a genuine festival (65).

If we adopt the standard definition of resentment ("Resentiment is the moral interpretation of the play of forces: I suffer therefore someone is guilty.") and reactive forces as slave morality, we are in danger of missing the point of Nietzsche's temporal logic. The idea that Christianity is a "slave morality" of the weak might suggest that the weak express a certain law for their advantage in order to have power over the strong. But this places the *position* of strength and weakness before the distribution of force. On this reading, the weak Christian is seen as one who uses or deploys a reactive morality. This implies that reactive strategy follows from a difference in power. But for Nietzsche the contrary is the case: the weak do not use reactive morality; weakness or slavery is effected through reaction. Reaction itself is a distribution of force, of which slavery is an effect. Reactive forces turn back upon themselves precisely because *what they effect*—their position—is not seen *as an effect or activity*. A reactive force *recognizes itself:* "I do this because of what I am." A reactive force regards its strategy as *effected from* its position. It does not see the strategic event of forceful becoming as that which marks out or constitutes the position. For Nietzsche, however, in the beginning is the force which constitutes the slave as slave; slavish forces are those which can only recognize their effects as causes: "I am weak because of the type of being I am" and not "I am the type of being I am only through my weakness." Overcoming resentment is a matter not of vanquishing slaves but of activating force. Strategy is not adopted according to one's position; a mode of strategy constitutes one's position. If the slave is an effect of resentment, or the turning of forces away from itself, mastery will be not just a shift in position but a shift in the quality of the force that determines position.

How might we see the human, as subject, as a reaction? The very idea of the human is reactive, of course, if it is seen as the given cause, truth, or ground of our being: if the human is an essence to be discovered. Just as a reactive force is an effect which takes itself as cause, so any recognition of essence or identity assumes that what one *is* is already given. The meek and mild Christian believes that he has chosen the path of humility and servitude *because he is a Christian*. But his identity as Christian is an *effect* of an original subordination to something other than himself (an ideal). Similarly, humanism turns to human (subjective) ideals to found its actions—ideals of the good moral subject—rather than seeing the human as the consequence of a certain way of acting. The human as the subject, at least in its philosophical or Platonic form, is defined against life. For the ideal of the subject is used to govern and justify existence, rather than being seen as an outcome of existence itself. Conceived as truth, cause, agent, or subject, the human is a reaction against life and becoming.

But this also opens the possibility that it is not the idea of the human per se that is reactive. What needs to be considered is the position the human occupies in the logic of truth and recognition. For alongside Nietzsche's disgust with the resentiment of human recognition there is also the affirmation of the over-man. This suggests that the "human" as the becoming-reactive of active forces might be an inevitable effect of becoming. If becoming does effect positions and modes of being—such as the human—then the human is not a cause of one's being but that which can also be affirmed as an event of becoming: not man as a rational animal or substance / subject, but man as the over-man, as the active assertion of the force or strategy that has asserted itself for so long as human while denying itself as force. If the human is a reaction against life, an effect of force that has taken itself as a cause, how can this reaction be made active? Not just by dispensing with the notion of the human, but by refiguring the relation of forces. The over-man is not a return to a presubjective unity or plenitude of chaotic becoming; nor is he a "posthuman" liberation into a field of pure difference. If the reactivism of the human subject is an effect of active becoming, then reactivism cannot be marked off as an evil that befalls activity. Rather, the reactive is an essential possibility of the active. The overcoming of reactive strategies cannot just be the assertion of a better or more worthy strategy; a critique of resentiment will need to address the *modality* of strategies. How do forces turn back upon themselves? How can the human reaction be overcome? These questions concerning the human cannot be answered by assessing this or that term according to a given strategy. Rather, we are compelled to address the character, style, or grammar of strategy as such. For, according to Nietzsche, resentiment is an event that has followed from not recognizing the strategic, positive, or effective nature of our grammar:

> A quantum of force is equivalent to a quantum of drive, will, effect—more, it is nothing other than precisely this very driving, willing, effecting, and only owing to the seduction of language (and of the fundamental errors of reason that are petrified in it) which conceives and misconceives all effects as conditioned by something that causes effects, by a "subject," can it appear otherwise. For just as the popular mind separates the lightning from its flash and takes the latter for an *action*, for the operation of a

subject called lightning, so popular morality also separates strength from expressions of strength, as if there were a neutral substratum behind the strong man, which was *free* to express strength or not to do so. But there is no such substratum; there is no "being" behind doing, effecting, becoming; "the doer" is merely a fiction added to the deed—the deed is everything (*Genealogy*, 45).

Nietzsche's early strategy—an overcoming of the human in a return to the force of life, a submersion in the music of the earth and loss of self-hood in Dionysian frenzy and becoming—is perhaps too close to being a reaction against reactive forces. The contemporary turn to a posthuman or prehuman chaos of pure becoming similarly risks defining itself against human identity. Nietzsche's later response, on the other hand, offers a genealogical repetition of reaction against life. Genealogy takes place as a positive repetition of becoming human; and it is through this repetition that human reactivism will activate itself as an effect. The effect of the human will be seen *as an effect*. In *On the Genealogy of Morals*, Nietzsche narrates a certain reaction: the way in which the primary forces of "festive cruelty" come to interpret themselves as grounded upon human moralism. In the beginning is an act of punishment or cruelty that *then* takes itself as justified by a prior ground of values or human norms. But Nietzsche's narration of this reactivism is itself an affirmation. For if moral values begin with a will that denies itself as will, a will that effaces the *event* of will by seeing will as grounded upon some foundational value, then narrating this effacement renders those values active. Values are not givens to which a will submits or responds; they are the becoming of will itself. A strategy does not organize itself around or according to values; values are effected through strategy. If the putative givenness or being of the human is a denial of life, a substitution of an effect of life for a cause, then a repetition of the will against life recognized *as will* activates the over-human. But this is not an overcoming of the human; it is a becoming human. As active, this will must take place as a perpetual repetition of its becoming, a continual willing of itself as effect. As active, it cannot rest with a recognition of itself as given.[2] And this activation of the reactive through genealogy will also demand a new *style*. It can no longer be a question of writing from the transcendental point of view in terms of conditions, grounds, and general possibilities. Rather, Nietzsche's texts assert themselves through the use of the first person singular, through the aphorism that parodies the collective wisdom of the proverb, and through imperatives that provoke dissent rather than seek legitimation. In many ways it is this style that both questions and reverses subjectivism. On the one hand philosophy's subject becomes avowedly subjective, asserting itself through explicit authorship, self-reference, and literary device. On the other hand, this hypersubjectivism is the very undoing of the subject; for the authorial subject of Nietzsche's text presents itself as nothing other than textual production.[3]

It is, then, a question not of deciding whether the "subject" or the human is good or bad, strategic or defeatist, but of asking about the character of the forces that take hold of the subject. The problem of the subject cannot be decided in the domain of the subject as such; it demands attention to the way the subject occurs as action or reaction to . . . what? If the subject occurs as reaction, what does it react against? Life? Will? Chaos? Power? Corporeality? Desire? In Nietzsche's terminology, reactivism occurs when an effect (of force) takes itself as a cause (the subject). But what are reactive effects *effects of*? What is it that becomes? For the overcoming of reaction will have to be an activation of what is denied; what, then, needs to be activated? Nietzsche's notion of "will," as Heidegger and many later feminists have perceived, might just be one more moment in a history of subjectivist representations of what is (Heidegger, *Nietzsche*, 15–21). Is it will, force, or punishment that turns against itself and moralizes by justifying itself according to some prior ground (*Genealogy*, 68)? Or are these ways of thinking about becoming still too human? Would any other strategy be possible?

FOUCAULT: SEXUAL STRATEGIES

It is precisely this question and the character of this question that occupy Foucault in *The Order of Things*. Foucault's archaeology of the human sciences locates the subject as an effect of a certain type of question. The modern task of providing a foundation for knowledge, the transcendental question, demands that any description of the human be located within its condition of possibility. The question of truth in general, a truth independent of any particular will or motivation, characterizes the western episteme.[4] This is what Foucault refers to in *Archaeology* as the "subjection to transcendence" (203): truth is seen not as an act of becoming but as submission to some already given (or transcendent) ground. But it is in the modern normalization of the human subject as the locus of truth that this subjection reaches its extreme decadence. If, in the premodern episteme, the question of truth was directed toward a world to be known, then there is still, Foucault argues, some room for thought, for there is still some difference between words and things. And it is this difference between words and things, so emphasized by Foucault, that allows for the manifestation of strategy: "Ought we not to admit that, since language is here once more, man will return to that serene non-existence in which he was formerly maintained by the imperious unity of discourse?" (*Order*, 386). If the world is not already meaningful, and if there is a gap between what we see and what we say, then any act of speaking or meaning will have to acknowledge its status as force, power, will, or strategy. In modern subjectivism, however, the *being* of language as exterior falls away, and man questions only himself. Once the question of truth turns back to the knower of order, so that knowing and what is to be known coincide, then the reactive and normalizing trajectory of anthropologism is complete. This results in the modern transcendentalism of recognition. If knowledge is self-knowledge, if truth is seen as the revelation of an interiority which is its own cause, then truth loses all its positivity, its will, its power and becomes the infinite unveiling of an ever-present condition. The transcendental character of the modern subject is the ultimate sign of reactivism. Defined not as a thing within the world or life, but as the infinite horizon, condition, or precondition for life, this subject empties itself of all power and all positivity. As purely formal and transcendental, the subject of modernity is both the ultimate condition or origin *and* not specifiable as any given thing. As the very possibility for truth or meaning, this subject is a denial of any specific will to truth, a denial of power. The subject who can turn back and know his finite being by reflecting on the horizon of his becoming is a subject who recognizes himself and recognizes himself as an origin. In so doing he masks, and reacts against, the positivity of life.

Foucault's endeavor is not to take the transcendental move back one step further—ask the condition of this self-questioning subject and locate it in a trace or anterior difference. His genealogy of the modern subject describes the subject in its (reactive) effects. The clearest example, of course, is the discourse of sexuality described in the first volume of *The History of Sexuality*. The task of revealing the inner sexual self, the origin and cause of all our being, regards itself as a liberation or the lifting of a repression. The discourse is clearly reactive in at least two respects. First, the self to be revealed is seen in opposition to a power of repression and is defined negatively against constraint, positive norms, and imposed impediments. Second, as the revelation of a truth *already there to be found*, the particular will to truth of this game of sexual disclosure, or its effect of power, is denied. Foucault's intervention was to demonstrate the positive effects of this discourse, its specific desire, and its particular force. Not only did sexuality create a certain type of self, but this self, in the very denial of its will to truth, disavows its power and takes itself as a subject in general. The reactive character of the modern subject produces not just a truth in general that denies its positivity, but also a subject in general that normalizes what it is to be a self. In this sense it is not so much a self (in its singularity) as a subject (to be revealed).[5]

Foucault's genealogical description of self-formation through techne, games of truth, and the regulation of desires is clearly set against the modern idea that the subject is the ground for truth, rather than an effect of a particular game of truth. Foucault's genealogy is more than a comparison of different ways of life, and more than a nostalgic return to Ancient Greek communitarianism. It is a diagnosis of subjectivism, an effective history that locates the inscription of the transcendental subject within practices of normalization, incarceration, moral edification, and interpretation. What Foucault's genealogy also suggests is a certain inevitability of the self as a game of truth. The subject as a reaction against life—interpreted as a condition for truth and existence—is seen as an effect of "games of truth." In the beginning is the strategy of becoming—practices of regulation, limitation, prescription, and description—with the self and its pleasures forming the substance of this strategy. The modern discourse of sexuality cannot help being a normalizing strategy, precisely because all effects are grounded on the prior cause of life, the truth of which is to be revealed: "A normalizing society is the historical outcome of a technology of power centred on life."[6] In such a society—with its notion of an underlying subject of life—law is not seen as an act of *decision*: it "operates more and more as a norm" (*History 1*, 144). Foucault's description of the ancient self uncovers a different modality of *becoming*. The ethics of ancient Greece have as their substance not an already given ground of life but a different mode of question: not "What is it that causes my being?" but "What sort of self will I be if . . . ?" Foucault's genealogical narration of the games, regularities, techne, and practices of truth and the self are not so much overcomings of the human as they are repetitions that emphasize the inherent locatedness, positivity, and specificity of the intimate play between self and truth.[7] Foucault's genealogical repetition of the beginning of reaction, like Nietzsche's narration of the will, is therefore a critical repetition that will activate the self as a game of truth.

Not surprisingly, then, the function of the self in Foucault's corpus is intimately tied to the strategy of genealogy. A repetition of reactive forces and their making-active concerns itself with the human, not as an overcoming but as a transvaluation. If the human is not something to be overcome but is to be relocated no longer as given cause but as positive effect, then genealogy will be a continual and critical procedure. This explains Foucault's sustained commitment to the self: its diagnosis in *The Order of Things* and its revaluation in *The History of Sexuality*. But it also explains Foucault's commitment to critique: given the inherent locatedness and position of any will to truth, the task of thought will be a persistent question as to how that position might be otherwise.[8]

Foucault's sustained commitment to genealogy is evidence of a recognition of the inescapable locatedness of any truth, statement, practice, or discourse in a self, will, way of life, or comportment. Given the inevitability of a *position* of thought or knowledge (in a self, body, subject, or enunciative point), the task of genealogy is to retrace the marking out or differentiation of that position:

> The analysis of the archive, then, involves a privileged region: at once close to us, and different from our present existence, it is the border of time that surrounds our presence, which overhangs it, and which indicates it in its otherness; it is that which, outside ourselves, delimits us. The description of the archive deploys its possibilities (and the mastery of its possibilities) on the basis of the very discourses that have just ceased to be ours; its threshold of existence is established by the discontinuity that separates us from what we can no longer say, and from that which falls outside our discursive practice; it begins with the outside of our own language (*langage*); its locus is the gap between our own discursive practices. In this sense, it is valid for our diagnosis. Not because it would enable us to draw up a table of our distinctive features, and to sketch out in advance the face that we will have in the future. But it deprives us of our continuities; it dissipates that temporal identity in which we are pleased to look at ourselves when we wish to exorcise the discontinuities of history; it breaks the thread of transcendental teleologies; and where anthropological thought once questioned man's being or subjectivity, it now bursts open the other and the outside. In this sense, the diagnosis does not establish the fact of

our identity by the play of distinctions. It establishes that we are difference, that our reason is the difference of discourses, our difference, far
from being the forgotten and recovered origin, is this dispersion that we
are and make. (*Archaeology*, 131)

The point of Foucault's genealogy is to overcome not the self but *subjectivism*: the idea of the subject as intention, horizon, foundation, or
ground. To narrate the formation of the subject through practices of the
self is not to do away with the subject so much as to reverse its logic and
causality; the subject is an effect of practice. In the beginning is a mode of
becoming: in subjectivism this becoming is apprehended as the *effect* of a
prior being. Foucault's idea of the self as produced through games of truth
is an attempt to activate what it means to think. In the western "subjection
to transcendence" (*Archaeology*, 203), truth is posited as that which is to
be discovered, as what is already there for the subject's apprehension; truth
is a presence to be re-presented. In contrast to this logic, Foucault's examination of the self as an effect of games of truth places becoming before
being. Rather than the already given presence of a subject who then encounters the truth of the world, there is a game of truth or an event of dispersion that effects a self and the substance which that self encounters. In
modern subjectivism the self becomes a self by locating truth within the
subject. Foucault's genealogy of the human sciences operates as a coun-
terdiscourse to, and a reversal of, this subjectivism. In *The Order of Things*
and *The History of Sexuality* the truth to be revealed about the human is
seen as the effect of certain knowledge practices. "These knowledge practices include institutional procedures, discursive boundaries, the empirical
conditions of technology and subject positions." Foucault's genealogy is,
therefore, a critical procedure. Genealogy uncovers the active forces of becoming from where we are, and from the forms have truth that have been
effected.

Considered in terms of feminist engagement with the subject, this suggests that a theory of sexual difference as a discovery of the constitutive
being of the sexual subject could only be reactive subjectivism. To reveal
or articulate femininity in general is already a denial of the specific games,
practices, articulations, and forces through which the various problems of
feminist ethics produce the feminine. Any positing of the feminine as a
site of innocence to be redeemed in opposition to the violence of the logos
is, as Marion Tapper has argued, a not too subtle manifestation of resentment.[9] For any claim or strategy that claims to be *nothing more* than an act

of self-recognition, the unveiling of an already existing and given subject or essence, is a denial of its own strategy *as strategy*. If the subject is a game of truth and an instance of power, then the reactive formation of subjectivity in general will be challenged and rendered active by the genealogy of its specific and constitutive techne. A feminist genealogy would be both a critical procedure—connecting the subject in general with the forces and techne that have made it possible—and an active becoming, through this encounter affirming the specific value of other techne and other values.

It is also possible, however, that certain forms of antisubjectivism will repeat the reactive strategy of the subject. If the foundation of the subject is dislodged by some other ground, then we have still posited a transcendent cause or "plane" from which the events of existence unfold. It is possible, for example, that we might think of the project of sexual difference in two senses: reactively (as a truth of the subject, self, or body to be revealed) or actively (as an event of differentiation or dispersion that then produces positions or perspectives from which revelation takes place). *The* question, of course, is whether such an active overcoming of the logic of subjectivism is possible. And the question has at least two answers within the Foucaultian corpus. *The Order of Things* charts a genealogy of those practices that produce the subject as the cause of our being (the human sciences and transcendental philosophy), and does so with the aim of liberating thought from "man":

> As the archaeology of our thought easily shows, man is an invention of a recent date. And one perhaps nearing its end.
>
> If those arrangements were to disappear as they appeared, if some event of which we can at the moment do no more than sense the possibility—without knowing either what its form will be or what it promises—were to cause them to crumble, . . . then once can certainly wager that man would be erased, like a face drawn in sand at the edge of the sea. (*Order*, 387)

But Foucault already expresses a doubt as to whether the human can be "overcome" and whether there can be a thought of anonymity, dispersion, and becoming: a *positive* thought that does not refer events to some prior ground (*Order*, 263). The later volumes of *The History of Sexuality* seem to ascribe inevitability to human reactivism. Given that desire does fold back upon itself to form a self, it might be better to explore the modalities of these foldings. There is not, then, a transcendental horizon (of being) that disperses itself. There are, rather, practices, events, or dispersions that produce the ground of dispersion in various modes (historical a priori) (*Archaeology*, 127). By describing the plurality of these modes, Foucault's genealogy demonstrates that while a certain folding into a self or ethical substance may be inevitable, a historical description of this folding desubstantializes or desubjectivizes any such ground. By asking about the *position* of truth—who speaks? what is the self or desire that undertakes this game of truth?—Foucault's genealogy moves back from the position of truth to the dispersion that produces this position (*Archaeology,* 54).[10] For Foucault, subjectivism is challenged by the *location* of truth in an art of the self, as an effect of specific modes of becoming, regulations, and techne. Foucault's project is an avowed antitranscendentalism; and the justification for his attempt to think about the self through practices, rather than a subjective ground, is explicitly affirmed through a Nietzschean ethics of active and effective becoming.[11]

Both Foucault and Deleuze can be read as responding to the Nietzschean problem of overcoming good and evil—values given in advance as transcendent. But rather than taking up Nietzsche's assertion of an irreducible perspectivism, they can also be seen as offering different paths from this problem. For in many ways, both Foucault's theory of power and Deleuze's emphasis on the prepersonal and the nomadic are criticisms of Nietzschean perspectivism. Not only is the subject, as Nietzsche argued, an accident of grammar—in order to speak of an event, attribute, or predicate I have to employ a subject, or a "doer" behind the deed. This grammar of subjectivism has also characterized a metaphysics of transcendence in which, as Foucault argued, events are always returned, domesticated and silenced by subordination to some general ground. In this regard, Foucault's genealogy attempts another project: an exploration of the ways of life and practices produced through the event of games of truth. As a genealogy of the subject, this would entail seeing the event—and the subject posited as the origin of that event—as simultaneous, as two sides of a certain folding. The "thinking otherwise" of Foucault's genealogy is a transvaluation of philosophy's own order: the self is produced in the inquiry it makes into itself.[12] And so, for Foucault, the mode of inquiry is evaluated according to the self it produces: the self of philosophy and transcendental subjectivity is a subject that recognizes itself as an already given ground; this self is a *reactive* strategy. A nonreactive self, however, would affirm itself though the questions it asks about itself—not in passive recognition but through self-formation: "Maybe the target nowadays is not to discover what we are, but to refuse what we are." ("Afterword," 216)

DELEUZE'S PHILOSOPHY AS *AMOR FATI*

If transcendentalism—the grounding of being in some foundation, presence, or subject—is at one with reactive strategy, how might we understand Deleuze's project of transcendental empiricism? Not only does Deleuze argue that we should no longer ask the interminable philosophical question of who speaks (*Logic,* 107); he also argues that it is Nietzsche who first liberates us from this question by thinking of a field of prepersonal singularities. In contrast to genealogy, Deleuze's focus on eternal return is not so much a critical short-circuiting of philosophy's path of "thought as recognition" as it is an attempt to think of thought as other than recognition.[13] If philosophy has always asked the question of who speaks and produces subjects accordingly, Deleuze asks whether we mightn't ask another question. We would, then, have not a genealogy, a critical repetition of philosophy's masked will to truth, but an attempt to write a grammar of life. The subject of philosophy has always been an effect of recognition: by asking who speaks, philosophy produces its own answers as the origin of thought. It follows, then, that the overcoming of philosophy as recognition will also be the overcoming of perspectivism. Nietzsche's perspectivism locates truth and the subject as the effect of the assertion of a certain position of force; it is not so much that the self is trapped by its perspective as that the self is *nothing other* than perspective (*Genealogy,* 119). Foucault shifts this emphasis slightly: one's self is not just a point of view or perspective; it is the modality of a question through bodily practices. We can, for example, ask who we are by asking about what we do—as in ancient ethics—or we can produce ourselves by questioning our subjectivity, as in the human sciences. But thought, for both Nietzsche and Foucault, is *located*; the self or the overman is nothing other than the character of this location. Deleuze's nomadology of dislocated thought, on the other hand, no longer begins from the self that produces itself as the effect of games of truth. Much of Deleuze's work will be taken up with the problem of the prepersonal character of Nietzsche's eternal return. And if eternal return is not to be seen as yet one more posited transcendence, one more explanation of existence determined in advance, then it will have to be encountered through a different question. Philosophy's question of who speaks, for Deleuze and Guattari, cannot help being a positing of the doer behind the deed. Perspectivism, point of view, locatedness, voice, and all the other devices for revealing the locatedness of position ultimately *situate* thought (and also suggest that thought might have a prior condition).[14]

The problem of transcendence—an outside to the subject that is given beforehand to be represented—is for Deleuze and Guattari a problem of philosophy's style (*Plateaus,* 97, 320). A certain subject-predicate structure produces a substance that then receives attributes, a subject that then acts, a world that is then valued, values that are then encountered, a thought that then thinks of something. A philosophy of immanence will be a nonreactive philosophy only through certain devices of grammar. For Deleuze and Deleuze and Guattari these include:

1. The infinitive—"to think," "to green," "to act," "to write," "to be"— does not admit of a division between what something is and what it does. There is the event itself and not some prior transcendence of which the event would be an act (*Logic,* 221).
2. The indirect speech act—the structure of "he said that . . . "; "it is said that . . . "; "one says . . . "—places the act of speaking outside the subject. No longer information (conveying a transcendence) or communication (thought conveyed from one subject to another), indirect speech shows speaking itself as an event that must be negotiated as act and performance and not seen as signification that can gesture beyond itself to some ever-receding signified:

It is for this reason that indirect discourse, *especially free indirect discourse,* is of exemplary value: there are no clear, distinctive contours; what comes first is not an insertion of variously individuated statements, or an interlocking of different subjects of enunciation, but a collective assemblage resulting in the determination of relative subjectification proceedings, or assignations of individuality and their shifting distributions within discourse. Indirect discourse is not explained by the distinction between subjects; rather, it is the assemblage, as it freely appears in this discourse, that explains all the voices present within a single voice (*Plateaus,* 80).

As Deleuze argues in *The Logic of Sense,* voice "comes from on high," not as a reflection of the world, nor as the expression *of* a subject, but as expression itself. If we think of thought as the owner of statements, as the producer of sense, as the condition of existence, we can do so only by virtue of a way of speaking, by asking certain questions that will always enable us to *recognize* what we understand thinking to be. But this is a denial of the life of *thinking;* for thinking is not a *being* (a subject), but the event "to think."

To understand eternal return as difference and distribution itself which continually affirms itself, as itself (and not as a transcendence determined in advance or as a *condition* of a subject that will understand itself), is at one with transcendental empiricism and a certain style. What sets transcendental empiricism apart from a history of reactive transcendental metaphysics is the radical character of the empiricism involved.[15] What is (or existence) is not determined in advance as so much matter. Seen as eternal return, it is continual differentiation. Affirming the return of that which differs demands that we see this difference not as difference *from*, nor as difference organized according to any aim other than difference itself (*Difference,* 28). The empiricism is transcendental because it does not take a part of what is—an object, a subject, thought, sense—to determine what is in general. Empiricism "goes all the way down" (or is transcendental), and so this needs to be distinguished from transcendental *realism*. There is not a domain of the real that is then given to a subject.[16] There is simply givenness, and the giving of the given cannot be located within the subject; this is not transcendental idealism. For Deleuze the given includes the effects of mind or differentiation by mind, but there are also prehuman "givings": the codings of genetics, bodily movements, spatial organizations, and random distributions of all forms of matter (*Plateaus,* 7). It is not as though there is a real world (realism) that is repeated virtually in the subject (as ideal). The actual is a constant becoming virtual. The peculiar virtual of the human, however, is that it reverses the actual-virtual order of becoming. A body becomes virtual by organizing itself into a subject (*Empiricism,* 92); this virtual effect then posits itself as the actual ground.[17] For Deleuze, then, the reactivism of the subject is overcome not by denying the subject—the death or critique of the subject—but by affirming the subject as a virtual effect, and then by *multiplying* movements of subjective "virtuality." This is why transcendental empiricism is connected to a multiplication of voices, not as expressions of a subject that speaks but as expressions per se. The expression is, then, an assemblage. And if expression is understood from the concept of eternal return, it is not located within the self-recognizing subject of time (a fold that turns back on itself) but distributed spatially, nomadically (an unfolding).

Deleuze's affirmation of nomadic distribution is an attempt to do something other than traditional transcendentalism's positing of a singular condition as the cause of existence, for empiricism is existence itself:

> Empiricism truly becomes transcendental, and aesthetics an apodictic discipline, only when we apprehend directly in the sensible that which can be sense, the very being *of* the sensible: difference, potential difference and difference in intensity as the reason behind qualitative diversity . . . a superior empiricism. (*Difference,* 56–57)

As such, then, transcendental empiricism is antisubjectivism. The transcendental subject as reaction is effected through a temporal folding back: as an effect of life, a product of active forces, it then takes itself as cause or ground, as what was there all along. Genealogy is, in a sense, an attempt to think of a different time, wherein the origin (the subject) is the effect of the cause (the act). And genealogy is also an attempt to think of time not as interpretation (a revelation of what was already there), but as *effective* history (the production of enabling origins). The self it effects is not an essence but an event. Deleuze's *geology* of morals is, alternatively, an attempt at a grammar of space: different series, planes, territories, paths, and maps. It is an ethology rather than an etiology (*Spinoza,* 27, 125). Before there is a genesis that can be traced back to an origin or condition, there is a multiple and synchronic stratification or structuring, not something located at a single point but a creation of possible points through the event of lines, striations, and articulations (*Plateaus,* 41).

What would the style of this ethology or geology be like? In addition to the infinitive and indirect speech, Deleuze suggests the exemplary character of free indirect style. If indirect speech puts language in its own place, as event itself, free indirect style emphasizes the character of language's place. Consider the classic work of free indirect style, James Joyce's *Dubliners.* Here, subjects do not speak. Speaking takes place. And speech does not mean what it says. The following sentence opens the final story in *Dubliners,* "The Dead." It does not appear in quotation marks.

> Lily, the caretaker's daughter, was literally run off her feet.[18]

Who is speaking? Not Joyce (an "artist" could not be guilty of such a solecism). Not Lily, for there are no quotation marks and she is the subject of the sentence. Nor are we given a clear meaning (for this is nonsense; Lily cannot *literally* be run off her feet). In the nonsense of this sentence we see an abandonment of speech. But we also see a carving out of a certain territory. Consider, also, the first lines of "A Painful Case," which begins in a voice of uptight bourgeois moralism: "Mr James Duffy lived in Chapelizod because he wished to live as far as possible from the city of which he was a citizen and because he found all the other suburbs of Dublin mean, modern and pretentious" (89). Here, Dublin is a way of speaking, an act of speech, a code, a territory. Its ethology is a locatedness of place as well as a certain voice, a voice that "no one" owns, a speaking.[19]

From the corpus of feminist theory Luce Irigaray's *Speculum of the Other Woman* might be read as a similarly free indirect location of philosophy's style, a style that produces certain subject positions. *Speculum* opens with a quotation from Freud and then begins, unusually, in the second person.[20] The text then oscillates between an explicit adoption of Freud's voice—"And I, Freud, am here to tell you . . . " (15)—and the author's commentary on Freud, "In fact, Freud goes on . . . " (16). But this oscillation between the voice of Freud and the voice of commentary is interspersed with general statements whose voice or position is uncertain. The sentence quoted below is unclear in its attribution. It is presented, not as a statement by Irigaray, but as the articulation of *philosophy's position*:

> Woman is nothing but the receptacle that passively receives his *product,* even if sometimes, by the display of her passively aimed instincts, she has pleaded, facilitated, even demanded that it be placed within her. (18)

It is not Irigaray who is asserting that woman is *actually* a passive receptacle. Woman is, however, in this position according to a certain way of seeing or speaking. If we repeat philosophy's own way of speaking—if we mime the voice of philosophy and mirror philosophy back upon itself—then all its attributed essences come to be seen as *events of attribution*. This explains, perhaps, the difficulty of essentialism and the difficulty, in general, of Irigaray's work. Philosophy is, in many ways, an unavoidable essentialism: it is a mode of self-questioning that refers the subject back to its own origin. In so doing, philosophy distributes the subject, the feminine, and essence equiprimordially through its style of questions. Irigaray repeats this style, through free-indirect discourse, in such a way that we are never sure *who* is speaking. In so doing she detaches style from the subject. The subject becomes an effect of style.

Deleuze's suggestion that philosophy might produce a style that would free thought from the subject is an outgrowth of his affirmation of transcendental empiricism and philosophy as *amor fati* (*What Is Philosophy?* 159). If there is only the given—if empiricism is transcendental—then there is not a subject to whom the given is revealed but only the "giving": a general becoming, articulation, or dispersion. And if philosophy is an *amor fati,* and not a justification of the given by some ground outside the given, then thought and speaking will be events in themselves, not re-presentations of some presence. Thought is a way of speaking, a style (*Plateaus,* 318). To free thought from the reactivism of a good subject decided in advance, to truly confront life, to really be a strategy and not an effect, philosophy must be an act of style: writing otherwise to think otherwise.

GENEALOGY OR GEOLOGY?

What does this mean for a politics of the subject? Is Foucault's genealogy of the self still human, all too human? Or is a self inevitably going to be posited as the subject of an explicit strategy? And how might we decide between Foucault's description of *strategy as self* and Deleuze's attempt to free the strategies of thought from the speaking subject? The problem might be tackled by looking at *Anti-Oedipus,* for this work is in many ways a genealogy of the subject that passes beyond itself to "schizoanalysis" and the opening of a geology. In *Anti-Oedipus* Deleuze and Guattari ask a quite Foucaultian question of the subject of psychoanalysis: ask not what it means but how it works (*Anti-Oedipus,* 109). Isn't the problem with psychoanalysis that it takes itself as an interpretive task, as the *finding* of Oedipus, as the *discovery* of castration, when all along it is the *production* of quite specific codings of desire? Psychoanalysis decides in advance what its material will do or mean, precisely because it conceives of itself as interpretive. Oedipus is there all along, waiting to speak for the analyst who listens. As a single story that expands itself into a story of stories, analysis is an elevation of perspective. The point of view of the analyst determines the truth of speech, and does so by asking who, *in general,* speaks. And the answer to this question is always the oedipalized unconscious; desire is seen as a meaning to be interpreted rather than an activation or becoming that analysis encounters. The subject of analysis, with its hidden depths, its silent grounds, its repressed origins, and its organized narrations, is a particular configuration of desire that substitutes its part for the whole. One virtual event within desire—the oedipal subject—is seen as the actual ground of desire in general (*Anti-Oedipus,* 129). Oedipus operates as a synecdoche that presents itself as the opening of all sense. All other events of sense are read from this point of the code.

But sense, Deleuze and Guattari argue, does not begin with figures and substitutions of equivalence; what is primary is not metaphor or tropes but the act of indirect speech (*Plateaus,* 76–77). There is not a presence that is then figured in speech, such that sense floats above the actual. Speech is one modality of becoming among others and is best represented not by the *substitution* of metaphor and interpretation (x = Oedipus) but by the proliferation of indirect speech ($x + y$). All speech is already quotation and already comes from elsewhere: "Every thought is already a tribe" (*Plateaus,* 377). An encounter with speech is not so much an interpretation, attribution, and relocation (to point of view, subject, or perspective), as another act of speech and the carving out of a new location. Schizoanalysis does not attribute speech to an expressive subject whose statements can be interpreted as so many metaphors; it sees speech as an act within which the subject is formed.

The genealogy of *Anti-Oedipus* turns back from the single coding of oedipal desire to the multiplicity of speech acts from which Oedipus has emerged. By demonstrating how a virtual effect (the fiction of Oedipus) has interpreted itself reactively (as an actual ground), the genealogy of psychoanalysis then calls for a new logic. Schizoanalysis will be not a hermeneutics but a proliferation of voices, fictions, codes, and connections. *A Thousand Plateaus* extends this demand in its manner of composition. Narrated partly in third person, explicitly fragmented and producing discontinuous series, *A Thousand Plateaus* also argues for a certain style. And in this sense there is still a demand, position, locatedness, and force in Deleuze and Guattari's project of becoming. The call for free-indirect style is explicitly the affirmation of a way of being and a certain strategy. Becoming "other than self" in *A Thousand Plateaus* is more than an event of speech, more than an act in its singularity: it is also, again, a certain coding, territorialization, and mapping. There is, then, a double method in *A Thousand Plateaus.* On the one hand, there is the performance of multiplicity through a proliferation of voices and planes, so that the work as a whole challenges the interpretive practice of attributing arguments to a specific position. On the other hand, there are also arguments about position as such: demands for free-indirect style, indirect speech, and infinitives. And this argument for a dislocation of thought can be, and is, *attributed* to the position of the authors. Nor is this problem of producing a philosophy of becoming denied by the text in question. The overcoming of perspectivism, point of view, voice, and attribution, as a battle of style, always risks reattribution. The passage toward a philosophy of becoming is, itself, always in the process of becoming: perpetually falling back upon being, being recoded, reterritorializing, taken as actual (*Plateaus,* 57–60). The ethics of *amor fati*—of not positing a value outside the given—is thought's ceaseless struggle (*Logic,* 149). In this regard transcendental empiricism is not so much a metaphysical theory as a constant question and demand directed to thought: the challenge of a thinking that does not *situate itself* in relation *to* a transcendent plane (*Spinoza,* 13; *What Is Philosophy,* 47).

The recognition of situation is, however, crucial to the critical project of Foucault's histories; in order to become we must write a history of the present. Recognizing where we are is the first step toward the question that will make us think otherwise:

> To reveal in all its purity the space in which discursive events are deployed is not to undertake to re-establish it in an isolation that nothing could overcome; it is not to close it upon itself; it is to leave one free to describe the interplay of relations within it and outside it. (*Archaeology,* 29)

Both Foucault and Deleuze, then, regard thought as a movement of becoming through the question. For Deleuze, a radical question is enabled only when we liberate voice from an intending ground. Hence, his writings are dominated by spatial metaphors of distribution, passage, flight, mappings, paths, and circuits. For Foucault, however, a question is always a way of life, position and *self*-questioning. For any event there is always a *particular* dispersion of the medium. This explains Foucault's visual and perspectival metaphors of light, optics, shining, and reflection. The problem of the visible in *The Order of Things* is inextricably intertwined with the task of disconnecting the putatively intimate connection between words and things. In so doing, words will be seen not as passive doublings or representations, but as acts, events, and movements of becoming:

> It is not that words are imperfect, or that, when confronted by the visible, they prove insuperably inadequate. Neither can be reduced to the

other's terms: it is in vain that we say what we see; what we see never resides in what we say. (*Order,* 9)[21]

How do we negotiate these different strategies? Can we locate thought beyond the position of the subject in an assemblage or multiplicity? Or is any such dislocation a failure to recognize the distribution of power that marks and locates any event of thought? Can we think from a "body without organs" (a desire not subjected to an already coded body-image)? Or is the body always a *site* for specific questions, questions that work with an "ethical substance"? Relating the problem to feminist ethics, we might ask: are an attempt to think otherwise than from a subject and a *feminist* articulation of such a demand not mutually exclusive? Isn't feminism, as a force that identifies itself and directs its strategy, always going to be a position, a coding, a demand for a certain style of territory? Was Foucault somehow right in staying within genealogy, in not attempting to step outside or justify a position, but, rather, emphasizing the positivity[22] of position? In some ways the Deleuzean task of thinking about the prepersonal, *the* plane of immanence, and the prehuman might be seen as one more move in a history of speculative system philosophy that attempts to think about the *ground* of thought. How might we decide between Deleuze's prepersonal geology (which always bears the risk of being posited as a speculative ground) and Foucault's genealogy (which carries the contrary risk of remaining within the perimeters of the subject)?

But expressing the problem this way—as genealogy or geology—is still perhaps a bit too like a distinction between good and evil. For the problem of strategy may not be capable of being decided according to an apparent opposition between strategies. A genealogy of the self, an overcoming of the subject's reactive transcendentalism, may allow, as Foucault thought it might, some room for thought. Not accepting what we are, we might think otherwise and not be subjected to an image of ourselves given in advance:

> If the discovery of the return is indeed the end of philosophy, then the end of man, for its part, is the return of the beginning of philosophy. It is no longer possible to think in our day other than in the void left by man's disappearance. For this void does not create a deficiency; it does not constitute a lacuna that must be filled. It is nothing more, and nothing less, than the unfolding of a space in which it is once more possible to think. (*Order,* 342)

However, Foucault also considered that genealogy would demand a certain way of writing. And it is notable that his own works are performances of the very style hailed by Deleuze and Guattari in *A Thousand Plateaus*: free indirect style. For what is *The Order of Things* if not knowledge speaking of itself: this text is, as it were, a mute description of ways of knowing. The "silence" of Foucault's style is not that it claims not to speak but that it speaks from within a style already given. And as the earlier positivism of *Archaeology* developed into a more explicit genealogy, we move from discourse distributed in space to the manifest foregrounding of anecdote, free indirect quotation, and immanent description, to the point where the question "Who speaks?" becomes increasingly difficult to answer in relation to Foucault's texts.[23] So, while Foucault's genealogy inevitably ties the style of knowledge to a certain self, his own texts never fully *own* their style. A classic example of this equivocation of voice concludes *The Archaeology of Knowledge*. After insisting on the anonymity of archaeological method, the text ends with a dialogue concerning the possibility of freeing voice from the subject and escaping "the attribution of transcendence" (202). As with so much free indirect style, it is so hard to tell where the author's voice ends and quotation begins. Conversely, while Deleuze and Guattari's *Anti-Oedipus* and *A Thousand Plateaus* are exercises in style, they are also locatable, although not completely, as propositions, utterances, and imperatives of a certain position.

This *double method*, whereby one asks *both* about the position of thought *and* about the field within which position is given, offers several benefits to contemporary social theory and philosophy of language. As Donald Davidson points out, if one is to talk about either a constructivist point of view or a conceptual scheme, then one will also be troubled by just what such a point of view is within, or what such a scheme is a *scheme of*.[24] One cannot assert an uncritical preconceptual ground (an essence), for this would raise the question of how the preconceptual or prehuman might be known. Nor can one assert a point of knowledge or construction as though this didn't raise the question of just what was being constructed. This is why philosophy and the question of style in philosophy can't be collapsed into "a kind of writing", to use Richard Rorty's phrase.[25] Nor, again to challenge Rorty, could the philosopher simply adopt the style of a language game with a permanent mode of irony or noncommitment.[26] What the oscillation between geology and genealogy indicates is that style is always more than itself. A grammar or way of speaking always effects a strategy, always produces or relates to that which exceeds style. To use

Deleuze's terminology, style institutes a plane or site of recognition (that retroactively then grounds the style). While this raises the challenge of a style that can itself think of style, it also raises the *responsibility* of thinking about the ways in which the idea of style organizes questions of grounding, position, and speaking. Richard Rorty's celebration of philosophy as a kind of writing is the fantasy of a style at one with itself, a style that produces no question of what it is a style *of*, or of how this "of" is produced through style. In contrast, then, to constructivism or aestheticism without ground, Deleuze and Foucault ask quite different questions about the *modes* of grounding that are inextricably intertwined with modes of style (Foucault) and the challenge of writing that would be more than a "kind of writing" (Deleuze).

CONCLUSION

What this suggests is that the genealogy of the self and the attempt to think about a style of collective assemblage are projects folded in on each other. And this is nothing other than the problem of the strategy of becoming. For strategy is the positivity of a certain position—a self, an enunciation, a style—but it is also, *as strategy,* never adequate to itself, never fully at one with the forces that enable and take hold of it. The (Foucaultian) genealogy of the sexual subject redistributes sexuality into a series of relations: no longer an inner self or subject, but a managed body. Deleuze and Guattari's geology of morals, schizoanalysis, and nomadology, on the other hand, in attempting to do *more* than undertake a genealogy, must also be, *in part* genealogical: a going over of philosophy's history as a series of events, a repetition of the transcendental subject as an effect within the given, an encounter with psychoanalytic coding and territorialization to open a deterritorialization. The ethics of genealogy and geology is not neither / nor but both / and: affirm thought in its event as self *and* think differently. There is no style that is not also an ethology, the carving out of a certain site or position. But there is no genealogy that is not also a force of style, a difference from any given ethos or habit, and the affirmation of the distribution that effects ethos.

Is it possible, then, for avowed positions, such as feminism, to be other than acts of self-formation? Would something like nomadology preclude the articulation of a specific ethical project? How might such an ethical project decide upon its strategy? If we take the idea of resentiment seriously, then we are confronted with the idea that strategy cannot be decided according to an already given position. It cannot be a question of feminism *deciding* the strategic value of the subject, the body, or the self. For this would imply a realm of intention or decision prior to strategy, an ethical origin to which the value of certain strategies might be referred. And it would also imply that some terms have a prima facie ethical value, regardless of the modality of their enunciation. If feminism *is* strategy, then it comes into its own as a certain style and a certain position. As such it will be both a genealogy and a geology. It will be both an affirmation of its position as position (and not as the innocent manifestation of essence, ground, horizon, "beyond," or absence) a question directed to itself as an event of style. Neither the subject nor the body is a good or evil idea in the service of a strategy given in advance. Rather, strategy itself is determined as active or reactive according to the style in which these notions are deployed.

8

KLOSSOWSKI OR THOUGHTS-BECOMING

Eleanor Kaufman

A striking feature of much critical writing today is the way in which the body is foregrounded in opposition to, or at the expense of, some notion of the mind or of thought, the latter deemed to be overly idealist, patriarchal, or metaphysical. It is the contention of this essay not only that there exists a materiality of thought but that this materiality can be linked both to feminist concerns and to extreme bodily states. Moreover, insofar as thought might be depicted as immaterial, incorporeal, or static, at issue here will be the movement-potential and materialization-potential of thought, the possibility that thought might become both something else and something new. And no writer better demonstrates the radical becoming-potential of thought than the French novelist-philosopher-painter Pierre Klossowski, whose fiction and philosophy stage thoughts as literal, active characters. Beyond delineating the otherworldly Klossowskian universe where thoughts are the major players, my aim is to examine the way in which such a universe is built upon and refracted against both the woman's body and the sick body of Nietzsche.

Michel Foucault concludes "Theatrum Philosophicum," his famous laudatory review of Gilles Deleuze's *The Logic of Sense* and *Difference and Repetition*, with a reference to the bodies of Nietzsche and Klossowski: "In the sentry box of the Luxembourg Gardens, Duns Scotus places his head through the circular window; he is sporting an impressive moustache; it belongs to Nietzsche, disguised as Klossowski."[1] This seemingly nonsensical conclusion articulates the dizzying lines of exchange between Deleuze, Foucault, and Klossowski, not limited to the three contemporaries but instead extending outward to encompass Nietzsche and Duns Scotus, among others. Furthermore, all partake, quite literally, of the same body: they share Duns Scotus's head, Nietzsche's moustache, Klossowski's simulacrum, and presumably Deleuze's thought (not to mention Foucault). In Foucault's evocative conclusion to "Theatrum Philosophicum," the body is no longer the marker of a single person but instead represents at once the breakdown of identity and the coming together of composite identities. It is precisely around this locus, that of the body (or the body as thought) as a means of complicating and overthrowing identity, that the works of Deleuze and Klossowski resonate and come together. I will look first at the body and thoughts as they are figured around the character of Roberte, the heroine of Klossowski's fictional trilogy *Les Lois de l'hospitalité (The Laws of Hospitality),* and second at the sick body of Nietzsche in Klossowski's monumental study of Nietzsche, *Nietzsche and the Vicious Circle,* focusing on how this work's dialectic of physical sickness and mental exuberance suggests the possibility of new and heightened forms of thought.

Klossowski begins his most extended tribute to Deleuze, "Digressions à partir d'un portrait apocryphe," in this fashion: "Deleuze is also assisted by his affinities with another exemplary spirit whose explorations reveal a common ground with his own: Michel Foucault. In every respect, they have this in common: the liquidation of the principle of identity."[2] Klossowski's own work (perhaps even more than Foucault's or Deleuze's), ceaselessly interrogates the principle of identity and in the service of this interrogation constructs a world of phantasms, simulacra, bodies, and spirits. This can be seen most notably in Klossowski's fiction, particularly the hospitality trilogy, and specifically in the disjunction of body and soul as they are figured in the character of Roberte.

Les Lois de l'hospitalité and Klossowski's oeuvre as a whole operate according to a logic of oppositional extremes. According to this logic, two radically different entities coexist without undergoing a properly dialectical synthesis. The synthesis obtains, if at all, in the differential of their difference. Such a logic of oppositions structures both the content and the form of Klossowski's fiction. On the one hand, there is a distinct narrative centered on a couple, Octave and Roberte, with other characters such as their nephew Antoine and the parachuting adventurer Vittorio della Santa-Sede (who takes on many identities and aliases) serving as foils for their continuous dialogue. Each volume of the trilogy is replete with fantastic twists of narrative, where two or more characters will turn out to be only one, where one chain of events is actually a pretext for an entirely different set of circumstances (e.g., a story focused on the Catholic church is also all about collaboration with the Nazis), and where unexpected and spontaneous sexual encounters are omnipresent. Yet, on the other hand, these twisted narratives are mixed with treatise-like discourses on such subjects as Scholastic philosophy, art history, and photography (usually through the mouthpiece of Octave, who is a professor). Klossowski's oscillation between bizarre narrative and esoteric treatise recalls the disjunctions present in Sade, though Klossowski is not nearly as predictable.

A similar disjunctive structure operates at the level of the personal characteristics of Roberte and Octave in *Roberte Ce Soir* and *The Revocation of the Edict of Nantes* (the first two books in Klossowski's trilogy *Les Lois de l'hospitalité* and the ones that will be discussed here), and later Roberte and the duo Théodore / K in *Le Souffleur*, the third book of the trilogy.[3] Roberte and Octave—and it is not incidental that they are in fact married—incarnate the cliché "opposites attract": Roberte is a young and striking woman with great social charm and much political savvy; self-characterized as "the most prominent woman in the radical party,"[4] she serves on the National Education Commission and is also Inspectress of Censorship; though descended from a long line of Protestant ministers, she is an outspoken atheist. Octave, a consummate esthete and art critic, is an aging professor of Scholastic philosophy who has been stripped of his position; he is an ardent, albeit rather heretical, Catholic who writes perversely erotic fiction and is a proponent of Sade. While these details are interestingly autobiographical with respect to Klossowski and his wife Denise Marie Roberte Morin-Sinclaire, what is noteworthy here is the disjunctive or oppositional nature of this coupling, which parallels and illustrates the similar disjunction that obtains between bodies and thoughts in Klossowski's work as a whole.

If these oppositions *within* the bonds of marriage are not enough, then it is all the more striking that Roberte and Octave also actualize within their marriage those infidelities that are commonly seen as antithetical to the very institution of marriage. Foremost among the infidelities is adultery, which consists in the master of the house giving over the mistress to engage in sexual relations with any and every guest who enters. Like marriage, these infidelities are governed by strict regulations, which Octave terms the "laws of hospitality":

> The master of this house . . . waits anxiously at the gate for the stranger he will see appear like a liberator upon the horizon. . . . For with the stranger he welcomes, the master of the house seeks a no longer accidental, but an essential relationship. At the start the two are but isolated substances, between them there is none but accidental communication. . . . But because the master of this house herewith invites the stranger to penetrate to the source of all substances beyond the realm of all accident, this is how he inaugurates a substantial relationship between himself and the stranger, which will be not a relative relationship but an absolute one, as though, the master becoming one with the stranger, his relationship with you who have just set foot here were now but a relationship of one with oneself.[5]

Under these laws of hospitality, a disjunctive synthesis, a bringing together of two differing entities—"two . . . isolated substances"—is effected. These two separate entities, the master of the house and the stranger, are brought into "substantial" relation through the body of a woman, Roberte. In "penetrat[ing] to the source of all substance beyond the realm of all accident," the stranger becomes one with the master; the host and guest are conflated. Such a conflation is perfectly conveyed by the French word "hôte," which means both "host" and "guest." Moreover, the English "host" ("hostie" in French) conveys the conflation of body and spirit through the medium of the body of Christ. By graciously usurping the role of the host, the guest, in actualizing this role of host, enables the host to take on the status of guest in his own house. Through the body of Roberte (just as, in what follows, through the sick body of Nietzsche), two opposed entities (husband and adulterer) are brought together, but brought together in a fashion that is not adversarial but rather "substantial." In other words, a body enables a conjunction of forces (here the host and the guest) that, when combined in such a fashion, rearranges given markers of identity (husband, adulterer) so that these identity formations are no longer absolute but instead in constant disarray (Klossowski's notion of the "liquidation of the principle of identity").

Apart from the guest / host disjunction, such a reconfiguration of identity occurs most prominently in Klossowski through the explicit medium of bodies and souls, or bodies and thoughts. The disjunction between bodies and souls is articulated in terms of purity and impurity. The undesirable conjunction is that of a pure body and impure thought, which can be passed off as general purity. Counteracting such a conjunction necessitates the enactment of a more shocking but ultimately more pure conjunction: that of the impure body and pure thought. In *Roberte Ce Soir*, Roberte is deemed guilty of the first offense. As a member of the Censorship Council, Roberte champions an effort to ban erotically explicit literature, including the work of her own husband. Yet when, returning home, she thinks about the literature in question, a discrepancy or impurity results. To counteract this, her thoughts fantastically become materialized as spirits (what Klossowski terms "pure breaths") that enact pornographic punishments upon her. As the spirits, in the form of a small Hunchback and a huge Guardsman, proceed to fondle and rape Roberte, they explain their grievances against her and give her ample time to recant:

> Your great sin in our eyes, Madame, is that you serve two masters, believing in one only so far as that belief is useful to you in disserving to the other, truthfully believing in neither of them. In relation to us, you attempt to maintain the fraudulent doctrine of dual substance. Are we the undesirable thoughts of your mind, then to us you oppose the muteness of a flesh to be withheld from our operations; why withheld, if you please, since by opposing it to your thoughts, tonight, which are nowhere else than in your spirit, it is from your very spirit you divorce this flesh; what now becomes of its integrity if it is not found in the principle of the resurrection of bodies? But in forbidding your poets, your artists, your players to describe, to paint, and above all to enact what we are operating upon you at the present moment, upon them you impose the muteness of integral flesh as if it were already the pure silence of spirits. Thus in relation to these composite substances, to these dual natures who employ speech to denounce their own duplicity, you have the nerve to act as a simple substance, that of the spirits who for lack of what is called passable flesh must be without hope of redemption and subsist valiantly in a spiritual death such as ours which you deny the instant you oppose to us the appearance of a flesh, as if it could be reborn incorruptible. Might you then be in agreement with us who refute this so-called mystery as a slur upon our dignity? Not a bit of it. For if a simple substance's pure silence is due to the absence of a speaking flesh, you clumsily confuse this silence with the muteness of a living flesh.[6]

Roberte, then, is guilty of keeping an impure silence. While speaking out against impure literature, she silently entertains impure thoughts about the very material in question. This situation fantastically causes the impure thoughts to materialize, and when they do so they effect exactly the opposite scenario: by performing impure actions on her body, the spirits hope to elicit in her a pure silence. In question here is a doubly dialectical reversal; instead of pure body / language at the expense of impure thought / silence, the oppositional and desirable dialectical structure is pure thought / silence at the expense of impure body / language. Such an opposition is based on a relation, which derives from Scholastic philosophy, between simple and composite substances. For Klossowski, a simple substance would be either pure thought or pure body, while a composite substance would in some way bring the two into conjunction. Because Roberte tries to act like a pure thought by denying her body, she is reprimanded by the pure spirits who work to elicit in her a recognition of the body's integral relation to thought.

The character of Roberte is in many ways the supreme locus of Klossowskian dialectics, the framework on which the fine points of the laws of hospitality are built and the breakdown of identity is effected. But in this structure, which sets up an economy of exchange between men, there remain troublesome gender dynamics, for clearly the enabling or catalytic force in this economy is precisely a rather essentialist notion of the woman (here Roberte) as body while it is the man who becomes more spiritual as a result of his encounter with the woman's body. Yet my contention is that Roberte's role is not to be dismissed out of hand for its misogynist implications, for it in fact raises some challenging questions from a feminist perspective.[7]

We might pause to consider the way in which Klossowski's system of hospitality is maintained at the expense of the very real body of the woman, here Roberte. It is easy to argue that such a construction is nothing more than another elaborate instance of "traffic in women." Indeed, Gayle Rubin's famous article of this title provides an exemplary gloss of the power relations that come to bear on the exchange of women between men:

> If it is women who are being transacted, then it is the men who give and take them who are linked, the woman being a conduit of a relationship rather than a partner to it. The exchange of women does not necessarily imply that women are objectified, in the modern sense, since objects in the

primitive world are imbued with highly personal qualities. But is does imply a distinction between gift and giver. If women are the gifts, then it is men who are the exchange partners. And it is the partners, not the presents, upon whom reciprocal exchange confers its quasi-mythical power of social linkage. The relations of such a system are such that women are in no position to realize the benefits of their own circulation. As long as the relations specify that men exchange women, it is men who are the beneficiaries of the product of such exchanges—social organization.[8]

On one level, Roberte fits all too well into the economy Rubin outlines, one where women are oppressed first and foremost because of their role as objects of exchange. And the fact that Roberte's body, particularly her omnipresent gloved hands, is itself the primary locus for such exchange makes this text hard to recuperate for a feminist analysis.[9] Yet the fact that such a potential for recuperation exists, that at its limit this text might be read as gesturing toward a new and alternative feminist space, is precisely its extraordinary appeal.

Such an alternative can be constructed from Rubin's later "Thinking Sex," the follow-up and companion piece to "Traffic in Women." At the outset of "Thinking Sex," Rubin depicts two concentric circles: the interior circle, called the "charmed circle," represents all that is "normative" in heterosexuality; the outer circle, called the "outer limits," mirrors each trait of normativity with its corresponding and outcast opposite. So, for example, in the inner circle we find such traits as "heterosexual, married, monogamous, procreative, noncommercial, in pairs, in a relationship, same generation, in private, no pornography, bodies only, vanilla" while the corresponding outer traits are "homosexual, unmarried, promiscuous, commercial, alone or in groups, casual, cross-generational, in public, pornographic, with manufactured objects, sadomasochistic."[10] What is striking about Klossowski's *Laws of Hospitality* with respect to these circles is that the relationship between Octave and Roberte, while assuming the first two traits of the normative inner circle—heterosexual and married—falls into the outer circle for all the other given traits. All of which is to say that here is no ordinary marriage, and Roberte is no ordinary wife. Insofar as Roberte has a role subservient to Octave in their unconventional heterosexual union, Roberte simultaneously opens up new possibilities of enacting and experiencing such a union. It is in this opening toward new possibilities that Roberte's character pursues what I would argue is a uniquely feminist project.

In outlining such a feminist project, it is useful to situate Klossowski's fiction in relation to the history of pornographic fiction in France. While Klossowski's fiction (and also his paintings, which often serve as illustrations to it[11]) might be classified as pornographic, it is also, in the vein of Sade, concerned with staging philosophical and religious dialogues, analyzing facetious works of art, and alluding more or less covertly to the political resonances of the Second World War. Thus, to call Klossowski's fiction pornographic does not sufficiently register many of its other nuances. Yet, if we locate Klossowskian pornography in a Revolutionary tradition of pornographic writing, these additional nuances begin to make more sense. As Lynn Hunt argues in "Pornography and the French Revolution," pornography underwent a substantial shift in register after the Revolution. In its Revolutionary incarnation, pornography incorporated aspects of materialist philosophy, worked to overtly subversive political ends, and was not inherently debasing to women; but all this changed after the revolution, when pornography was depoliticized and also infused with pejorative moral overtones.[12]

Hunt stresses the central role of Sade in the shift from politicized to pejorative pornography:

> Sade's novels marked an important transition in the 1790s. He took the politically and socially subversive possibilities to their furthest possible extreme and, at the same time and perhaps by the same act, he paved the way for the modern apolitical genre of pornography. His attack on every aspect of conventional morality undermined the use of pornography for political ends in the future. Pornography was now identified with a general assault on morality itself, rather than a specific criticism of the irrationalities of the ancien regime moral system.[13]

Like Sade, Klossowski also takes "politically and socially subversive possibilities to their fullest possible extreme." Though Klossowski's fiction is arguably bolstered by misogynist modes of representation, it is simultaneously an attack on all that is most sacred to conventional morality, particularly the institution of marriage. Instead of presenting an alternative to the marital institution that is beyond or outside it, Klossowski explodes it from within. Instead of presenting an anarchistic world of free play where all sexual mores are acceptable, Klossowski institutes a system of laws just as rigid as those surrounding marriage, though this new system of laws works to precisely the opposite effect. In lieu of attempting to protect the marital bond from the ever-present threat of adultery, Klossowski makes the adulterous prostitution of the wife into the supreme law of the household, the law of hospitality. Instead of being constrained to sexual encounters with only her husband, Roberte is constrained to sexually encounter all other men *but* him. It is as if Octave ensures his wife's fidelity by imposing on her a law of infidelity—whereas he might have waited fearful of Roberte's infidelity, he instead anticipates it and outwits it by insisting upon it. In this regard, Klossowski employs the disjunctive extremes of adultery and fidelity as they are figured around the woman's body to give the sacrament of heterosexual union a strange new identity, one that paradoxically upholds the laws of marriage and fidelity by reversing them and thus pushing these laws to their limits. While such a refashioning of marriage is in some sense carried out at the woman's expense, here it is complicated by the fact that Roberte indefatigably seeks out and embraces each new adventure that awaits her.

Roberte's active, aggressive attitude might be explicated once again by considering the role of women in Revolutionary pornography. As Kathryn Norberg argues in "The Libertine Whore: Prostitution in French Pornography from Margot to Juliette," French pornographic writings from the Revolutionary period refuse to depict women merely as victims of men or as morally inferior creatures. She writes that:

> virtually all of the works included in this group present a particular picture of the prostitute, what I call the "libertine whore." This whore . . . is independent, sensual, sensible and skilled. She is healthy and possessed of a very healthy . . . sexual appetite. She is a businesswoman and an artist who provides "varied" sex for men who can afford it. She is a courtesan who lives in luxury and abides by "philosophy," usually materialist philosophy. Intelligent, independent, proud and reasonable, she is *not* diseased or monstrous; she is not humiliated or victimized either by life or by her clients.[14]

This positive depiction of the "libertine whore" is strikingly like Roberte. She is an important radical political figure; she is supremely intelligent, elegant, and self-composed, even while being repeatedly submitted to surprise sexual encounters.

While Roberte is indeed "submitted" to such encounters in *Roberte Ce Soir*, the division between the aggressor and the one attacked, between initiator and initiate, is far from clear in *The Revocation of the Edict of*

Nantes. Like the libertine whore whom Norberg characterizes as actively seeking out her pleasure and as narrating her story in the first person rather than through the mediating voice of a man, Roberte herself initiates encounters and narrates them through a series of journal entries (presented in alternation with journal entries by Octave). In one such encounter, Roberte seduces a young bank clerk who has come to their home to see Octave. In front of her husband, Roberte makes overtures to the young man, and the two soon retreat to a separate room. Then the phone rings; it is a call for Octave, and he must retrieve the receiver form underneath the very chair on which Roberte and the clerk have planted themselves. Apart from the clerk, everyone privy to this scene appears to be singularly unphased. In further journal entries entitled "The Roman Impressions," which are actually flashbacks to a time ten years earlier, Roberte narrates her encounters with wounded soldiers while she was serving as a Red Cross volunteer in Rome just before the city's liberation in 1944. It appears that much of Roberte's interest in such an enterprise is in fact bound up with the possibilities (for sexual transgression) that such a situation offers.

Roberte's journal entries not only narrate her various encounters but also reflect critically on them. In these entries, Roberte meditates both on her own situation and on the situation of women in general. In one entry, she expounds a philosophical argument *against* Octave's theology, one in which she discusses how the conjunction of woman and the body can be used to ends that would abolish the distinction between body and soul:

> Yes, Octave, we [women] are natural-born atheists; and atheism's progress in the world of today may perhaps have its true source here: the growing importance of the hand we are taking, the weight we are exerting in present affairs. Yet our basic refusal to *believe* is as different from that of a knowingly and determinedly atheistic male as the latter's bias is from the faith of a nun. I'll go still further: my own cousin, converted to Catholicism, today in an Ursuline convent, is nearer to me in her attitude than my friend Sarah, an out-and-out materialist. The feeling she has for her body, more profoundly inherent in woman than in man, is also the reason why she is better able to stifle the senses, to attain insensibility, than the ascetic; no more body, no more soul; perfect death; an extinction with which, however, we have an almost sweet relationship, a tender one; our nothingness is as *warm* as our body; *sang-froid* is nothing but virile vanity.[15]

According to such an analysis, the body, and specifically the body of the woman, serves as a conduit or means of access to another realm (here, explicitly antitheological) where the identity of the body is transformed into "insensibility," "extinction," and "nothingness." In this regard, Roberte serves as a "porte parole" for—indeed, a dramatization of—the Klossowskian principle of the "liquidation of identity."

These lines reveal the complexity of Roberte's experience of the laws of hospitality. While confessing to feelings of dishonor and shame, Roberte also experiences keen enjoyment from this debasement, a debasement which for her marks an outpost of fantasy and unreality in a world burdened by responsibility.[16] If Octave's laws of hospitality are deemed perverse, then Roberte's mode of complying with them is equally perverse. In her essay on Klossowski in *Intersections*, Jane Gallop writes that "the perversion of the notion of prostitution to a point where the prostitution endangers the identity of the client makes the question of which is the greater whore" and then that "the whore in her radical femininity has the potential for the Nietzschean superman."[17] Similarly, Roberte's actions lead us to question who is really more perverse: the instigator of the law of hospitality or she who, in her subjection to this law, conforms well beyond the call of duty, and in this radical conformity pushes the law itself to its outer limits. Moreover, Gallop's reference to Nietzsche is altogether fitting, for, as Klossowski himself makes explicit in his analysis of Nietzsche, the experience of the body in its extreme states (sex, sickness) provides access to an otherwise inaccessible realm of lucidity, one where the distinction between body and thought, between matter and energy, is momentarily suspended.

Just as sexual encounters allow new thresholds of thought-eroticism in the hospitality trilogy, the sick and convalescent body[18] serves a similar function in Klossowski's study of Nietzsche, *Nietzsche and the Vicious Circle*. Klossowski's analysis of Nietzsche is unique in that it takes Nietzsche's ill health as well as his letters describing his condition as fundamental to an understanding of his philosophy. In this sense, the physical and the personal are part and parcel of the philosophical oeuvre. As Klossowski puts it, "[I]t may seem absurd to read Nietzsche's successive texts as so many 'migraines' inverted in words. Given the way Nietzsche was compelled to describe the various phases of his conscious states, however, he was unable to avoid the mechanism of such an inversion."[19] Klossowski's study of Nietzsche works to decode this mechanism of inversion. Indeed, Klossowski characterized his approach as attuned to physiognomy and not to ideology.[20] Such an approach focuses on how the condition of being sick or convalescent allows new and altered states of being. These altered states might be called *becomings*, especially as they entail fundamental shifts in perception. Becomings reflect the new aesthetics of living, one perceived only from a vantage point that is exterior to the normal parameters of healthful living.

Nietzsche carefully documents these altered states, and Klossowski makes this the focus of *Nietzsche and the Vicious Circle*, in which he fully reproduces and comments on many of Nietzsche's letters to friends, physicians, and family members. Most of these letters, written during periods of ill health, give detailed depictions of Nietzsche's physical and mental states. Not only are these states related, but indeed physical incapacity and pain allow previously unimagined states of mental joy and freedom.[21] Nietzsche puts it thus in a letter written in January 1880 to Doctor O. Eiser:

> My existence is a *dreadful burden*: I would have rejected it long ago, had I not been making the most instructive experiments in the intellectual and moral domain in just this condition of suffering and almost complete renunciation—this joyous mood, avid for knowledge, raised me to heights where I triumphed over every torture and all despair. On the whole, I am happier now than I have ever been in my life. And yet, continual pain; for many hours of the day, a sensation closely akin to seasickness, a semi-paralysis that makes it difficult to speak, alternating with furious attacks (the last one made me vomit for three days and three nights, I longed for death!) . . . My only consolation is my thoughts and perspectives.[22]

As Klossowski glosses this passage, "[T]he act of thinking became identical with suffering, and suffering with thinking. From this fact, Nietzsche posited the *coincidence of thought with suffering*, and asked what a thought would be that was deprived of suffering. Thinking suffering, reflecting on past suffering—as *the impossibility of thinking*—then came to be experienced by Nietzsche as the highest joy."[23] While all the forces of sickness would serve to withhold or deplete energy and lucidity, there is a counterforce at work that responds with a new and enhanced form of lucidity. What results is an enabling disjunction—not unlike that outlined above with respect to Roberte and the pure soul / impure body—in which physical excess, here in the form of sickness, allows for an unprecedented mental purity and freedom. As with Roberte's body in *Les Lois de l'hos-pitalité*, the body once again serves as a medium for attaining altered mental states, states that would be impossible were it not for the inextricable conjunction of the body and mind and, *at the same time*, the capacity to dissociate them. If there is one theme in all of Klossowski's oeuvre, it is this, and nowhere is it expressed more forcefully than in the study of Nietzsche.

Throughout his work, Klossowski underscores the disjunction between the body and the identity of the person, a disjunction in which the body can be instrumental in breaking down the identity of the person, and this in a positive and joyous fashion. With respect to the sick body, the mind unleashes thought-energy that runs contrary to the negating forces of the body's sickness. This thought-energy is the product of a disjunctive process of becoming, which Klossowski describes in exuberant terms:

> Nietzsche experienced this dissolving confrontation between somatic and spiritual forces for a long time, and he observed it passionately. The more he listened to his body, the more he came to distrust *the person the body supports*. His obsessive fear of suicide, born out of the despair that his atrocious migraines would never be cured, amounted to a condemnation of the body in the name of the person being diminished by it. . . . By studying the reactions of his nervous system, he would come to conceive of himself *in a different manner* than he had previously known—and indeed, in a manner that will perhaps never again be known. Consequently, he developed a mode of intelligence which he wanted to submit to exclusively physical criteria. He not only *interpreted* suffering as energy, but *willed* it to be so. Physical suffering would be livable only insofar as it was closely connected to joy, insofar as it developed a voluptuous lucidity: either it would extinguish all possible thought, or it would reach the delirium of thought.[24]

The virtually unprecedented state that Nietzsche attains is achieved through a separation or oscillation between the body and the "person the body supports." This process of becoming is catalyzed by a mind-body disjunction, or more nearly the mind's separation from a body in some state of sickness or impurity. It must be stressed that sickness or impurity is *not* a negative state to be overcome but rather a positive enabler that is never actually separate from its thought counterpart. The change of state, or becoming, is that from a bodily sensation to a thought-sensation infused with corporeal energy. Such a becoming might be called an eroticization or a materialization of thought. It is thus all the more fitting that Klossowski frequently refers to Nietzsche's sickness-induced lucidity as "voluptuous lucidity." It seems that a similar voluptuous lucidity results from Roberte's repeated sexual encounters. While these are in one sense preeminently scripted heterosexual encounters, they are interesting in that the voluptuousness lies not in the physical sex but rather in the altered mental states that arise from the disjunction of bodies and identities.

Klossowski best characterizes this process of disjunctively induced becoming not in the language of becoming as such but rather by the terms "new cohesion" and "corporealizing thought." Klossowski expresses this most succinctly when he writes that Nietzsche "struggled at one and the same time with the to-and-fro movement of the impulses, and for a *new cohesion* between his thought and the body as a *corporealizing* thought."[25] Provoked by the body, thought ascends to a space where it can revoke the body, but not without being energized by the body's very materiality. Materiality transported into the realm of thought permeates thought to such an extent that a new cohesion results: corporeal and spiritual materialities are no longer distinct.

Although the explicit language of becoming belongs more expressly to the philosophy of Deleuze,[26] Klossowski's periodic gestures toward a Deleuzian framework at once demonstrate his profound affinities with Deleuze *and* demarcate another order of thought-becoming—Deleuze's thought and Klossowski's thought merging into one singular "corporealizing thought." It is thus of no small significance that Klossowski's study of Nietzsche is dedicated to Deleuze. Moreover, in the analysis of Nietzsche's sickness discussed above, Klossowski draws on without explicitly citing Deleuze's work on Nietzsche. Klossowski does this by actually using the term *becoming* to describe the dynamics between the body and thought, and also by using the Deleuzian notion of "active" and "reactive" forces.[27] Klossowski writes: "Nietzsche says that *we have no language to express what is in becoming*. Thought is always the result of a momentary relation of power between impulses, principally between those that dominate and those that resist."[28] In expressing the production of thought as a function of a power relation between active and reactive forces, Klossowski further echoes the following analysis in Deleuze's *Nietzsche and Philosophy* of the power of reactive forces:

What Nietzsche calls an active force is one which goes to the limit of its consequences. An active force separated from what it can do by a reactive force thus becomes reactive. But does not this reactive force, in its own way, go to the limit of what it can do? . . . A reactive force can certainly be considered from different points of view. Illness, for example, separates me from what I can do, as reactive force it makes me reactive; it narrows my possibilities and condemns me to a diminished milieu to which I can do no more than adapt myself. But in an other way, it reveals to me a new capacity, if endows me with a new will that I can make my own, going to the limit of a strange power. . . . Here we can recognise an ambivalence important to Nietzsche: all the forces whose reactive character he exposes are, a few lines or pages later, admitted to fascinate him, to be sublime because of the perspective they open up for us and because of the disturbing will to power to which they bear witness.[29]

In this passage, Deleuze overturns the hierarchy between active and reactive forces, arguing with Nietzsche that the reactive force of sickness can be its own form of activity and can inaugurate new and interesting states of being. Klossowski pushes Deleuze's reading still further by focusing even more squarely on the positive newness of the perspective opened by the reactive force of sickness. While Deleuze highlights this fascination with sickness as "an ambivalence important to Nietzsche," Klossowski makes this fascination the cornerstone of his exegesis of Nietzsche. Though Deleuze's tone is more muted—and Klossowski's more exuberant—Deleuze's and Klossowski's readings of Nietzsche nonetheless intersect strikingly on the question of the sick body and its ability to open new perspectives and unleash new energies.

It is indeed through the medium of Nietzsche, and specifically the oppositional relation between bodily sickness and mental health expressed in Nietzsche's letters, that Deleuze and Klossowski engage most actively with each other. In this fashion, Nietzsche, like Roberte, is a medium of exchange between men. Just as Roberte actualizes the relation between host and stranger in Klossowski's fiction, so too does a Nietzschean framework of bodies and thought actualize the literary-philosophical relation between Deleuze and Klossowski. Deleuze explicitly uses such a framework in his laudatory essay on Klossowski, "Klossowski or Bodies-Language." Here, the title encapsulates the central disjunction between body and thought in the Klossowskian oeuvre. Deleuze reads this disjunction once again in terms of active and reactive forces that ultimately dislocate personal identity. The forces are now called "provocation" and "revocation":

> Does Klossowski simply mean that speaking prevents us from thinking about nasty things? No; the pure language which produces an impure silence is a *provocation* of the mind by the body; similarly, the impure language which produces a pure silence is a *revocation* of the body by the mind. . . . More precisely, what is revoked in the body? Klossowski's answer is that it is the integrity of the body, and that because of this the identity of the person is somewhat suspended and volatilized.[30]

The body is once again central to this interplay of forces, whose ideal outcome is "pure silence," or the "revocation of the body by the mind." Revocation, then, linked simultaneously to the body, the mind, Nietzsche, and the woman (all of which are, at different points, both hailed and revoked[31]) is, for Klossowski, not pejorative but instead a positive space of opening. And it is Deleuze who brings out this positivity in Klossowski most forcefully. Just as Deleuze shows that the Nietzschean reactive forces are capable of working toward the most exhilarating of ends, so too does Deleuze in turn transcribe all that Klossowski revokes into a positive force. For Deleuze, Klossowski's depiction of oppositional extremes surpasses the realm of dialectics and negativity and instead inaugurates its own realm of positive purities, which might also be called intensities. Deleuze notes how "the couple Octave-Roberte refers to a pure difference of intensity in thought; the names 'Octave' and 'Roberte' no longer designate things; they now express pure intensities, risings and falls."[32] Octave and Roberte are not merely opposites caught up in a dialectical logic but rather disjointed thought-entities that, in the affirmation of this disjunction, paradoxically assume a uniquely positive presence.[33]

Deleuze's reading of Klossowski forcefully locates Klossowski's oeuvre within a realm of intensities and disjunction. And through this network of readings, Deleuze and Klossowski themselves converge as a thought-intensity around the force field of the sick body, while at the same time maintaining unique philosophical tonalities that serve as their space of disjunction from one another. This parallels in much more subtle fashion the dynamics between Octave and Roberte. As extreme opposites in a heterosexual union, Octave and Roberte on the one hand embody all that is most pernicious and oppressive in patriarchal hierarchies. Yet, from another perspective, when considered as disembodied intensities, intensities enabled, like Nietzsche's sublime visions, by a distinct form of corporealizing thought, Roberte and Octave—above all Roberte—become something altogether different. This something, not exactly a person and not exactly a pure spirit, might be described best as an incitement or provocation toward thought. This thought, whose newness is always unexpected, materializes like the hunchback who comes to accost Roberte, materializes just at the moment where it is both most provoked and least anticipated.

PART

3

Global Futures

9

THE DURÉE OF THE
TECHNO-BODY

Gail Weiss

The implosion of space into time, the transmutation of distance into speed, the instantaneousness of communication, the collapsing of the workspace into the home computer system, will clearly have major effects on the bodies of the city's inhabitants. The subject's body will no longer be disjointedly connected to random others and objects through the city's spatiotemporal layout; it will interface with the computer, forming part of an information machine in which the body's limbs and organs will become interchangeable parts. Whether this results in the "crossbreeding" of the body and the machine—whether the machine will take on the characteristics attributed to the human body ("artificial intelligence," automatons)—or whether the human body will take on the characteristics of the machine (the cyborg, bionics, computer prosthesis) remains unclear. Yet it is certain that this will fundamentally transform the ways in which we conceive both cities and bodies, and their interrelations. What remains uncertain is how.

ELIZABETH GROSZ

Almost daily, we are bombarded with news of innovative technologies capable of repairing bodily injuries (e.g., laser surgery), replacing body parts (e.g. prostheses), and now cloning animal bodies to create genetically identical but anatomically distinct beings. These innovations have met with ambivalent responses from the public at large, (which usually hears of them via the media), from the scientists who have developed them, and from academics who have theorized about them. On February 23, 1997, the front page of that icon of respectability, the *New York Times*, was em-

Elizabeth Grosz, "Bodies-Cities," *Space, Time, and Perversion: Essays on the Politics of Bodies* (New York: Routledge, 1995), 110.

blazoned with a headline that seemed more in keeping with its tabloid döppelganger, the *National Enquirer*: "Scientist Reports First Cloning Ever of Adult Mammal / Researchers Astounded / In Procedure on Sheep, Fiction Becomes True and Dreaded Possibilities Are Raised."[1] In the days that followed, more and more articles appeared in newspapers and magazines confirming the initial report, providing evidence of similar procedures that have been successfully performed with monkeys, and raising questions about that most horrifying but tantalizing possibility—could humans be next?[2]

The answer to a crucially different ethical question—*Should* humans be next?—was, at least in early articles and interviews, a resounding, and seemingly unanimous "no." Indeed, the scientists who had produced "Dolly" by cloning hastily assured us that they are not in favor of extending these technological feats to human beings. Rather, we were told, these technologies are intended to be used primarily for animal husbandry; for instance, cloning will allow us to increase the milk output on dairy farms by cloning cows that are "superproducers of milk." One "expert," Dr. Neal First, clearly oblivious of the impact of his pronouncement on a general audience, has gone so far as to proclaim that "if—and it's a very big if—cloning were highly efficient, then it could be a more significant revolution to the livestock industry than even artificial insemination."[3]

Although I have never been an advocate of animal rights, Dr. First's sanguine pronouncement plunged me into speculation on the existence of those future female bovine "superproducers" whose lives will be technologically regulated from birth (by cloning) through maternity (artificial insemination by donor [AID] pregnancies), lactation (the milking machines which will be the only way for them to relieve their super-full udders, since their calves are not allowed to nurse), and finally, in death (through the technological apparatus of the contemporary slaughterhouse, which kills, packages what is edible, and efficiently disposes of all waste).

My reflections on the cow's intimate relationship to technology led me next to those human scientists and farmers who are making it possible, and to the recognition that these cybernetic possibilities can in no way be construed as affecting only cows; rather, they are directed toward *us*, toward human beings who drink cows' milk, eat their flesh, wear their skin—in short, consume them. So, to restrict the questions raised by cloning purely to animals such as sheep, monkeys, and cows fails to eliminate the "human" factor. Moreover, since cloning is itself a reproductive technology, the issues it raises seem to implicate some human beings more than others, namely, those females whose reproductive experiences are capable of being radically altered by these procedures and the related procedures that are likely to follow such as ectogenesis (gestation and birth outside the female body). Of course, cloning and ectogenesis will alter the reproductive experiences of males as well as females, especially since they may, through genetic engineering, allow for male-male reproduction in the absence of a female or even of her egg. Now, whether or not these technologies are ever developed for humans, the question I asked earlier—*Could they be?*—is itself enough to cause us to interrogate anew the interface between bodies and machines, to explore the significance of an intercorporeality that defies any attempt to affirm the autonomy of the body apart from other bodies or from the disciplinary, technological practices that are continually altering and redefining them.

This is itself a vast project, which is being carried out on several different fronts and with several different (but largely unstated) political agendas. The barrage of statements (which themselves often appear to be clones of one another) from scientists (all of whom seem to be male) who appeal to medically "neutral" language to discuss these techno-bodily possibilities, implicitly deny the economic, metaphysical, sexual, and racial implications these new body technologies involve; and the futuristic, hypothetical language used in their descriptions also can seduce us into believing that these technological developments and their potential consequences affect merely an impossibly distant, imaginary future—not the present, much less the past.

The specific question I would like to take up here has to do with the temporality of the techno-body, which is certainly not a future body but is our own bodies and bodily possibilities to the extent that they are discursively represented, psychologically constructed, and physiologically reconstructed through technological processes which include the pen, the analyst's couch, the speculum, forceps, the surgeon's knife, the computer, the city and its abjected other, the suburb, as well as the unassuming petri dish, that all-important maternal substitute, which has displaced the female as the "originary" site of genetic experimentation and reproductive speculation.

In *Nomadic Subjects: Embodiment and Sexual Difference in Contemporary Feminist Theory*, Rosi Braidotti argues that our new biotechnologies—which make organs interchangeable (through organ transplants), give us babies without sex (through in vitro fertilization) and sex without babies (through contraceptives)—reduce bodies to organisms, organisms

to organs, and in the end, evacuate human (and especially female) agency
by doing away with the very notion and experience of durée or becoming
in time:

> Stuck between the archaic material power and the postmodern mother-
> machine, between the mystical-hysterical body and the test tube, we run
> the risk of losing our most precious ally: time. The time of process, of
> working through, of expressing transformations of the self and other and
> having them implemented socially. This is the time of women's own be-
> coming. It can be taken away before it could ever be actualized; it could
> be short-circuited, aborted.[4]

More particularly, Braidotti argues that these new biotechnologies
"freeze" time, thereby affirming not life but death. This freezing is enacted
through what she depicts as an equally frozen, masculinist figure: namely,
the contemporary biotechnician, who:

> as the prototype of high-tech power, represents the modern knowing sub-
> ject: "man-white-Western-male-adult-reasonable-heterosexual-living-in-
> towns-speaking a standard language."
> Under his imperious gaze the living organisms, reduced to an infinitely
> small scale, lose all reference to the human shape and to the specific tem-
> porality of the human being. All reference to death disappears in the dis-
> course about "biopower"—power over life. What seems to me at stake in
> the biopower situation is the progressive freezing-out of time, that is to say
> ultimately of death. The living material that comes under the scrutiny of
> the medical gaze is beyond death and time—it's "living" in the most ab-
> stract possible way. (*Nomadic Subjects,* 47)

In marked contrast to her depiction of these allegedly frozen, deathlike
biotechnologies (which themselves rely quite heavily on the freezer in
order to promote their "timely" effects), Braidotti describes woman's excess, her "monstrosity," the monstrosity of (Deleuze's) becoming-woman,
a becoming that has made her a site of fascination and horror, and which
is in danger of being transubstantiated into a marketable and possibly even
dispensable product. Indeed, Braidotti likens this transformation to a
perennial, alchemic fantasy:

> On the imaginary level . . . the test-tube babies of today mark the long-
> term triumph of the alchemists' dream of dominating nature through their

self-inseminating, masturbatory practices. What is happening with the new reproductive technologies today is the final chapter in a long history of fantasy of self-generation by and for the men themselves—men of science, but men of the male kind, capable of producing new monsters and fascinated by their power. (*Nomadic Subjects,* 88)

For Braidotti, contemporary reproductive technologies, such as in vitro fertilization, represent a flight from the excesses of both maternal desire and maternal imagination; they collapse the spatiality and temporality of the relationship between mother and fetus into a "homunculus, a manmade tiny man popping out of the alchemist's laboratories, fully formed and endowed with language" (*Nomadic Subjects,* 87). While clearly disparaging these alchemic biotechnicians' fascination with their own power and with the new "monsters" they have created, Braidotti also disparages the transformation of woman as a site of excess, horror, and fascination to a reproductive instrument or machine.

Nostalgically, Braidotti asks, "Where has the Cartesian passion of wonder gone?" Paradoxically, this wonder for her turns out to be the very mixture of horror and fascination that she claims men are fleeing from *through* their fascination with the transformative possibilities offered by contemporary biotechnologies. Braidotti is seemingly oblivious of this tension in her position, a tension that appears insofar as horror and fascination are escaped through a new fascination which brings its own horrifying possibilities. Rather than provide a justification for her implicit and extremely problematic distinction between a "legitimate" subject of horror and fascination (women before reproductive technologies existed) as opposed to an "illegitimate" one (cybernetic fetuses), Braidotti ignores these difficulties and concludes that it is impossible to see our contemporary reproductive technologies as anything other than "a form of denial of the sense of wonder, of the fantastic, of that mixture of fascination and horror that I have already mentioned" (*Nomadic Subjects,* 89).

Even if we set aside this tension, which threatens to undermine her entire account, it would seem that Braidotti is calling for a return to an imaginary time when this horror of and fascination for women's bodies accorded them dignity and respect. I think it is indeed an imaginary time because it is not clear when the combination of horror and fascination that she is valorizing has ever been advantageous to those who have been designated as "monstrous." Braidotti blames "the massive medicalization of scientific discourse" for eliminating the "marvelous, imaginary dimension of the monster," yet I would argue that this "marvelous, imaginary dimension" has never been quite so marvelous for those individuals whose monstrosities have been constructed through this phantasmic site.

Basically, Braidotti is conflating several issues that need to be considered separately: (1) Are these new biotechnologies really "freezing time," technologies of death as opposed to life? (2) Is death adequately understood as "frozen time," fundamentally opposed to the flowing temporality of life? (3) Are contemporary reproductive technologies indeed diminishing the horror and fascination Braidotti identifies with a Cartesian passion of wonder before that which escapes our control? These questions lead, in turn, to further questions about Braidotti's own analysis: (4) Is this mixture of horror and fascination advantageous for those who are its objects, that is, is it a mixture of passions we want to privilege? (5) Does this fascination and horror, and Braidotti's corresponding reification of these passions, serve to intensify, in oppressive ways, the monstrosity of the monstrous?

Before addressing these questions, I should first note that in a more recent essay, "Signs of Wonder and Traces of Doubt: On Teratology and Embodied Differences," Braidotti attempts to deconstruct the historical understanding of the monster as the radical "other"; rather, she argues that:

> The peculiarity of the organic monster is that s / he is both Same and Other. The monster is neither a total stranger nor completely familiar; s / he exists in an in-between zone. I would express this as a paradox: the monstrous other is both liminal and structurally central to our perception of normal human subjectivity. The monster helps us to understand the paradox of 'difference' as a ubiquitous but perennially negative preoccupation.[5]

The paradox, then, is that the organic monster is a liminal, phantasmic site that refuses straightforward categorization or description and, at the same time, it is "structurally central to our perception of normal human subjectivity" insofar as it serves to establish difference by constituting an abject domain generated through the fantasies of a historically evolving, racist, and sexist imaginary. For, she tells us,

> This mechanism of 'domestic foreignness', exemplified by the monster, finds its closest analogy in mechanisms such as sexism and racism. The woman, the Jew, the black or the homosexual are certainly 'different' from the configuration of human subjectivity based on masculinity, whiteness,

heterosexuality, and Christian values which dominates our scientific thinking. Yet they are central to this thinking, linked to it by negation, and therefore structurally necessary to upholding the dominant view of subjectivity. The real enemy is within: s / he is liminal, but dwells at the heart of the matter. (*Between Monsters,* 141)

Ultimately, I would argue, Braidotti is profoundly ambivalent in her response to the paradox of the monster, and this ambivalence can perhaps be attributed to her tacit recognition that the monster's subversive potential as a liminal entity, always threatening to disrupt established (social) order, can be maintained only to the extent that, in a process well described both by Mary Douglas and by Julia Kristeva, we disavow our own monstrous excesses by reincarnating them in the body of the abject other.[6] That is, the subversive potential of the monster is inseparable from its marginalization. In horror and fascination, Braidotti implies, we recognize that *we* are the monster, or at least are born of the maternal monster; and her concern about contemporary biotechnologies is that they give us an illusory sense of control over the monstrous / maternal, domesticating our horror and fascination, but, in so doing, create new monsters, nonmaternal, cybernetic monsters who may end up controlling us. For, she concludes, the monster as the embodiment of difference:

> moves, flows, changes; because it propels discourses without ever settling into them; because it evades us in the very process of puzzling us, it will never be known what the next monster is going to look like; nor will it be possible to guess where it will come from. And because we *cannot* know, the monster is always going to get us. (*Between Monsters,* 150)

Let us return, at this ominous point, to the questions I raised earlier, to see, by disentangling the complex and contradictory threads of Braidotti's analysis, if her concerns about contemporary biotechnologies are indeed well-founded. Let me first take up my initial question and restate it as follows: Are these new technologies "freezing" time as Braidotti suggests, by diminishing the power of maternal imagination and maternal desire and replacing them with a masculinist, misogynist, parthogenetic fantasy? Braidotti's own evolving understanding of the monster as a "shifter, a vehicle that constructs a web of interconnected and yet potentially contradictory discourses about his or her embodied self" and, as "a process without a stable object" already calls into question such a reductive claim

(*Between Monsters*, 150). For, as a moving, flowing, changing, embodiment of difference, the monster will itself subvert any attempts that are made to "neutralize" it by "fixing" or "freezing" it. However, one may always respond that although these reproductive technologies will not succeed in freezing time or eliminating the monster, this is still what they are aiming at and actively trying to achieve. Yet I would challenge this claim as well. To support this challenge, I will turn not to an examination of the technologies themselves (though this is an important project in its own right), but to what is being presupposed but left uninterrogated in Braidotti's own discussion: an understanding of temporality as lived time, embodied time, in contrast to the disembodied, "frozen" time that she claims is the goal of biotechnological practices and their scientific / medicalized discourses.

No one, I think, has offered a more profound account of this distinction between lived temporality and "objective" time than Henri Bergson, in his well-known (but all too often overlooked) essay "An Introduction to Metaphysics."[7] Here, Bergson argues that temporality or "inner time," is irreducible to "outer" or "clock" time, and that any analysis of the latter will fail to grasp the essence of the former. To support the irreconcilability of temporality and time, Bergson appeals to the intuition each of us has of her or his own durée, that is, to the sense we possess of our own personality flowing through time. Bergson argues that this experience of continual becoming or durée cannot be captured in discrete moments of time; our durée is itself a continuous flux or flow that is accessible to intuition but eludes analysis and its conceptual symbolizations. Durée, Bergson maintains, violates the "law" of noncontradiction; it is both a unity and a multiplicity because it "lends itself at the same time both to an indivisible apprehension and to an inexhaustible enumeration" (*Metaphysics,* 23). Despite its contradictory nature, Bergson argues that we can and often do grasp our durée as an absolute by a "simple act" of intuition. "By intuition," he claims,

is meant the kind of *intellectual sympathy* by which one places oneself within an object in order to coincide with what is unique in it and consequently inexpressible. Analysis, on the contrary, is the operation which reduces the object to elements already known, that is, to elements common both to it and other objects. To analyze, therefore, is to express a thing as a function of something other than itself. All analysis is thus a translation, a development into symbols, a representation taken from successive points of view from which we note as many resemblances as possible between the new object which we are studying and others which we believe we know already. In its eternally unsatisfied desire to embrace the object around which it is compelled to turn, analysis multiplies without end the number of its points of view in order to complete its always incomplete representation, and ceaselessly varies its symbols that it may perfect the always imperfect translation. It goes on, therefore, to infinity. But intuition, if intuition is possible, is a simple act. (*Metaphysics, 24*)

One way to understand Braidotti's claim that contemporary biotechnologies "freeze" time is to view them as attempting, through an analytic medicoscientific process, to gain control over the durée of both maternal and fetal bodies. Moreover, one might argue that procedures such as cloning challenge the integrity of this durée and make it impossible to grasp by any "simple act" of intuition. Although I think Bergson might well have been sympathetic to Braidotti's suspicions about contemporary biotechnologies, especially insofar as they seem inevitably to tamper with our sense of time, I also think that his account of both durée and intuition provides a means of countering Braidotti's overwhelmingly pessimistic analysis.[8]

If, as Bergson suggests, intuition is a matter of "placing oneself within the object in order to coincide with what is unique in it and consequently inexpressible," then it would seem that intuition can always occur as long as there is a unique temporal experience there to be intuited as well as a temporal being who is capable of intuiting it. Later on in the essay, Bergson reinforces and elaborates on this point by claiming that intuition need not be restricted to our own durée, since in the very act of intuiting our own durée, we are brought "into contact with a whole continuity of durations which we must try to follow, whether downwards or upwards; in both cases we can extend ourselves indefinitely by an increasingly violent effort . . . we transcend ourselves" (*Metaphysics, 48–49*)

In claiming that we are able, with effort, to transcend our own durée and participate in the durations of others, Bergson is trying to show that a metaphysics based on intuition is not solipsistic. However, his claim that one duration is always in contact with a whole continuity of durations is provocative in its own right. More specifically, by invoking this "continuity of durations," Bergson seems to be arguing for the imbrication of our individual durées and, even further, for an intertemporality that need not be restricted to human experiences. Indeed, one of his most striking examples of intuition in *An Introduction to Metaphysics* is an intuition of Paris, a city with its own unique durée, which, he argues, cannot be intuited "even with an infinite number of accurate sketches" if one has never seen the city oneself. Setting aside his problematic claim that one must see the city oneself in order to have an intuition of its durée—a claim that rings true only if we lose sight of the power of both art and literature to evoke the durée of a city and its various inhabitants—I would like to turn to his suggestion that durées are never isolated but always interconnected and that, through a "violent effort," we can extend ourselves indefinitely, even transcend ourselves by intuitively grasping this continuum.

If, as Bergson argues, analysis is impotent before durée, incapable of grasping it except through "ready-made concepts" that "never actually give us more than an artificial reconstruction of the object" (*Metaphysics*, 29), a corresponding analysis of the durée of the techno-bodies produced by contemporary biotechnologies via an exploration of the desires and fantasies that motivate their practitioners will also fail. Ultimately, for this particular purpose, it is irrelevant what the desires and fantasies of contemporary biotechnicians turn out to be; if they indeed see themselves, as Braidotti suggests, as contemporary alchemists capable of dispensing with that horrifying and fascinating object of desire, the maternal body, once and for all, this does not mean that their productions will fulfill their "fathers'" wishes. For, as Donna Haraway notes in "A Cyborg Manifesto," "illegitimate offspring are often exceedingly unfaithful to their origins. Their fathers, after all, are inessential."[9]

The durée of the techno-body—whether this body be that of a newly cloned sheep; a "test-tube" baby; a woman in labor hooked up to technological devices that record fetal movement, fetal heartbeat, maternal blood pressure, and contractions; a boy with a liver transplant; a woman with a prosthetic leg—arises out of a violent effort and requires a violent effort in order to see the interconnections that link this durée with our own. Indeed, what is most violent, I think, is the recognition that technology is part and parcel of our own durée—the monster will "get us" precisely to the extent that we view it as a threat from the "outside," incarnated in demonic biotechnologists and their allegedly masturbatory fantasies, rather than recognizing that it is not "out there" but within our own bodies, facilitating the death of solipsism by affirming the intercorporeality of time. As Haraway notes, "The machine is not an *it* to be animated, worshiped, and dominated. The machine is us, our processes, an aspect of our embodiment" (*Reinvention*, 180).

One danger of emphasizing the gulf between temporality and time, as I have done thus far, is that it makes us likely to forget the ways in which our own lived experience continually traverses the divide between them. For surely it is overly simplistic to say that time, as measured by calendars, watches, sundials, and the movement of planets and stars, is "out there" while our temporal experience is within us; rather, we "inhabit" time and are inhabited by it, through our own bodily rhythms and movements, and through the interconnections between our own durée and the durée of all that we encounter. Indeed, to the extent that the conventions of clock time are themselves based on the movement of the earth around the sun, clock time is not merely an external, analytical device that helps us negotiate our everyday affairs; it is based on corporeal movement, movement that is inscribed in our own bodies. "Freezing time" would lead to a corresponding freezing of temporality; it would require the severing of the continuum that unites one durée with another durée and would collapse an instant into an eternity. This leads us to the second question I asked earlier on, is this frozen time, which seems so counter to the "rhythms of life," the time of death, as Braidotti suggests?

"Freezing time" is itself a conundrum, because there is no way to imagine how time could be "frozen." People, rich people like Walt Disney, for instance, can be frozen; embryos can be frozen; but time itself cannot be frozen without time itself being transformed into something it is not: a specific entity rather than a fluid, corporeal process. Sometimes, these liminal entities (frozen embryos and cyrogenetically preserved people) are referred to as existing in "suspended animation," and I think this term expresses their temporal existence more accurately than saying that they are instances of "frozen time." Dead bodies that are not preserved in this way decay, a temporal process which leaves tangible effects on those bodies (and less tangible effects on other bodies), and which eventually transforms them into nonorganic matter.[10] Death is therefore not a stopping of time, though it is indeed a disruptive alteration of bodily temporality, an alteration which can be intuited through the interconnections between our own durée and the durée of others who have died. So, in a certain sense, Epicurus was wrong to proclaim that the experience of death is impossible, since when death is, we are not; and when we are, death is not. Death occurs not outside time, but in time; death inhabits time as a virtuality which is continually embodied or actualized.

"Freezing time," I would argue, is not the goal or even the outcome of a deathlike biotechnology, but a metaphorical strategy in the Ricoeurian sense, a strategy that is productive to the extent that it shatters and increases "our sense of reality by shattering and increasing our language."[11] To the extent that we acknowledge the compelling force of this contradictory metaphor, and to the extent that we view it as applicable to the contemporary biotechnologies Braidotti discusses, we must recognize its power to disrupt our understanding and experience of durée, a durée that extends, transforms, and transcends itself through these very technologies, technologies which, whether we actively make use of them, ignore them, or even avoid them, actively retemporalize our lives.

Braidotti's use of the metaphor of "freezing time" is rendered even more complex by the ambiguity and ambivalence in her discussion of a related metaphor, which I have already mentioned: the metaphor of the monster. As we have already noted, she privileges (in problematic ways) the monster as a site of wonder which she identifies with fascination and horror and valorizes the power of the monster as the maternal body or even the "freakish" body of those whose corporeality resists normalization. Yet she also appeals to the metaphor of the monster to characterize the destructive, death-inducing, time-freezing fantasies of contemporary biotechnicians, who, she argues, are creating organs without bodies—that is, who are decorporealizing bodies in order to control, manipulate, and exchange them. Can she have it both ways? Do contemporary biotechnologies signify the erasure of the monster of old in favor of genetically engineered cyborgs, which in turn take their place as the new monsters, monsters that threaten to "get us"? This leads me back to my third question: Are contemporary reproductive technologies indeed diminishing the horror and fascination Braidotti identifies with a Cartesian passion of wonder before that which escapes our control?

In a strange sense, there seems to be an almost natural progression in the category of the monstrous. Once we have ceased to be horrified and fascinated by alleged pathologies of the human, the impetus to create new monsters, new sites of horror and fascination, seems almost inevitable. Moreover, this follows from, rather than challenges, Braidotti's own valorization of the monster and the fascination and horror it invokes. In her essay "Between Monsters, Goddesses and Cyborgs: Feminist Confrontations with Science," Nina Lykke extends the metaphorical domain of the monster by claiming that it:

> can perform as a representation of boundary phenomena in the interdisciplinary or hybrid grey zone between the cultural and natural sciences. In

this zone, boundary subjects and boundary objects, monsters which cannot be defined as either human or non-human, challenge established borders between the sciences. This is a zone where confrontations between feminism and science take place.[12]

To make these confrontations productive, it is essential, I think, to recognize that, as Patricia Bayer Richard notes, we cannot "put the technological genie back in the bottle."[13] Nonetheless, to recognize that these technologies are here to stay does not mean that we should simply endorse them or overlook the racist, classist, and misogynistic presuppositions that may underlie and motivate them. On the other hand, I would argue that the metaphor of the monster or even the metaphor of "freezing time" won't work to capture what may be pernicious about these technologies. These technologies and the new, virtual realities that they have spawned—the virtual realities of frozen embryos, cyrogenetically preserved "corpses," and even their "cyborgian cousins," the virtual realities that "inhabit" cyberspace—replicate, rather than efface, the horror and fascination that has always accompanied the interpellation of the monster. To the extent that they offer themselves as a way of reconfiguring our own corporeal possibilities, they may indeed serve as sites of wonder and of passion. But what we often find through these technologies is not an escape from the conventional, but a reinscription of convention, whether this reinscription takes the form, through reproductive technologies, of Richard's "tailor-made child" or, in the domain of virtual reality, of "cyberspace heroes" who, as Anne Balsamo notes, are "usually men, whose racial identity, although rarely described explicitly, is contextually white."[14] Their counterparts, "cyberspace playmates," she observes, "are usually beautiful, sexualized, albeit sometimes violently powerful women" (*Technologies,* 131). For Balsamo:

> Cyberspace offers white men an enticing retreat from the burdens of their *cultural* identities. In this sense, it is apparent that although cyberspace seems to represent a territory free from the burdens of history, it will, in effect, serve as another site for the technological and no less conventional inscription of the gendered, race-marked body. So despite the fact that VR [virtual reality] technologies offer a new stage for the construction and performance of body-based identities, it is likely that old identities will continue to be more comfortable, and thus more frequently produced. (*Technologies,* 131)

If, as Haraway argues, "communication technologies and biotechnologies are the crucial tools recrafting our bodies," then we need to think carefully about the ways in which the latter reinscribe, rather than oppose, challenge or subvert, the patriarchal status quo (*Reinvention,* 164). As Balsamo suggests in the passage just cited, cyberspace may seem to promise an escape from one's cultural identity, but it may end up reinforcing that identity through the replication of the aesthetic ideals that help to constitute and solidify its normative, hegemonic structure. So, far from leaving the body behind, or absorbing "the material into the semiotic" in a process according to which "the material is constructed as potentially changeable by semiotic, sign-producing acts, by programming and reprogramming," the cyborg may turn out to be both less and more monstrous than we have imagined; less monstrous insofar as its reprogramming may lead not to radical innovation but to fairly conventional repetition, more monstrous insofar as oppressive corporeal practices are reinscribed in a more ubiquitous, virtual register.[15]

The metaphor of the monster, I would argue, has become so pervasive that it has lost its potency; more specifically, it has lost the "shattering" power which Ricoeur identifies with a metaphor's ability to create a novel reality through its redescription of reality. "The strategy of metaphor," he proclaims, "is heuristic fiction for the sake of redescribing reality" (*Ricoeur,* 85). To the extent that the metaphor of the monster has drawn much of its power from the mixture of fascination and horror that the figure of the monster has evoked, the time has come to think long and hard about the consequences of privileging responses that may stem more from bad faith than from a "genuine" sense of wonder in the face of that which refuses normalization. As Beauvoir reminds us in *The Second Sex,* it is a bourgeois luxury to view the "other" as mysterious, as beyond our comprehension.[16] And, for those all-too-numerous others whose various "excesses" or "lacks" or both are constructed as mysterious, as monstrous, the price of this "heuristic fiction" may be far too high. For Beauvoir, it justifies a refusal to recognize the concrete situation of the mysterious or monstrous other by appealing to a mythical understanding that refuses to give way to any reality that conflicts with it.

So, my response to the fourth question I asked earlier—Is this mixture of horror and fascination advantageous for those who are its objects, that is, is this a mixture of passions we want to privilege?—is a resounding "no." If contemporary biotechnologists and the techno-bodies they help to produce are indeed replacing the monsters of old with new monsters, this may be advantageous for the former, but the advantage will be relative to the disadvantageous position of the latter. Too much focus on how these technologies are instruments of control runs the danger of transforming the technologies themselves into agents rather than recognizing that, as Balsamo reminds us, "technologies have *limited* agency" (*Technologies,* 123). It also takes our collective attention away from the ways in which women and men who fail to comply with society's corporeal ideals are themselves controlled and regulated by both technological and nontechnological practices.

If Bergson indeed teaches us, as Deleuze argues, "that my duration essentially has the power to enclose other durations, to encompass the others, and to encompass itself ad infinitum," then we can move beyond what Haraway has called "an informatics of domination" toward an understanding of technology as offering new ways of linking bodies up to one another, expanding their interconnections, and, in so doing, increasing their intercorporeal potentialities.[17] Such a view does not, as I have already stated, lead to a wholehearted endorsement of each and every new technology that is proposed or developed; rather, it displaces the focus from the technology as such to a careful examination of its corporeal effects and, in turn, to the discursive practices that situate it as desirable, inevitable, or horrifying.

If, as I believe, fascination and horror, and Braidotti's corresponding reification of these passions, oppressively intensify the monstrosity of the monstrous (in response to my fifth question), the answer will be not to condemn the passions themselves as oppressive, but rather to recognize that passions are always passions *for* something or other and are not capable of being analyzed in the absence of the objects (or persons) that arouse them. The passion for technology need not lead to the technologization of passion. But if it does, we should hesitate to call this a new monster until we have interrogated its intercorporeal implications and effects. And, to the extent that we are embedded and encompassed within the techniques and practices we critique, such an interrogation can never point the finger at a monster without a mirror being present. One day, perhaps, this mirror will itself be technologically transformed so that it reveals not a frozen, alienating, monstrous image of otherness, but the lived, intercorporeal durée of our own techno-bodies.

10

SPECTRAL NATIONALITY: THE LIVING-ON [SUR-VIE] OF THE POSTCOLONIAL NATION IN NEOCOLONIAL GLOBALIZATION

Pheng Cheah

In the late twentieth century, nationalism is probably one of the few phenomena that we associate most closely with death. The end of this millennium is marked (and marred) by an almost endless catalogue of fanaticist intolerance, ethnic violence, and even genocidal destruction that are widely regarded as extreme expressions of nationalism: patriarchal fundamentalism in Afghanistan and other parts of the Islamic world; the atrocities designated by the proper names of Rwanda and Bosnia; the recent revival of the nuclear race in South Asia as a result of religious official nationalism in India and Pakistan; etc. Indeed, one might even say that in our age, nationalism has become the exemplary figure for death. The common association of nationalism with recidivism and the desire for the archaic implies that nationalism destroys human life and whatever futures we may have because its gaze is fixed on the frozen past.

Yet the nation's seemingly inevitable affinity with death is paradoxically inseparable from the desire for life. For the destructive, or better yet, sacrificial tendencies of nationalism are part of an attempt to protect or maximize the capacity for life. In nationalist discourse, the nation is not only

Note: This chapter is part of a book in progress entitled *Spectral Nationality*.

conceived in analogy with a living organic being; it is also regarded as the enduring medium or substrate through which individuals are guaranteed a certain life beyond finite or merely biological life, and hence, also beyond mortality and death.[1] The nation, in other words, guarantees an eternal future. Its alleged organic power of birth and origination is intimated by its etymological link with "nativity" and "natality." What is presupposed is a vitalist ontology that opposes life to death, spirit to matter or mechanism and, ultimately, living concrete actuality to abstract ghostly form.

We would, however, be mistaken to assume that this vitalist ontology is peculiar to nationalist discourse. As I will suggest, this ontology of life underwrites the discourse of revolutionary decolonization and contemporary theories of postcolonial nationalism regardless of whether they are organicist or sociological or whether they defend the nation-form or denounce it as an ideological construct. Indeed, the familiar thematic oppositions we use to describe all forms of political community—oppositions that either pit the state against the nation, the people or civil society; or capital against labor—rely on ontological metaphors that subordinate the dead to the living.

In this chapter, I want to explore whether this vitalist ontology, which conceives of the future in terms of eternal present life, provides an adequate basis for understanding the persistence of the nation-form in the current neocolonial global conjuncture and the future of postcolonial nationalism as an emancipatory project. I will argue that the modality of becoming of the decolonizing and postcolonial nation cannot be understood in terms of any human, natural, or even organic form of life in the conventional meaning of these terms. I make this argument by way of a critical analysis of Derrida's provocative and illuminating reflections on spectrality. Derrida's *hauntology* is the thought of radical finitude, and I want to outline some of its implications for theories of political community. But if Derrida's reflections are invaluable to my understanding of the spectrality of the postcolonial nation, he is also dismissive of the spectrality of the nation-form, especially in his use of the figure of the *arrivant* and a discourse of hospitality to characterize the challenges posed by contemporary globalization. For him, nationalism is without promise. It can promise nothing and has no future to-come. In my evaluation of this gesture of repudiation, I suggest that in this respect at least, Derrida inherits the Marxist determination of nationality as a subcase of ideology. Thus, even though his analysis of spectrality is a questioning of Marx's vitalist ontology, like Marx, Derrida also wishes to exorcise the spectrality of the nation. I conclude with a brief look at the future of the postcolonial nation-state in contemporary globalization.

1. THE NATION-PEOPLE AND ITS ONTOLOGY OF LIFE

Let us begin with an exemplary instance of how the discourse of revolutionary nationalism relies on an ontology of life: Frantz Fanon's description of the Mau Mau uprising in Kenya. "Every native who takes up arms," Fanon writes, "is a part of the nation which from henceforward will spring to life. . . . The national cause goes on progressing and becomes the cause of each and all. . . . Everywhere . . . we find a national authority. Each man or woman brings the nation to life by his or her action."[2] This idea of the spontaneous organic dynamism of the nation-people is essentially an ontotheology. Fanon conceives of the people via an analogy with a self-causing Absolute Being (*causa sui*). Put another way, the eternal source of ever-present life has become embodied in the transfigured human agent as national subject.[3] The state is merely the incarnation of the national spirit, for the nation-state is only a secondary institutional manifestation or by-product of national consciousness. The state is established when the cultural forms expressing nationhood require political-institutional embodiment as the condition of their survival.[4]

Fanon's biogenetic schema for understanding the relation of the nation-people to the state makes explicit the ontological metaphors of life and death underpinning the sociological topography that opposes the nation-people to the state. Like the political party from which it grows, the state is similar to dead letters without intentional significance. It is mere matter or mechanism awaiting animation by the national-popular will: it "is not an authority, but an organism through which the people exercise their authority and express their will." (*Wretched,* 185). An authentic nation-state is one that is truly popular-national. Only then will it be an organic whole that exhibits an immediate unity of the government, the people, and the task of nation-building. In contradistinction, indigenous bourgeois nationalism and political institutions that resort to spurious forms of nativism as a cover for their failure to express popular social consciousness are merely "the hollow shell of nationality," an empty form of national consciousness that lacks real life.

The bourgeois leaders of underdeveloped countries imprison national consciousness in sterile formalism. It is only when men and women are in-

cluded on a vast scale in enlightened and fruitful work that form and body
are given to [national] consciousness. Then the flag and the palace where
sits the government cease to be the symbols of the nation. The nation
deserts these brightly lit, empty shells and takes shelter in the country,
where it is given life and dynamic power. (*Wretched*, 204)[5]

Obviously, Fanon's thought is informed by the familiar sociological oppositions of state and nation; the party leadership and the common
masses; the indigenous urban bourgeoisie and the rural peasantry; the capi-
ital and the country. We should already know these oppositions by rote,
since they saturate the entire discursive field of the social sciences. However, Fanon's deployment of these oppositions makes very explicit something that largely remains implicit in their repeated usage in the social sciences: namely, that these oppositions, which we take as positive social
facts, are constitutively imbricated with the metaphysical oppositions of
empty form and concrete actuality, sterile artifice and creative organic
work, death and life.

Of course, these metaphysical oppositions have a long philosophical
history. Their widespread usage to characterize forms of political organization, however, stems from the modern conception of freedom that arose
in the wake of the separation of mechanism from human reason effected
by the Newtonian or Cartesian predication of the natural or material world
as the sum-totality of objects governed by arational mechanical laws.
Henceforth, freedom is precisely what is not or cannot be blindly determined or given by something else, for example, past events that are part of
the mechanism of nature. The mechanism of nature also includes human
techne or instrumental reason, since this is considered a lesser or degraded
form of reason, the causality of which is also governed by mechanical
laws. Freedom is fundamentally linked to the possibility of a living future
that is not determined by the past. In contradistinction, the mechanical lies
on the side of death, even if, like the automatons of Vaucanson that profoundly haunted Kant's account of the spontaneity of moral freedom, the
mechanical can simulate life.[6]

This sundering of the realm of human freedom from the material world
of mechanism is, of course, part of the larger shift from a cosmological to
an anthropologistic view of the world. Ideal models of political community in the contemporary world, which aim to provide the optimal institutional basis for the realization of freedom, attempt to reconcile freedom
with the arational world of mechanism. They almost invariably do this by
means of an analogy between organic life-forms and the technic of social

and political organisation in which techne is sublated into intelligible organic life, and the artificial is seen as ultimately working in the service of life. It is important to remember that the organic is not just brute nature or matter devoid of life. It is organized matter, matter imbued with animating purposiveness, which thereby becomes an organism that possesses life. Insofar as political organization makes nature organic or organized matter by imbuing it with an internal vitality and a purposiveness that exceed mechanism, insofar as political organization is a form of the actualization or objectification of rational ideas through purposive willing, it would be an exorcism and sublation of death. It is in this spirit that Kant thinks of "natural purposes" as organized beings and constitutional political organization as an analog of organic life, and Fichte characterizes the German nation as "a truly original and primary life."[7] Similarly, Hegel describes spirit [*Geist*], the highest objective appearance of which is the ideal state, in the following terms:

> To say that spirit exists would at first seem to imply that it is a completed entity. On the contrary, it is by nature active, and activity is its essence; it is its own product, and is therefore its own beginning and its own end. Its freedom does not consist in static being, but in a constant negation of all that threatens to destroy freedom.[8]

The same vitalism informs the idea of creative labor that underwrites Marx's account of the formation of the proletariat as a universal class.

Now, this ontology of life is ubiquitous and extremely tenacious. Its fundamental metaphysical oppositions resurface in discourses about postcolonial nationalism across various disciplines. For instance, in his sketch of the troubled life of the postcolonial nation in *Culture and Imperialism*, Edward Said characterizes the genesis of the postcolonial nation not so much as a stillbirth but as the monstrous birth of a pathological chauvinism:

> Nationality, nationalism, nativism: the progression is, I believe, more and more constraining. In countries like Algeria and Kenya one can watch the heroic resistance of a community partly formed out of colonial degradations, leading to a protracted armed and cultural conflict with the imperial powers, in turn giving way to a one-party state with dictatorial rule. . . . The debilitating despotism of the Moi regime in Kenya can scarcely be said to complete the liberationist currents of the Mau Mau up-

rising. No transformation of social consciousness here, but only an appalling pathology of power duplicated elsewhere—in the Philippines, Indonesia, Pakistan, Zaire, Morocco, Iran.[9]

Said's cautionary moral narrative is the all too familiar story of a fall that informs most postcolonial cultural theory. Coming after the formal success of political independence, postcolonial nationalism is the anticlimactic betrayal of the promise of freedom in decolonization where, as a result of its consummated marriage to the postcolonial state, the nation-people becomes subordinated to particularistic state imperatives. The path of becoming that is charted out here—Said calls it a "progression"—is linear. Its violent outcome is not unpredictable because it follows the inherently constraining logic that is proper to the nation as an artificial–technical construct. To this manipulative and hierarchical essence of nationalism, unfolded and realized as statist ideology, Said opposes the spontaneous populism of decolonization movements. We only need to scratch a little at the surface to see that this opposition between spontaneity and instrumental manipulation is essentially the opposition between life and death.

This thematic opposition between the spontaneous dynamism of resisting peoples and their institutional capture by the techne of reactionary class and state apparatuses informs almost all theories of postcolonial nationalism, and it can take the form of different sociological permutations. Even accounts as opposed as Partha Chatterjee's neo-Marxist critique of Indian nationalism as a statist ideology and Benedict Anderson's well-known defense of the nation as an "imagined political community" are governed by this opposition. In the conclusion of *Nationalist Thought and the Colonial World*, Chatterjee follows the orthodox Marxist rejection of cultural nationalism as a discourse that inevitably ends up as a statist ideology. Relying on Antonio Gramsci's theory of passive revolution, he argues that in the Third World, anticolonial cultural nationalism is the ideological discourse used by a rising but weak indigenous bourgeoisie to co-opt the popular masses into its struggle to wrest hegemony from the colonial regime, even as it keeps the masses out of direct participation in the governance of the postcolonial state.[10]

The topography Chatterjee sketches is of the subsumption of populist forces by the nation-form so that this dynamism can be captured by the bourgeois state *qua* relatively independent instrument of capitalist development. Simply put, the *nation-form* is an ideological cultural community used to yoke the people to the bourgeois state. Postcolonial nationalism and national culture would therefore be a false resolution of the contradiction between the people and capital:

> The conflict between metropolitan capital and the people-nation it [nationalist discourse] resolves by absorbing the political life of the nation into the body of the state. Conservatory of the passive revolution, the national state now proceeds to find for the 'nation' a place in the global order of capital, while striving to keep the contradictions between capital and the people in perpetual suspension. All politics is now sought to be subsumed under the overwhelming requirements of the state-representing-the-nation. . . . Any movement which questions this presumed identity between the people-nation and the state-representing-the-nation is denied the status of legitimate politics. Protected by the cultural ideological sway of this identity between the nation and the state, capital continues its passive revolution by assiduously exploring the possibilities of marginal development, using the state as the principal mobiliser, planner, guarantor and legitimator of productive investment. (*Nationalist,* 168–169)

In subsequent work, Chatterjee suggests that the opposition between state and civil society in Western social and political theory ought to be rejected in favor of an opposition between capital and community, on the ground that the former inevitably confines radical political action to the debilitating nation-state form.[11] My point here is that regardless of whether we see the fundamental contradiction of social existence as between civil society or the nation-people and the state or as between community and capital, the fundamental opposition is always between popular spontaneity and its ideological manipulation.

This opposition also informs Benedict Anderson's *Imagined Communities,* even though it is an impassioned defense of nationalism against Marxist critiques such as Chatterjee's. Anderson argues that in its initial emergence, the nation is a mass-based imagined political community induced by a constellation of historical forces in the late eighteenth and early nineteenth centuries such as the rise of print-capitalism and a new mode of homogeneous empty time. But to this pioneering style of emancipatory popular national consciousness, he counterposes a second style of nationalism—the reactionary official nationalism deployed by European dynastic states to naturalize themselves in response to the challenges of popular nationalism.[12] The problems of postcolonial nationalism are then explained in terms of a Janus-like modulation between good and bad, popular and statist models of nationalism adopted by each decolonizing nation after it achieves statehood.

These influential accounts of postcolonial nationalism therefore insist on a strict demarcation between organic spontaneity and technical manipulation: between the nation-people and the state in Anderson's case, and between the people / community and capital in Chatterjee's case. And this limit or line separating the spontaneous people from the state or capital ultimately turns out to be the line between the organic and the artificial, life and death. For Chatterjee, the nation is an artificial, ideological extension of the bourgeois state, a tool of dead capital. And Anderson, even as he suggests that the nation is a political community imagined in language, nevertheless stresses the organic nature of patriotic love:

> Something of the nature of this political love can be deciphered from the ways in which languages describe its object: either in the vocabulary of kinship (motherland, *Vaterland, patria*) or that of home (*heimat* or *tanah air* [earth and water, the phrase for the Indonesians' native archipelago]). Both idioms denote something to which one is naturally tied. . . . [I]n everything 'natural' there is always something unchosen. In this way, nation-ness is assimilated to skin-colour, gender, parentage and birth-era—all those things one cannot help. And in these 'natural ties' one senses what one might call 'the beauty of *gemeinschaft*'. (*Imagined,* 143)

Thus, like Chatterjee, Anderson also views the vicissitudes of postcolonial nationalism as the consequence of the contamination of spontaneous life by artifice and manipulative technomediation. "Often," he writes,

> in the 'nation-building' policies of the new [decolonised] states one sees both a *genuine,* popular nationalist *enthusiasm* and a *systematic, even Machiavellian*, instilling of nationalist ideology through the mass media, the educational system, administrative regulations, and so forth. . . . One can thus think of many of these nations as projects the achievement of which is still in progress, yet projects conceived more in the spirit of Mazzini than that of Uvarov. (*Imagined,* 113–114, emphasis added)

Decolonizing nationalism is thus a spontaneous project of becoming that is perverted in the aftermath of independence when the postcolonial nation becomes possessed by the state it thinks it controls. Anderson evokes this possession and stultification of the living national body by official nationalism through images of the ghostly technical infrastructure of a house and suffocating anachronistic garb that are strikingly reminiscent of Fanon's images of the palace as a brightly lit empty shell and the flag as an empty symbol of the nation.

> The model of official nationalism assumes its relevance above all at the moment when revolutionaries successfully take control of the state, and are for the first time in a position to use the power of the state in pursuit of their visions. . . . [E]ven the most determinedly radical revolutionaries always, to some degree, inherit the state from the fallen regime. . . . Like the complex electrical system in any large mansion when the owner has fled, the state awaits the new owner's hand at the switch to be very much its old brilliant self again.
>
> One should therefore not be much surprised if revolutionary *leaderships*, consciously or unconsciously, come to play lord of the manor. . . . Out of this accommodation comes invariably that 'state' Machiavellism which is so striking a feature of post-revolutionary regimes in contrast to revolutionary nationalist movements. The more the ancient dynastic state is naturalized, the more its antique finery can be wrapped around revolutionary shoulders. (*Imagined,* 159–160)

From my reconstruction of Chatterjee's and Anderson's theories of decolonizing nationalism, we can see that regardless of whether one is for or against the nation, regardless of whether one sees it as an ideological phantasm of the bourgeois state or as a dynamic growing body, one is always on the side of the open-ended and spontaneous becoming of the people conceived either as a community of language or as the collective agent of class struggle. And one is always against the territorial state, which is regarded as an artificially bounded entity that seeks to impose stasis on the becoming of the people by diverting this dynamism in the service of dead capital.

Now, the metaphysical oppositions between life and death, the organic and the artificial, or *physis* and *techne* structure Chatterjee's and Anderson's provocative theories of postcolonial nationalism in a complex way. Neither author simply dismisses the artificial in favor of the organic. Indeed, both are critical of simplistic organicist theories of the nation that regard it as a natural genetic principle. Instead, what we see is a more complicated gesture that tries to reconcile the artificial to the organic, death to life, to subordinate the former to the latter through an organicization of the technical that puts it in the service of life. Anderson suggests that the nation is a sociological organism, an artificial product of modern sociological conditions that is nevertheless experienced as an organic form of community; Chatterjee suggests that popular struggles against capital can "subvert the ideological sway of a state which falsely claims to speak on behalf of the nation" if they become performatively constituted as the universal subject of class struggle through the technic of consciousness-raising.

The technical becomes a source of perversion and death only when it cannot be organicized. It is here that Anderson and Chatterjee reveal themselves as heirs to the vitalist ontology that Fanon inherited from German idealism and Marxist materialism. For even though their approaches to nationalism appear to be irreconcilably opposed to each other, they are united by an admirable belief in an uncompromised or pure collective subject of resistance, an ever-present and self-originating source of life that renews itself through purposive collective self-actualizing action. Both share a basic distrust of the state as an instrument of dead capital and its corollary, a basic belief in the spontaneous transfigurative power of the people.

Of course, both of these contemporary theories of decolonizing nationalism are disillusioned and sobering. They do not exhibit the catastrophism and eschatology of thinkers like Marx and Fanon. They are formulated in the wake of the betrayal of the ideals of decolonization, and they attempt to account for this betrayal. As we saw earlier, for Fanon, the state is a techno-phantomatic object, something formed by a secondary process of the people's self-objectification. The state can be inspirited by the nation-people precisely because it is the work of the people that has become estranged or alienated from the people during the process of externalization or objectification. This estranged or alienated object, this techno-phantom, needs to be reappropriated and returned to its original living source. In contradistinction, although Chatterjee still regards the entire civil society-nation-state complex as a superstructure, he is forced to concede that in its malignant turn against its creator, this phantomatic edifice has become a more tenacious external fixture that may have completely escaped the grasp of its creator. At the very least, its exorcism is not possible in the present. Anderson goes even further by suggesting that the state is completely foreign to the nation-people. It is an evil foreign body that cannot be reappropriated without contaminating revolutionary nationalism.

However, if Anderson and Chatterjee both touch on the historical obstacles that stood and still stand in the way of the actualization of nation-people as a free collective subject, they do not actually question the idea of actualization or self-objectification itself. In the final analysis, all obstacles to the actualization of freedom remain external to the process of actualization. Indeed, these obstacles are by definition contingent because the actualization of freedom in and by a pure uncompromised collective body is the removal of all obstacles for that collective body. Thus, Anderson's figuring of the relation between nation and state via a simile of the possession of the human occupant by the ghostly infrastructure of the house may be a despairing view of the transfigurative power of the people, but it is nevertheless a pessimism that tries to hold this power of becoming in reserve as a future horizon. A revolutionary leadership, he notes, may inherit the secondhand switchboards and palaces of the previous state, but people are *never* the beneficiaries of this spectral legacy (*Imagined,* 161)—which is also to say that the living people never willingly receives the ghost of techne into its home.

I want to be as precise as possible about where I agree with and differ from these two provocative contemporary theories of decolonizing nationalism. On the one hand, it is clear that the vicissitudes of nationalism issue from the necessary relation between the nation-form per se and the state, as Chatterjee suggests, rather than from a fundamental qualitative difference between a popular nationalism that is completely free of the state and an official nationalism that emanates from the state. This is because the line between state and nation-people is especially fuzzy in Asian and African decolonization. Since the nation-people as a bounded community is arbitrarily generated from colonial state frontiers, popular national consciousness is initially weak and needs to be actively fostered through the artifice of political organization, which can always be monitored by the state. Furthermore, the masculinist and patriarchal nature of revolutionary nationalist movements such as the FLN in the Algerian struggle for liberation indicates that nationalism is not a completely egalitarian force even in its popular phase.[13] The contaminated nature of popular nationalism indicates that one can no longer point to the technical apparatus of the state as the sole source of the postcolonial nation's oppressive practices. In any event, any analytical separation between an oppressive, hierarchical nationalism and a good, demotic nationalism needs to account for the common element or continuity between these two forms. It is this continuity that allows nationalism as such to modulate between its good and bad faces without any sharp transition.

But, on the other hand, as Anderson suggests, political love for the nation is not reducible to an ideological mystification that the state inculcates in the minds of its citizens. Marx himself missed the tenacity of nationalism so badly because he hastily deduced the ideological and phantomatic nature of nationality from the economic and cultural nationalism of the European states of his time, thereby foreclosing the popular dimension and emancipatory potential of nationalism. This popular, emancipatory side of nationalism, which is exemplified in decolonization (linked by Anderson to the "good" nationalism of Mazzini), is especially important in view of the uneven globalization of capital.[14] Echoing Hegel's description of patriotic sacrifice as a form of self-consciously willed death in which the transcendence of human finitude is achieved, Anderson suggests that the endurance of the nation as a political community ought to be thought of in terms of the quasi-religious moral pathos of purification through death:

> [T]he great wars of this century are extraordinary not so much in the unprecedented scale on which they permitted people to kill, as in the colossal numbers persuaded to lay down their lives. . . . The idea of the ultimate sacrifice comes only with an idea of purity, through fatality.
>
> Dying for one's country, which usually one does not choose, assumes a moral grandeur which dying for the Labour Party, the American Medical Association, or perhaps even Amnesty International can not rival, for these are all bodies one can join or leave at easy will. (*Imagined,* 144)

But these two positions—rejecting the nation as an ideological extension of the state and affirming it as the source of popular emancipation—are irreconcilable only if we assume, as Chatterjee and Anderson apparently do, that the nation or the people can only be *either* contaminated *or* pure. Chatterjee and Anderson make this assumption because, as we have seen, their work is irrigated by a vitalist ontology according to which techne, if it is not to infect and contaminate the transfigurative power of the living people, must be sublated and put into the service of life. To reiterate, if the technical cannot be organicized and made part of the body of the people in its self-actualization, it must be expunged. Otherwise, it will remain as a source of perversion and death. The historical vicissitudes of postcolonial nationalism and its enduring imperativity in the current neo-colonial global conjuncture, I want to suggest, render untenable this on-tology of life. For the fact that the nation or the people *qua* source of trans-figurative power is utterly compromised at the origin suggests that the possibility of contamination is inscribed in the very structure of the people's actualization.

To put this another way, I am suggesting that the relationship between the people and the postcolonial nation-state (Chatterjee, Said) or the people-nation and the postcolonial state (Fanon, Anderson) cannot be adequately understood in terms of the contamination of a living spirit by techne, in terms of a perverse diversion, detour, or deferral of a true be-coming as the result of the intrusion of an external or contingent artifi-cial foreign body. For if the people and living national culture need the state to survive, and the state comes into being and continues to exist within a neocolonial capitalist world order the transcendence of which is not in sight, then the contamination of national culture by the bourgeois state is not a matter of the intrusion of an artificial alien body that can be either sublated or permanently removed. It involves a more original susceptibility to contamination by the technical: an a priori receptability of the people, its opening out onto that which is other to it, its welcom-ing of an other that dislocates even as it constitutes the self-identity of the people.

The questions I have posed about these influential accounts of post-colonial nationalism amount to a philosophical problem insofar as I have attempted to question the ontology of life that underpins them. When the state is characterized as an abstraction, or when national culture is de-scribed as an ideology, we think of them as creatures of death or phantoms that invade the living body of the people and obstruct its life. However, if these prostheses turn out to be necessary supplements to the living na-tional body, then the line between life and death can no longer be drawn with clarity because death would be inscribed within the heart of life. The living people would be constitutively susceptible to a certain kind of death that can no longer be thought within a vitalist ontology that asserts the un-equivocal delimitation of death by life and the victory of the latter over the former. It is a death that must be interminably negotiated. I want now to turn to Derrida's reflections on spectrality because they help me figure the peculiar living-in-dying of the nation.

2. OF LIFE-DEATH: DERRIDA ON SPECTRALITY

Derrida's recent work on spectrality is an important intervention in discussions about the future of nationalism for at least two reasons. The more obvious reason is that a discourse on death necessarily involves a rhetoric of borders. As Derrida observes, because death delimits "the right of absolute property, the right of property to our own life," it is the ultimate border, a border "more essential, more originary and more proper than those of any other territory in the world."[15] Indeed, as we have seen, the line between the nation-people and the neocolonial state is always a line between life and death. Derrida will figure the subject's aporetic experience of its own finitude and futurity—an experience of the impossible—in terms of absolute hospitality and an opening up to the *arrivant*. In *Specters of Marx*, Derrida will denounce the nation-form as ontopologocentric because it fails to practice this absolute hospitality that keeps alive the promise of the messianic without messianism.

However, it seems to me that the most interesting aspect of Derrida's recent work for understanding the peculiar life of the postcolonial nation-state is not his critique of nationalism but his notion of spectralization as a general process of paradoxical incorporation, a state of originary prosthesis that needs to be distinguished from ideology even though it is the condition of possibility of ideology. I suggested above that attempts to characterize the relationship between the people and the postcolonial nation-state in terms of the incarnation of life-giving spirit or the animation of finite corporeality by spirit, and the subsequent corruption of this spirit by that technical-artificial (ideological) body, missed the constitutive interpenetration of the two terms in neocolonial globalization. Derrida helps me to understand this mutual haunting between the nation and the state because he suggests that spectralization is an irreducible possibility in any incarnation of spirit, since it is the constitutive condition of incarnation as such.

What does Derrida mean by spectralization? Spectralization is the incarnation of autonomized spirit in an aphysical body, which is then taken on as the real body of the living subject.

> The specter is *of the spirit*, it participates in the latter and stems from it even as it follows it as its ghostly double. . . .
> The production of the ghost, the constitution of the *ghost* effect, is not simply a spiritualization or even an autonomization of spirit, idea or

thought, as happens *par excellence* in Hegelian idealism. No, once this au-
tonomization is effected, with the corresponding expropriation or alienation, and only then, the ghostly moment *comes upon* it, adds to it a sup-
plementary dimension, one more simulacrum, alienation or expropriation.
Namely, a body! In the flesh (*Leib*)! For there is no ghost, there is never
any becoming-specter of the spirit without at least an appearance of flesh,
in a space of invisible visibility, like the dis-appearing of an apparition.
For there to be ghost, there must be a return to the body, but to a body that
is more abstract than ever. The spectrogenic process corresponds therefore
to a paradoxical *incorporation*. Once ideas or thoughts (*Gedanke*) are detached from their substratum, one engenders some ghost by *giving them a
body*. Not by returning to the living body from which ideas and thoughts
have been torn loose, but by incarnating the latter *in another artifactual
body, a prosthetic body*, a ghost of spirit.[16]

The specter would thus appear to be a negative by-product or undesirable residue, the waste of culture as human self-objectification self-actu-
alisation, or collective rational work (*Bildung*). It is the incorporation of
an idealization "in a body without nature, in an *a-physical* body, that could
be called, if one could rely on these oppositions, a technical body or an institutional body" (*Specters*, 127).

However, Derrida emphasises that a specter is not an ideologem in the
Marxist sense. It is not merely a mystification that is confused with and
lived as concrete reality. Whereas an ideologem is an illusion that begins
from the living body and ought, in the final instance, to be referred back
to its material historical conditions by immanent political critique, spectrality is a process without beginning or end because it is the movement
that constitutes all finite bodies. Thus, Derrida writes,

> all the grave stakes we have just named . . . would come down to the ques-
> tion of what one understands, with Marx and after Marx, by effectivity, ef-
> fect, operativity, work, labour [*Wirklichkeit, Wirkung*, work, operation],
> living work in their supposed opposition to the spectral logic that also gov-
> erns the effects of virtuality, of simulacrum, of "mourning work," of
> ghosts, *revenant* and so forth. . . . [D]econstructive thinking of the trace,
> of iterability, of prosthetic synthesis, of supplementarity, and so forth,
> goes beyond this opposition and the ontology it presumes. Inscribing the
> possibility of the reference to the other, and thus, of radical alterity and
> heterogeneity, of differance, of technicity, and of ideality in the very event

of presence, in the very presence of the present that it dis-joins *a priori* in order to make it possible [thus impossible in its identity or its contemporaneity with itself], it does not deprive itself of the means with which to take into account . . . the effects of ghosts, of simulacra, of "synthetic images," or even, to put it in terms of the Marxist code, of ideologems, even if these take the novel forms to which modern technology will have given rise. (*Specters,* 75)

For Derrida, the process of spectralization is intimately connected to our radical finitude as beings in time. He suggests that the persistence, survival, or living-on of the *form* of a present being through time—the form which makes something actual, which allows it to be materialized, and the persistence of which represents a momentary arresting of our dying in any given instance[17]—is a minimal idealization before idealization proper because this persistence allows us to identify this present being as the *same* throughout all its possible repetitions. This differing-deferral (differ*a*nce) of a present being in the living-on of its form is a type of automutism. But this automutism, while it is clearly not an effect of *human* reason, society, culture, techne, or language, is also not an affect of the mechanism of nature. As the iterability that constitutes the present in general, that which makes any and all presence possible, this minimal idealization is the trace of the inhuman and unnatural spectral other within the present in general. But, more important, spectrality is also the condition of possibility of the externalization of ideas proper, of their incorporation in an external body *qua* present object, etc., as well as the condition of possibility of ideologization. This is because spectrality is the originary opening up of any present being by and to the other. It is precisely this internal vulnerability of any present being to alterity—its pregnancy with the movement of altering—that allows something to alter, change, or transform itself in time, or to be changed, transformed, or altered by another in time.

It would not be excessive to say that we are broaching the condition of possibility of causality as such, since spectrality is that which allows something to act on and affect itself or another (and also to affect itself as an other) or to be acted on or affected by another (and also by itself as an other). It is that which allows any action (transitive and intransitive) or event—which is to say, any production and also any creation—to take place. This is why, among other things, spectrality also inscribes technicity within the organic because it opens up every proper organic body to the supplementation of artifice.

Derrida's idea of spectrality goes to the heart of the vitalist ontology that underwrites the theories of the postcolonial nation we have considered above. We need to remember that generally speaking, the nation is either affirmed as a vehicle for the transcendence of human finitude or rejected as an ideological apparatus of the bourgeois state, which is an instrument of dead capital. As such, nationalist discourse is a secularized version of a traditional religious discourse of finitude that contrasts our finitude as creatures of nature with an infinite self-causing divine Creator who gives us our being. We justify our finite existence and give meaning to it through our faith in the infinite. In a secularized world, the sphere of culture, which sometimes takes the form of the political community of the nation, has become a substitute for the infinite.

In contradistinction, spectrality is co-extensive with our *radical* finitude, which should be rigorously distinguished from any traditional understanding of finitude. Our radical finitude refers to our sheer persistence as beings in temporality, our continuing temporalization. It refers to the fact that our continuing presence is given (to us) by an alterity which is so radical that it is not a thing or another present being, not even an infinite and absolute self-causing presence called God. This alterity is absolutely contingent, but it is at the same time the absolutely necessary condition of our existence. Radical finitude is nontranscendable because there is no refuge of eternal presence into which we can cross over.

What then are the political implications of radical finitude? The aporia of radical finitude is not a logical impasse or blockage that would lead to nihilism or apolitical quietism. It is a practical experience of the impossible—that which is impossible but which is nevertheless given to experience—that has to be endured interminably. The experience of radical finitude is an experience of the impossible because the imminent possibility of our own death remains something that is fundamentally undecidable for us, something that is unpresentable to us and that we can never know.[18] By the same token, this ordeal, in which we are exposed to undecidability, has to be interminably endured because our own persistence in time beyond any given instant can never be guaranteed. In each and every instant, we live only in and through the possibility that in another instant, perhaps the next, we might die. But at the same time, the experience of radical finitude is a practical experience. Without our persistence in time, no decisive action or incarnational work (*Bildung*), and therefore, no politics, can take place. The experience of radical finitude is the origin of imperativity and responsibility insofar as this impossible other, which is not of the realm of presence, nevertheless enjoins us to act in the here and now (which is no longer even as we speak), without waiting and thinking too much, before it is too late. And, perhaps, our actions will always have been too late. *Perhaps* it will already be too late. *Always* perhaps, because unless we resolve to act immediately, we will never know if it is indeed too late for us to act, for our actions to make a difference, for them to alter present conditions of existence. As Derrida notes in his reading of Marx's *The Eighteenth Brumaire of Louis Bonaparte*,

> This anxiety in the face of the ghost is properly revolutionary. If death weighs on the living brain of the living, and still more on the brains of revolutionaries, it must then have some spectral density. To weigh [*lasten*] is also to charge, tax, impose, indebt, accuse, assign, enjoin. And the more life there is, the graver the specter of the other becomes, the heavier its imposition. And the more the living have to answer for it. . . . The specter weighs [*pèse*], it thinks [*pense*], it intensifies and condenses itself within the very inside of life, within the most living life, the most singular (or, if one prefers, individual) life. The latter therefore no longer has and must no longer have, insofar as it is living, a pure identity to itself or any assured outside: this is what all philosophies of life, or even philosophies of the living and real individual, would have to weigh carefully. (*Specters,* 109)[19]

Thus, at the same time as spectrality constitutes the present, it is also the condition of (im)possibility which disjoins the present. It disjoins even as it renews the present in one and the same movement. The *revenant* or returning spectral other tears time conceived as a continuous succession of "nows." But it is precisely the rending of time that allows the entirely new to emerge. Hence, at the same time that spectrality contaminates and compromises all our rational efforts at incarnating ideals—or, better yet, precisely because it compromises all these efforts—it also generates the unerasable promise of a "future to-come." This future to-come is not the future present promised by Hegelian or Marxist teleology. It is a future which is always arriving but which never arrives finally.

Strictly speaking, of course, the lesson in the affirmation of the future to-come that Derrida draws from his hauntology is not a modality of becoming, since it is not of the order of "being." The "to-come" is precisely not a be-coming, a coming-to-be, a reaching toward a future present. Yet, even though development and industrialization *are* modalities of becoming, Derrida still brings us very close to the mutual haunting of the nation-people and the state. Commenting on the ontology of life in Marx and Stirner, Derrida writes:

> Both of them love life, which is always the case but never goes without saying for finite beings: they know that life does not go without death, and that death is not beyond, outside of life, unless one inscribes the beyond in the inside, in the essence of the living. They both share, apparently like you and me, an unconditional preference for the living body. But precisely because of that, they wage an endless war against whatever represents it, whatever is not the body, but belongs to it, comes back to it: prosthesis and delegation, repetition, differance. The living ego is auto-immune, which is what they do not want to know. To protect its life, to constitute itself as unique living ego, to relate, as the same, to itself, it is necessarily led to welcome the other within (so many figures of death: differance of the technical apparatus, iterability, non-uniqueness, prosthesis, synthetic image, simulacrum . . .), it must therefore take the immune defenses apparently meant for the non-ego, the enemy . . . and direct them at once *for itself and against itself. (Specters,* 141)

Derrida points out that Marx wants to get rid of this ghostly other within life, "as if he still believed in some de-contaminating purification in this regard, as if the ghost were not watching the spirit, as if it were not haunting the spirit, precisely, from the threshold of spiritualization, as if iterability itself, which conditions both the idealization and the spiritualization of the 'idea,' did not erase any critical assurance as to the discernment between the two concepts" (*Specters,* 123–124). This schema of the irreducible inscription of death within life, of living on with, in, and through a certain kind of death, I want to suggest, describes precisely the relation of the living national body to the bourgeois postcolonial state: the opening up of the proper body of the living nation-people to technicity as instantiated by the formative role played by modern knowledge, technomediation, and organization in the genesis of the nation; the importance of literature and culture in the narrow sense as image-creating phenomena in the formation (*Bildung)* of a national public sphere; the penetration of the state by the light of public reason; and conversely, the opening up of the nation by the very same formative technics to monitoring and manipulation by the state in the service of dead capital; and the stifling of the national will to overcome the current world order by the global circulation of neocolonial cultural images, etc.[20]

But speaking more generally, if we consider the precarious life of the postcolonial nation-people in terms of the current economic conditions within which this body, conceived in analogy with a living body, has to maximize its capabilities and well-being, then its relation via the bourgeois state to the outside in uneven globalization—technological flows, flows of foreign direct investment, flows of cultural images, etc.—is a case of spectrality or the interminable experience of the aporia of life-death. For uneven globalization produces a polarized world in which national development in the periphery is frustrated because of state adjustment to the dictates of transnational capital. But in a global capitalist system the transcendence of which is not in imaginary sight, transnational forces are also a means for the development of the national body. However, the state can resist capitulation to transnational forces only if it is transformed from a comprador regime into a popular national-state. This is the hope we saw in Fanon, Anderson, et al., the belief that popular rearticulations of the nation can be ethically imperative and not automatically dismissed as ideologies, even though the exclusionary dimension of popular nationalism can always be manipulated by state-elites.

The point here is not to reject these projects of postcolonial national *Bildung* as ideologies. For if I understand Derrida correctly, the specter is neither living nor dead, neither ideology nor the spontaneous will of the people but the sliding movement or flickering between the two. And the spectrality of the nation is especially pronounced in contemporary globalization. As long as we continue to think of "the people" or "the people-nation" in analogy with a living body or a source of ever-present life, then the postcolonial state *qua* political and economic agent is always the necessary supplement of the revolutionary nation-people, the condition for its living on after decolonization. The nation-people can come into freedom only by attaching itself to the postcolonial bourgeois state. It can live on only through this kind of death. The state is an uncontrollable specter that the nation-people must welcome within itself, and direct, at once *for itself and against itself*, because this specter can possess the nation-people and bend it toward global capitalist interests.

However, this line of thought would not be sanctioned by Derrida. Regardless of how contentless he purposely leaves the future to-come, it is definitely antinationalist. For even though this is a quasi-transcendental argument that "deduces" the messianic to-come from the structural openness of finite beings, Derrida dresses the place of spectrality up as the scene of migrancy and transnationalism:

> awaiting what one does not expect yet or no longer, hospitality without reserve, welcome salutation accorded in advance to the absolute surprise of the *arrivant* from whom or from which one will not ask anything in return and who will not be asked to commit to the domestic contracts of any welcoming power (family, State, nation, territory, native soil or blood, language, culture in general, even humanity) . . . messianic opening to what is coming, that is, to the event that cannot be awaited *as such* . . . to the event as the foreigner itself, to her or to him for whom one must leave an empty place, always, in memory of the hope—and this is the very place of spectrality. (*Specters,* 65)

I want to be as precise as I can about what I understand Derrida to be saying here. Derrida does not say that the specter is a migrant to whom we must play absolute host. He does not put it so vulgarly or bluntly. In *Aporias*, he is quite careful to say that the arrivant is indeterminable, does not cross a threshold separating two identifiable places, and is therefore not to be reduced to a traveler, an émigré, or a political exile, refugee, or immigrant worker (*Aporias,* 33).[21] Nevertheless, the place of spectrality is definitely not national, because nationalism is dismissed as a discourse and a project that will not allow for the promise of the messianic.

Writing in reference to contemporary interethnic wars, Derrida argues that nationalism cannot give place because it is an ontopology, an outmoded doctrine or discourse of self-present place:

> Inter-ethnic wars are . . . proliferating, driven by an *archaic* phantasm [which is presumably not a specter because it is tied to a past present] and concept, by a *primitive conceptual phantasm* of community, the nation-State, sovereignty, borders, native soil and blood. Archaism is not a bad thing in itself, it doubtless keeps some irreducible resource. But how can one deny that this conceptual phantasm is, so to speak, much more outdated than ever, in the very *ontopology* it supposes, by tele-technic dislocation? (By *ontopology* we mean an axiomatics linking indissociably the ontological value of present-being [*on*] to its *situation*, to the stable and presentable determination of a locality, the *topos* of territory, native soil, city, body in general). For having spread in an unheard-of fashion, which

is more and more differentiated and more and more accelerated (it is ac-
celeration itself, beyond the norms of speed that have until now informed
human culture), the process of dislocation is no less arch-originary, that is,
just as "archaic" as the archaism that it has always dislodged. (*Specters,*
82)

Not only have population transfers in contemporary globalization rendered the nation-form obsolete; the current age also attests to its violence:

> In the virtual space of all the tele-technosciences, in the general dis-
> location to which our time is destined—as are from now the places of
> lovers, families, nations—the messianic trembles on the edge of this event
> itself. It is this hesitation, . . . It does not "live" otherwise, but it would no
> longer be messianic if it stopped hesitating: how to give rise and to give
> place [*donner lieu*], still, to render it, this place, to render it habitable, but
> without killing the future in the name of old frontiers? Like those of the
> blood, nationalisms of the native soil not only sow hatred, not only com-
> mit crimes, they have no future, they promise nothing even if, like stupid-
> ity or the unconscious, they hold fast to life. (*Specters,* 169)

Strictly speaking, of course, an ontopology is not an ideology in the
Marxist sense. Yet the archaic phantasm of the nation is definitely not the
life-death of the specter. It is simply on the side of eternal death and cannot cross over the undecidable border between life and death because it
can promise no life. My point here is that in this respect at least, Derrida
inherits the Marxist treatment of nationality as a subcase of religion and
mysticism that has been rendered effete by globalization even though he is
critical of the Marxist ontology that opposes rational work to mystical belief. Thus, Derrida notes that Marxist internationalism is "in principle non-
religious, in the sense of a positive religion; it is not mythological; it is
therefore not national—for beyond even the alliance with a chosen people,
*there is no nationality or nationalism that is not religious or mythological,
let us say 'mystical' in the broad sense*" (*Specters,* 91, emphasis added).
   But why is the nation-form so resolutely ideological and not spectral?
We ought to pause before arriving at Derrida's conclusion, for at least
three reasons. First, the decolonizing nation is not an archaic throwback to
traditional forms of community based on the blind ties of blood and kin-
ship but a new form of political community engendered by the spectrality
of modern knowledge, technomediation, and modern organization. Sec-

ond, the persistence of the national question in Marxism indicates that the nation is not a mere ideological formation, exorcised as easily as Marx thought it to be.

Finally, one should note that *neocolonial* globalization does not necessarily render the nation-form obsolete because notwithstanding increased transnational labor migration in the contemporary era, the deterritorialization of peoples remains limited for reasons that are structural in the global political economy. As the Marxist political economist Samir Amin has argued, in an uneven capitalist world system, the most deprived masses of humanity are largely confined to national-peripheral space. The globalization of production—liberalization of trade and capital flows—involves the global integration of commodities and capital but stops short of an unlimited integration of labor—the unrestricted opening of the centers to labor migration from less industrialized or unindustrialized peripheries where the bulk of capital's "reserve army" is located.[22]

Consequently, "the mobility of commodities and capital leaves national space to embrace the whole world while the labor force [largely] remains enclosed within the national framework" (*Re-Reading*, 74). Thus, Amin argues, instead of producing large groups of deterritorialized migrant peoples who prefigure the nation-state's demise and point to a postnational global order, *uneven* globalization makes popular nationalist movements in the periphery the first step on the long road to social redistribution.

The question I want to pose is whether, in light of the failed promises of postcolonial nationalism and, as Samir Amin and others have argued, also its continuing imperativity as an agent of ethicopolitical transformation in neocolonial globalization, Derrida's dismissal of nationalism as an ideology may be hasty. In any event, this dismissal is limited in focus because Derrida understands transnationalism and globalization only in terms of the broad figure of migration. His predication of the future as transnational migrancy forecloses the unevenness of capitalist globalization and its effects on postcolonial nationalism. For instance, what does it mean for a country in the south to practice hospitality without reserve as a host for transnational capital? If as Derrida suggests, globalization brings about "new forms of a withering or rather a reinscription, a re-delimitation of the State in a space that it no longer dominates and that moreover it never dominated by itself" (*Specters,* 94), then instead of dismissing examples of popular nationalism in the postcolonial South that arise in response and resistance to economic transnationalism as essentially and irredeemably ontopologocentric, one might see them as instances of spectrality.

ENVOI: THE SPECTRALITY OF THE NATION IN POSTCOLONIAL SOUTHEAST ASIA CIRCA 1997–1998

I have argued that we might see the postcolonial nation as a creature of life-death because, by virtue of its aporetic inscription within neocolonial globalization, the neocolonial state stands between the living nation-people and dead global capital, pulling on both even as it is pulled by both. I want to end an essay as speculative as this with a brief coda, a concrete example that is also a promise of work to come. As is well known, the financial crisis that is still sweeping across Asia today "began" in June 1997, triggered by a massive attack on the Thai baht by currency speculators on May 14–15, 1997. This crisis has become a free fall into deep economic recession across industrialized and industrializing Southeast Asia and East Asia, indicated by increased inflation, declining production, and rising unemployment. What is so surprising about the collapse of the "Asian economic miracle" is its suddenness. Almost overnight, the strong economic fundamentals of many of these countries—the economic well-being of the nation conceived as an organic body—widely regarded by international financial and economic authorities such as the World Bank not only as sound but also as models for less developed countries to follow,[23] were driven down by global financialization.

Clearly, the ghost of money has contaminated the realm of real production. But, more important, these rapidly developing postcolonial national bodies have been spectralized by the ghost of foreign money, which they cannot not welcome within themselves in order to develop, even though this autoimmunization is precisely also a certain kind of death. Indeed, prior to the collapse, in their official cultural self-representations in the international public sphere, these countries had, ironically, colluded with the Northern liberal picture of the fiscalization of the globe, world trade liberalization, and foreign direct investment—"growth for all, leading to transnational solidarity"—by touting themselves as success stories of flexible or disorganized global capitalism.

Here are instances of both sides of the aporia, where the postcolonial national body must accept the other within itself but cannot clearly discriminate between what it welcomes into itself: on the one hand, as Dr. Mahathir Mohamad, the Prime Minister of Malaysia, noted even after the crash, Malaysia regards "genuine foreign direct investors as *vital* contributors to the country's industrial development. We have always treated them as *special guests* of the country."[24] On the other hand, the very conditions that can secure future foreign direct investment, such as acquiescence to IMF directives, are themselves harmful. Using Indonesia as an example, one commentator notes that "some of the IMF policies are wrong and deadly. Asking the IMF for assistance may well cause a moderately sick patient to develop a serious and life-threatening disease that will take much suffering and many years to get out of, if at all."[25]

Far from being rendered obsolete by globalization, the living-on of the postcolonial nation in the wake of the currency crash can be seen in the rise of both popular and official nationalisms in Southeast Asia in response to economic neocolonialism and IMF manipulation: protest by the Malaysian state against unregulated currency speculation, peasant protest in Thailand, and student radicalism in Indonesia that led to the ousting of Suharto. The postcolonial nation must be seen as a specter of global capital (double genitive): it always runs the risk of being an epiphenomenon or reflection of global capital to the extent that is originally infected by the prosthesis of the bourgeois state *qua* terminal of capital. But it is also a specter that haunts global capital, for it is the undecidable neuralgic point within the global capitalist system that refuses to be exorcised.

11

INNOCENCE

Alphonso Lingis

You, Nancy Gilvonio, a *charapa*, half Indian, were born near the town of Tarapoto on the Amazonian side of the Peruvian Andes. How extremely improbable is your existence! There had been the chance encounter of that woman with that man, then she happened to please him and he her, and it happened that they disrobed and embraced, and then out of how many times two hundred million spermatozoa streaming into her vagina there was the infinitesimal chance that this *one* met with and got absorbed into this ovum! At any turn of the million chance encounters the path is made of, it would have been someone else, and not you, that was born.

For you, Nancy Gilvonio, to look back to the time before your birth is to look upon an abyss in which you are utterly absent, nowhere programmed, nowhere preexisting in potency. In that abyss of past time, there is nothing that forecast you, demanded you, required you. Growing up near the town of Tarapoto, on the Amazonian side of the Peruvian Andes, you did feel this void. The cement and the board buildings of Tarapoto, the parched laterite roads, the cleared fields, and the trees beyond exist because they have existed. To see them is to see their past, full of them. Before the fullness of their past, you cannot shake loose a sense of inner insubstantiality. You exist as a precarious stirring with nothing behind to give you momentum, existing in defiance of this void. There is something ineradicably heroic about your bare existence. You are seduced by your own heroic existence born by chance from the void. That is why something understands, something quickens in you, whenever you hear of a heroic act.

What a stupendous marvel, your birth in a hut in the Amazonian town of Tarapoto! What a marvel, the newborn, the born new! And what innocence! How light is your birth, not laden with the weight of a past it has to answer for! In the past with all its crimes, all its outrages and villainy, there was nothing whatever of you.

You open your eyes. Everything is new! The immense white light floods you. Where there was nothing at all, there is suddenly this vision, these endless landscapes, these fathomless skies!

"My child," says your mother. She cannot help seeing in you her body, which composed and nourished your body. As you begin to coordinate limbs and senses and pick up patterns of doing things in the house and in the town, she and your father cannot help seeing "our" in you—our child, ours like our project, our work is ours. She and he are you, but you are not she and are not he. It is not in your physical traits and sense of what you are—a girl, a *charapa*—but in your existence that you are a stranger to them.

For you existence is not a burden and a task. A child, you are, without being on your own. You leave the burden of carrying on the projects initiated in the past and the task of securing resources for the future to your parents. You play out your existence. One day you can take on responsibility for the past they are carrying forward. But your birth, the innocence and newness of existence in you, is of itself irresponsibility and revolt against the past.

You, Nancy Gilvonio, awoke in a shanty near the town of Tarapoto in the Amazonian rain forest that extends below the icy mists of the Andes. Years later you awaken in a night truck lurching around bends in the mountain road to Lima. You wake up in the cold misty silence of an abandoned peasant hut in the high mountains. You, Nancy Gilvonio, wake up alone lying on the ground under an immense solitary tree. You wake up in the middle of the night, wake up to the immense solitary purity of the night.

To be born is to awaken to the world. Is not every awakening a birth? Your luminous consciousness, Nancy Gilvonio, that awakens in the morning to the room is flooded with light. The dark of the night with its confused intrigues and sorceries has passed away without leaving a trace. The unconsciousness of sleep is disconnected; the empty space in which it existed is utterly lost, and your eyes cannot see where it has gone. Light, warmth, air, resonance, a supporting depth of ground are there by incessant oncoming. The light of yesterday and of a minute ago is utterly passed away; there is no residue of it in this light. The light, the air, the warmth are so fully there they have no horizons where their future is visible. They are there without reserving anything for tomorrow, without guarantees, there gratuitously and by grace.

Once awakened, you move on, noting only the familiar patterns and general lines of the house, the landscape, and the workplace. By noting continuities and recurrences, your awareness endures and becomes redundant. It persists as a state of awareness. The state of awareness is listless and phlegmatic, as though drunk. But in the course of a day there are dozens, hundreds of soberings up, awakenings. It is one thing to take note of things, of landmarks and benchmarks, your glance passing lightly over them as you pass among them. It is something else to wake up to something, say to one of those very things. While kneading the cornflour dough, to wake up to a hummingbird sizzling in the sheets of sunlight. To wake up to the huge eyes of the grazing alpaca, enigmatic as a song brooding over a love lost centuries ago.

The spring force with which awakening vaults is not the momentum of continuities and recurrences; awakening is a leap out of that momentum. The flow of the limitless night or the continuum of appearances in the day and the flow of duration are interrupted. A cut, a break is made, and across this gap the past passes out of reach. The awakening awakens as from nowhere. You shake your head and peer about to find where you are.

Awakening is a bound, not weighted down with the past that inculpates the present and demands compensation from the future, a bound out of the drunkenness of remorse and resentment. Awakening is a commencement. It is a point of departure. You come alive, you become alive to the dragonfly, to the twist of cloud over the twilight mountain, to the gleaming cheeks of a boy. Awakening is a birth.

Awakening is joyous. The innocence of awakening, the active disconnection of the past, make possible this joy. How good to be alive! How refreshing is this silence! How calm the evening is! How pungent it smells! In every joy there is an awakening.

Joy surprises you, waking you up out of the state of awareness become listless and phlegmatic by the continuities and recurrences. How truthful is joy! You Nancy Gilvonio cannot not believe in the visions delight illuminates. Joy gives you the strength to open your eyes to all that is there without being foreseeable or understood. Where, if not from this joy, did you find the strength to see so far into the darkness? To see as far back and as far away as the tyrants held sway?

Your awakening is innocent and just, even if it has no consequences, even if it subsides, even if it fails.

You, Nancy Gilvonio, were born and each day awake in a shanty in a muddy clearing. This shanty is your home. It is a zone of tranquillity and intimacy. Space divides between the zone of the intimate and the outlying stretches of the alien. Your home is a zone of extraterritoriality from the paths and roads extended by accountings demanded and produced. You recognize your home each day upon awakening, and years later when you return to it, by the warmth and tranquillity that pervades this retreat from the affairs of the town and the forest. Years later, to awaken in this shanty is to be born innocent and irresponsible, the alien world kept at a distance.

Awakening can stop and silence you, freezing the continuity and momentum of movements. You can be held in thrall to the clouds swiveling in the blue, the leaves of the trees braiding the wind, the birds clattering and murmuring in the downpouring night.

Awakening can also give rise to action. To awaken can be to wake up to what has to be done. Because the home is a zone of tranquillity and rest, a zone of innocence, action can have starting point, can begin.

Your father, Nancy Gilvonio, and your two older brothers worked on a plot of the cleared and so quickly leached out ground to grow food, and went off on whatever labor jobs turned up down the river or in the forest. Your mother went out to work in the fields, and she went to collect laundry from the town to scrub at the well. As soon as your childish limbs acquired coordination, you began to work. You washed and dressed your younger brothers and sister; you prepared food for them during the day when your mother was away. Each year you took on more and more tasks about the house, then in school. You worked hard at your lessons and began dreaming of going on to higher education. And one day, against all odds, you set off to San Marcos University. With but one change of clothes in your bag, you climbed onto a truck, and three days later you arrived in Lima. You made sociology your major. You worked as a cleaning woman in the upper-class neighborhoods of San Isidro to pay your rent and buy books. You were short in stature, lean, with a narrow face and very broad and deep eyes. Your black hair was straight and long. Your skin was pale brown flushed with clay-red, as though always lit by a twilight sun.

The work your father, your brothers, and your mother did was not really participating in the immemorial rhythms of peasant life in its eternal recurrence. They interrupted field work to take whatever labor jobs turned up, some legal with road construction and logging gangs, some involving smuggling merchandise and coca. The field work, the meals, and the laundry your mother scrubbed have the nature of tasks that must begin in the morning after the discontinuity of the night, tasks that come to an end. Even if they begin again as though they had never been done, they must begin still again because they were finished the day before.

What we call our action, in the intense sense, is not simply an adjustment to compensate for what passes and passes away—an inhalation that compensates for an exhalation, a stabilizing step forward that compensates for the destabilizing of the gait. Our action rises upon an interruption, a break, of the continuity of operations, biological, physiological, and also laborious, that go on in us.

Philosophies of history, whether reactionary or radical, see actions as shaped by values, which are predicates put on things, predicates constructed in the categorical system of an industry, action a meaning which can become determinate only within the vocabulary, grammar, and rhetoric of a semiotic system. They see in the driving force of an action the momentum of accumulated skills and habits. They explain an action out of an evolving environment where everything is already social, significant, and historical.

But our action, in the intense sense, is an interruption of the continuous dialectic of history, an awakening from the drowsy murmur of the semiotics of a culture. Its bound of energy comes from a cut in the continuity of skills and habits. One day in a forgotten corner of the tsarist empire, my father, who had never been to school at all, the son of a peasant who was the son of a peasant who was the son of a peasant, burrowed into a hay wagon and crossed the border into East Prussia, there to confront and deal with whatever confronted him. One day in the town of Tarapoto on the Amazonian side of the Peruvian Andes, Nancy Gilvonio climbed in a truck with strangers. Two innocents, two children.

The interruption of continuity makes possible the leap, with all the forces of the present, into what is ahead. It makes possible hope, awaiting what is beyond all expectation. Hope is hope by rejecting the evidence of the past, by being against all odds.

Each moment of awakening is a return to youth, to the insolence, impetuousness, brashness of youth. In our action there is festivity, license, and puerile pleasure. There is an element of lubricity, of wickedness in the innocence of action.

You, Américo Gilvonio, were growing to the threshold of manhood in Tarapoto, with the woozy sense of how much your body—your size, your voice, your hirsuitness, your musculature, your genitals—had developed by contrast with the body of your brother Raúl, two years younger than you. You vividly felt how much your knowledge, your know-how, your thinking had changed each year, so that you found it awkward that there was always a gap between what you thought and what those two years or even a year younger than you thought. And new possibilities, new thrills, new escapades, new undertakings beckoned to you each week. You felt your past to be a succession of stepping-stones you had crossed; you felt your present to be open upon the paths of a future whose stepping-stones are already visible and beckoning. Your future lay before you, a circumscribed field of work awaiting you in Tarapoto.

Things and events in your environment impose themselves or pass lightly. Things and events do not show themselves without exhibiting their importance. There are things that are the best not just on a continuous scale, but on a level utterly above all the others of their kind, as well as incomparable with one another. There are immense, solitary trees in the forest that are not cut down, that shelter and guide you when you walk through the forest. You, Américo Gilvonio, listened to the voice that is under the earth and in the heavens; it knows what matter the stars, all types of roots and waters, insects, birds, and worms are made of, and this knowledge it, embracing you with its shadows, extends to you. There are sacred places—cascades, mountains, gorges, places marked by the enclosures of Sacsayhuamen and Machu Picchu. It is not you who assign importance to such things and events with a ready-made scale you would carry with you, nor is their importance assigned relative to your needs and wants. They make you forget yourself in the drumroll of their epiphany. The day you came upon a jaguar, free, sprawled over the limb of a tree not ten feet over the ground, the jaguar opening only half of one eye but contemplating you, contemplating some wild and lordly animal in you. The day you watched the columns of minuscule ants, who have made a home for themselves in the sweet dead core of a tree, streaming over the leaves of that tree to clean it of fungis and diseases and glittering like red stars in those dark green leaves.

The flowering plants about the home are wilting in the sun. The weeds are choking the rows of beans. Things and events expose their needs. A child you come upon is crying from hunger or cold. The dog has a thorn in his paw. The immense, solitary tree requires you to stop and hear the music, wisdom, counsel, and immortality it whispers.

Your own hunger and thirst awaken you to what you have to do. The hunger and thirst of what is important awaken you to what has to be done; the urgency and immediacy of those needs impose what has to be done on you. Strolling in the drowsy afternoon, you come upon the ashes of a cooking fire that have flared up in the breeze and are spreading greedy flames in the grass. You are there, and what has to be done has to be done right away. But also you must do it—because you can. You have the strength, which the old couple who stopped you do not have, to free the tapir caught in the branches of a tree in the flooding river. Someone having cramps or panicking is in danger of drowning, and you are the one who can swim. You, Américo Gilvonio, *charapa*, half-Indian, are growing strong in waking up to what you have to do. You know that what you have to do may require all fierceness in you and unyielding hatred.

After the Great Rebellion of 1536 and the final conquest of Qosqo by Pizarro, Manco Inca retreated to a stronghold in the inaccessible fastness of Vilcapampa. Four Incas held their people together there until, in 1572, the Inca Tupac Amaru was lured out for battle and hunted down in the Amazon jungle. He was given written assurances by Felipe II of Spain that if he surrendered he would be treated as a prisoner of war. Tupac Amaru surrendered to save the lives of his people, and was dragged in triumph to Qosqo, where, in the cathedral square under the eyes of the Viceroy Francisco de Toledo and the bishop and the priests of the Inquisition, his wife was mangled in front of him and his head then struck off and stuck in a pole set up before the cathedral rising on the foundations of the residence of the founder Inca Viracocha.

Before the sinister spectacle of the superstition and error, greed and despair, complicity and betrayal, cynicism and brutality that is the history of our species, philosophies of history claim to track a pattern, plan, or meaning. Then historical events and processes become understandable or explainable. Looking back, what looks like crisis, violence, and chaos has to be assigned instrumental significance. This historical understanding would not be accessible to individuals whose field of action is staked out by their urgent needs, their poverty. It is naturally claimed by those whose wealth or institutional power gives their action the greatest scope.

Armed with neoliberal political doctrines, the strong man sets out to impose sense on the cacophony of party politics, the muteness of marginals, and the subversion of agitators. The alleged rationality of the world market economies does not put an end to the violence of class and race conflict; it institutionalizes its own violence and implants itself by violence.

In far-off Lima, president Alberto Fujimori abruptly shut down the parliament, arrested hundreds of opposition leaders and journalists, and launched an all-out military campaign to exterminate the armed opposition, the Sendero Luminoso and the Tupac Amaru Revolutionary Movement.

An army unit arrives in Tarapoto. People are stopped, interrogated, disappeared. For you, Américo, the horizons abruptly widen and you see the field of your life inserted into the broad expanse of the lives of the cholos, charapas, zambos, Quechuas, Aymaras of Peru. Everything you think of doing begins to take account of the changes affecting your country. You know someone in the next village who has contacts with the Tupac Amaru Revolutionary Movement. You abruptly decide to join the armed rebellion. You confide in Raúl, who passionately declares that he will go with you. You will fight, with all your strength, for the defeat of the oppressor, for the overthrow of the oligarchy, for a renewed birth of your people delivered to a stronger, nobler future by the arms of your united comrades. With what fierce joy this vision awakens in you!

An awakening awakens emotional forces which drive action. Emotions rise up and break through the webs of meanings spun by ideologies, preconceptions, and justifications.

All the most ancient emotions awaken, are newborn, as though there had never been history. Before the death of our child, mourners gather in a tragic chorus, as though there had never been the Christian doctrine of individual immortality or the secular doctrines of the biological insignificance of any individual of the species. In the heart of the rain forest, we feel the emotions hunters and gatherers a million years ago felt in campfires, rituals, and dances. By night the computer programmer and office manager dream of the sacred and demonic rationalized, corporate society; we feel the fierce passions of outlaws and bandits.

The spectacle of stupidity and deceit, pillage and torture can arouse a vehement repugnance that thrusts one from it. But in this very repugnance, the vision of the exorbitant, the grand scale of the violence, can, like the vision of the terrible in nature's floods and storms, attract us, and can arouse the power to act on one's own. Out of this disconnection, action can arise that consists in endowing one's life and the lives of one's comrades with a meaning for which one is fully responsible.

In 1988 you, Nancy Gilvonio, learned that soldiers had arrived one day at the hut in the muddy clearing near Tarapoto; they were looking for Américo and Raúl. They repeatedly beat your father, pouring water to waken him each time he sank into unconsciousness. They left him crippled. You, Nancy, left your studies at the university and returned to Tarapoto in a truck to try to earn money so that your parents and sister would survive.

An initiative consists in a discharge of forces. You happened to be there at the right time, somehow found the right thing to say or to do. But does it not leave a trace of itself on you, a diagram that can be varied, can be stabilized as a skill and a habit? And does not a successful action fill one with pleasure or at least with satisfaction, a good deed with glory? But in reality you are left the next day emptied of your burden, left not with strengthened powers but with harnessed powers, not knowing if new powers, the right powers, will be there when the time comes. Action of itself produces discontinuity, a return to emptiness, to innocence.

You, Américo, learn how to exist and operate clandestinely; you do everything possible to conceal your activities and those of your comrades; you do everything possible to escape from a raid unharmed and unidentified, for your fundamental obligation, to your cause, is, even when you are undertaking the most dangerous of subversive activities, to preserve that precious and invaluable agency of resistance, your life. But you are captured. You are tortured; you do everything to hold strong, lest in a moment of weakness you involuntarily betray your comrades. You know that when your torturers finally come to think they will get nothing from you, you will be shot or bludgeoned to death. Your torturers tell you that your brother Raúl has cooperated with them, and that if you cooperate you can see your brother. You wonder in despair, Has Raúl already been disappeared? You lie on the floor of this cell, waiting for them to return, to torture you once more, or this time to bludgeon you to death. You are alive only in this waiting, these hours of waiting.

We live our lives on the surface of the planet, among things we can detach and manipulate; to survey them we rise from the earth skyward. The sky is without surface, without shape, without inner structure, ungraspable. We rise further upward to view the course of things we see in the sky, the sovereign realm of chance. Chance confounds the intellect, the reasoning, reckoning intellect that identifies possibilities on the basis on past regularities. In acting we discover that our initiatives are so many dice throws. In the empty sky above us, we see also a realm of terror, terrorist death that strikes at random, strikes without consideration of innocence or guilt, strikes anyone who just happens to be there.

It also seems to us that the sky is a bond uniting us to all who breathe under its expanse, uniting us to all who are born and shall be born under the sky. You and I, and Nancy and Américo and Raúl Gilvonio.

You, Américo, no longer have any reason to will to live. You could try to gain your life, but only at the cost of betraying your comrades. To live, then, is inconceivable to you; what such a life would be, could be, you cannot imagine in any other way than repugnant, to others but more deeply to yourself. Were you to try to imagine yourself surviving, living by collaborating with the secret police, betraying one after another your comrades, forever distrusted and despised by the secret police themselves, you could not identify that image with the one, in the deepest core of yourself, you feel and know as yourself. You will die. You do not suddenly give up the will to live and wish to die, but, confronted with the inevitability of your execution, you no longer struggle to put off your death. You assent to your fate.

Now, as you are led to the court of the prison where you will be tied to a stake and shot, you feel a strange lightness. You are not standing on a scaffold, a stage, where the people have assembled to hear your last words of courage and defiance and witness how you die; it is dark and all about you the thick walls of the prison will muffle the shots so that they will not be heard even by your fellow prisoners. You will be "disappeared," your mother will never be told by the police that her son was captured. Yet, in the dark, you feel something like exaltation; you are floating on light, as though the future and the past had fallen from you, with all their weight, and left these last moments disconnected, buoyant, and with all their energies intensified. Strange, miraculous buoyancy and lightness, miraculous elation as you feel yourself falling, falling upward into the sky.

You realize that you recognize that this buoyancy, this lightness, this elation. You felt it on the night when you and Raúl slipped out of Tarapoto to meet your contact, who would lead you to the jungle camp of the Tupac Amaru guerrillas. Do not all guerrillas who enter into a clandestine struggle against the regime of oppression know that it may end for them before the firing squad and that their cause may end in defeat—and do they not know, or believe, that in joining the guerrillas they will be able to laugh in the face of the firing squad? They know that strange, that extraordinary lightness of entering into the struggle against all odds.

The will drawn to chance is what we call love. Love is awakened only by chance. In the fugitive, suffocating beauty of a woman's body, of a man's body, astonishment greets the utterly improbable. In the inexplicable splendor of a woman's courage, a man's heart, love welcomes the unknowable. Nothing is more contrary to love than to wish unfavorable chances excluded, to interrogate, to tremble before the most extreme risks. In the force of the passion for justice, love quickens.

One night a man covered in filth sought out the hut in Tarapoto where he woke you, Nancy Gilvonio, who lay in an exhausted sleep, but a sleep always threatened by terror. He had come to tell you what he knew of your brothers. He grew up in Balconcillo, a working-class slum in Lima. He had been arrested during a strike at a textile factory, where before his eyes his closest friend, Hemigidio Huerta, had had his eyes gouged out with a rifle butt and then been beaten to death by the police. He had fled prison and fled Lima into clandestinity, where he had known Américo and Raúl. His name was Néstor Cerpa Cartolini. When he left the next night to make his way to the Tupac Amaru hideout, you, Nancy Gilvonio, went with him. Always clandestine, always moving, always ever more in love, your life was raids with the Indians in the mountains and flights into the trackless wilderness they knew. How proud was your love! That year, 1988, a son was born to you. A second born was in 1993. You, Nancy, cannot help thinking of your dead brothers when you look upon your sons.

The interruption of continuity, the effacement of the past—innocence—makes pride possible. Men would like to think that they become functionally male with the mounting saps of natural evolution; it gives them the confidence now that they are males by nature. Women would like to think that they have a female nature, which becomes evident in the growing accumulation of natural biological signs and developments. But in truth the story of a boy becoming a man is a tale of one awkwardness, failure, and castration after another. How a woman forgets now the ignorance and incompetence in which as a girl she groped! None of us could today know one sole moment of sexual happiness, one moment of pride in our animal sexuality and nature, if we remembered, if we did not have the power to forget. What will always vacate the orgasmic ecstasy is the memory that this night compares you with the woman last night or last month or the fifteen-year-old of my first summer of love. What fades the presence of the other is the performance that makes the kisses and caresses we squander on her or him a demonstration of something that had been in doubt or a compensation for the stresses and distresses of the day and of the years. The force to cut off from us that melancholy succession of mortifications which is the history of each of us is the great power that makes us able to make love to this person this night as though we had never made love to anyone before, to make love to this person this night as though there will never be anyone again. This is the ecstasy that says I was born to be here, in your arms; I could die now.

On November 30, 1995, Nancy was arrested. Her arrest, as a terrorist, was announced to the press, but she had been beaten so badly she was never shown. Nancy Gilvonio did not reveal the whereabouts of Néstor Cerpa Cartolini. One day she was dragged before a hooded judge who sentenced her to life imprisonment in Yanamayo Prison, a frigid redoubt on top of a 13,000-foot mountain in southern Peru. Her unheated cell is six by ten feet, with a tiny open window that lets in icy wind but no beam of sunlight. Her bed is a cement slab, the latrine a crude hole in the floor. She is locked in there for twenty-three and a half hours a day. She is allowed to receive a visitor for fifteen minutes once every two months. She is allowed no reading matter or exercise. If Nancy Gilvonio is still alive, she is there as we wait with our words.

How much succeeds that is made of greed and stupidity, deceit and betrayal, plunder and torture! What succeeds finally comes to be deemed beneficial. About what fails, one says, retrospectively, that those who risked that did the wrong thing and were wrong to think they were justified in acting as they did. But we also see how others take up the flame from the fallen ones, to torch the barracks of the oppressor in another place, another time. Every generation in Peru, the enslaved and oppressed Indians have risen against the white oligarchy in the name of Tupac Amaru. But what of those who fail and are disappeared, buried by night in unmarked graves, their very names lost in the night and fog?

But there is a fundamental innocence in their act. In its failure, if it left no beneficial consequences, it left no consequences. And the passion for justice that flared in it is the whole of its meaning.

In death, every life fails. It disconnects from the processes of history. If it is true that its enterprises may go on by themselves, one no longer pilots them and they are vulnerable to being taken over or brought to a halt by others who live. In letting go of the controls, in disconnecting, in dying, there is a fundamental innocence. That is why the corpses of criminals too are treated with respect. That is why disappearing them is an exasperated effort of monsters to wipe out innocence from their regime.

Nancy Gilvonio, half-breed, improbably born somewhere in the Amazonian side of the Peruvian Andes, entombed, disappeared. *Nancy Gilvonio, mistress of Néstor Cerpa Cartolini, alias camarada Huerta, alias camarada Evaristo, alias El Gordo. Terrorist of the Tupac Amaru Revolutionary Movement,* which military and civilian experts on terrorism judge is now down to not more than thirty to forty members still at large.

Courage courses in the resolve of one who, before the imminence of death, seizes hold of all that is possible by mobilizing all his or her powers. When there are no adequate resources and you have no forces you can count on, when you stand under the empty, terrorist sky, what surges up in you is bravado.

In pursuing actions that expose us to the blows of chance, we know in exhilaration what we have received by chance, what we are by chance. There is something infantile about bravado. Bravado turns your eyes upward into the sky empty of you as was the surface and depth of the earth below when you were born. Bravado swells in feeling seduced by your heroic existence born by chance in the void.

With the capture of Tupac Amaru in 1572, the conquest was complete. With the beheading of Tupac Amaru before the cathedral of Qosqo, the conquest was launched, extending for the subsequent four hundred years to our day.

Under President Alberto Fujimori, the oppression of the Tupac Amaru Revolutionary Movement of this generation has been no less determined than Pizarro's. Thousands of guerrillas, civilian leaders, dissidents, and Indians have been massacred. Those taken prisoner are sentenced by hooded judges. Lawyers are not allowed to present a defense or cross-examine witnesses. Maximum-security jails today hold 442 militants of the Tupac Amaru Revolutionary Movement, including 89 women. Among the most notorious of these jails is Yanamayo Prison.

Can we spend our whole lives ensuring that no extraordinary or grand demand would ever be made of us, that we could answer every situation with ordinary decency? Can we live our whole lives doing only the comfortable and secure work we do, putting forth our powers and energies and feelings only to a measured and prudent extent? How doing so extends throughout our years an inner desolation that will become irremediable when old age irreversibly diminishes those powers and energies and feelings!

We may well refrain from blaming those who have never defied the impossible, because we recognize the uselessness, indeed the harm, of inflicting guilt on the one who failed to do the extraordinary thing, or because we fear we too may fail when the time comes. Yet the death from a hideously painful disease that may well await us will require no less heroism than that of the guerrilla in battle or before the firing squad; the accompaniment of our dying lover or child may require of us the unimaginable strength and resolve of those who go on rescue operations in glaciers or medical missions in refugee camps. And when the time for these deeds comes, though all the others be silent and without reproach toward us, we will know that the heroic was obligatory for us.

At 8:14 P.M. on December 17, an elegant garden party honoring Japanese Emperor Akihito's birthday at the Japanese ambassador's residence in Lima was overflowing with more than 600 guests sipping whisky, nibbling on sushi, exchanging *abrazos*. But an ambulance had just unloaded a handful of people into a house next door. A moment later, a powerful explosion silenced the festivities. Through the dynamited wall of the adjacent building Tupac Amaru guerrillas burst upon the garden party. At once a firefight erupted between the police in and in front of the compound and the masked guerrillas. Holding off the police, the guerrillas herded the 600 guests inside the embassy and sealed it. How many were these guerrillas who had taken 600 hostages without killing or even injuring anyone? The press counted between twelve and twenty. They were men and also women.

The hostages included thirty-five Japanese businessmen, eight military and police generals (including the chiefs of intelligence and antiterrorism), seven foreign ambassadors, six national congressmen, five supreme court justices, two government ministers, and President Fujimori's mother, sister, and younger brother. The Japanese businessmen included top executives for Mitsubishi, Mitsui, Toyota, and Panasonic. The entire top power structure of the oligarchy and the police of this police state had been seized in a feat unprecedented in the whole of history.

At eleven o'clock that evening, 280 women and older people, including Fujimori's mother and sister, were released. In the days that followed all but 72 hostages were released.

The guerrilla commando was led by camarada Hermigidio Huerta. Hermigidio Huerta is the nom de guerre of Néstor Cerpa Cartolini, Nancy Gilvonio's husband.

The commando set forth its unique demand: that the 442 Tupac Amaru prisoners, including 89 women, be released, in exchange for the freedom of the 72 hostages.

Prime Minister Hashimoto of Japan flew to meet with President Fujimori in Canada, to pledge him not to endanger the lives of the hostages. Each day the Red Cross delivered food to the hostages, including meals from Lima's best Japanese restaurants for the Japanese. The cardinal archbishop of Ayacucho, the Canadian ambassador—who had been one of those at the Japanese ambassador's reception but had been released the first night—and a representative of Fujimori's government were instructed to negotiate with the Tupac Amaru guerrillas. But Fujimori offered safe conduct out of the country to the "terrorists" only if they released all their hostages unharmed.

Meantime Fujimori ordered a SWAP commando to be constituted and trained by the U.S. special forces, and miners to be recruited to tunnel from a distance toward and under the grounds of the Japanese ambassador's residence. In the prisons, journalists and the Red Cross were denied access to the 442 Tupac Amaru prisoners.

Four months passed. To break the nerves of the guerrillas, the police blared military marches at top volume toward the residence. Negotiations were intermittently broken off. The guerrillas released two more hostages, who had developed health problems. One was General Luis Valencia Hirano, commander of the state antiterrorist police, who had a stomach ulcer.

In every act of bravado the action is launched much more by the apparition and magnitude of the impossible than by the dimensions of the possible. In many cases it is necessary to hope for nothing in order to undertake any action.

Lives that have been shattered and irreparably broken sometimes find singularly little bitterness and instead, somehow, beyond explanation, an immense affirmation. There is an ultimate bravado, in people made great by their endurance of affliction, uncomplaining and undaunted and finally laughing. Their affliction and their bravado have made them deep but also childlike, innocent, insolent, and impetuous.

In March, the guerrillas detected, through the blare of the military marches, a sound of tunneling under the residence. They moved all the hostages to the second floor of the building. After four months, it was clear that the negotiators had instructions to concede nothing. Inside the residence, the guerrillas felt the future and the past fallen from them, with all their weight, and experienced these last moments disconnected, buoyant, and with all their energies. They spent their afternoons playing soccer.

On April 22, in midafternoon, while the guerrillas were playing soccer, multiple explosives opened the tunnels, and the government SWAT team broke through. The troops shot dead all the guerrillas, including two unarmed women. They were found to be fourteen. In the pandemonium one of the hostages, a supreme court judge, died of a heart attack. The thirty soldiers of the SWAT team circled around the bodies of the slain guerrillas, each one firing shots into the head of each corpse. After President Fujimori, before the cameras of the press, stepped triumphantly over the mutilated bodies, they were taken to the army base and then buried in unmarked, unrevealed graves.

A letter was found, written the day before by Néstor Cerpa Cartolini, to his nine-year-old son, whom French sympathizers had been able to spirit out of Peru to France. The letter read:

> If I ever leave this Japanese residence it will be because I have achieved what you are waiting for and dreaming of: having your mummy out of prison, being able again to see her, touch her, play with her and be in her arms.

NOTES

Chapter 1. Grosz / Thinking the New

1. Rémy Lestienne (*The Creative Power of Chance* [Urbana: University of Illinois Press, 1998], 2–3) argues, following Roger Penrose, that if there is to be a unified physical theory of the kind Einstein dreamed about, it would not be the hyperdeterminism of Laplacean models (perhaps best exemplified today, ironically, by chaos theory) but would require both unpredictability in principle and (temporal) irreversibility.

2. See Michel Foucault, "The Discourse on Language" in *The Archaeology of Knowledge*, trans. A. M. Sheridan-Smith (New York: Harper Colophon, 1972).

3. This position, now regarded as the causal theory of time, is committed to temporal irreversibility on the ground of the irreversibility of causal relations; it is represented perhaps most clearly in the writings of Leibniz and Kant. It is a position that has also been forwarded in the more contemporary work of Reichenbach and Carnap. See Adolf Grünbaum, *Philosophical Problems of Space and Time* (Boston: Reidel, 1973), chap. 7, "The Causal Theory of Time."

4. See Jacques Derrida, *Limited Inc.*, trans. Samuel Weber (Evanston, Ill.: Northwestern University Press, 1988).

5. "To the biologist as to the philosopher the great inadequacy of determinism is its inability to account for the appearance of novelty. Biology above all seems rich in new and more complex structures and functions; the rigid determinist must either deny the reality of these novel appearances or claim that they are somehow derivable from general laws. . . . The feeling grew that biology would have to choose either to follow physics and live with determinism or to strike out on its own. To many it seemed that biological phenomena were so different from physical that some element of indeterminism would have

to be admitted. The schism thus established lasted well into this century and produced some notable debates. However, at the present time controversy has faded in perspective and a very different atmosphere prevails; physics and biology are together edging toward a unified theory. . . . The fact [is] that the generation of mutational novelty . . . by the random or chance chemical modification of the informational molecules, which are the genetic store of organisms . . . underlies the evolutionists' stress on the creative contribution of pure chance and the impossibility of predicting the results of its intervention." (Mercer, quoted in F. Eugene Yates, "Quantumstuff and Biostuff" in F. E. Yates, Garfinkel, Walter, and Yates, *Self-Organizing Systems: The Emergence of Order* [New York: Plenum, 1987], 11.)

6. Duration should not be conflated too readily with becoming, though it remains an abiding condition of becoming. Not all duration induces becoming; conversely, not all becoming necessarily involves duration. For the purposes of this chapter, I understand *becoming* to imply active transformation; while *duration* may designate a state of preservation or conservation as readily as a mode of transformation.

7. This burgeoning area contains many initial attempts to chart parallels between the sciences and humanities. See Arkady Plotnitsky, *Complementarity: Anti-Epistemology after Bohr and Derrida* (Durham, N.C.: Duke University Press, 1994); and N. Katherine Hayles, *Chaos Unbound: Orderly Disorder in Contemporary Literature and Science* (Ithaca, N.Y.: Cornell University Press, 1990).

8. Lyotard describes the refiguring of matter in contemporary technoscience as a fourth blow (following Copernicus, Darwin, and Freud) unsettling the privilege of the human. Matter can be seen to exhibit desire, if by desire is understood divergence and complexification. If we proceed beyond anthropomorphism, even if cells, stars, and chemicals cannot read or desire in one sense, they can in another:

> . . . in the current state of science and techniques, resort to the entity "Life" to cover what I call, for want of a better term, desire [*conatus, appetitio* for others], i.e., the complexification which disavows—de-authorizes so to speak—all objects of demand in turn: resort to this term seems still far too anthropomorphic. To say that Life is responsible for the formation of systems such as the atom or the star or the cell or the human cortex or finally the collective cortex constituted by machine memories is contrary, as are all teleologies, to the materialist spirit. . . . (Jean-François Lyotard, "Matter and Time," in *The Inhuman,* trans. Geoffrey Bennington and Rachel Bowlby [Stanford: Stanford University Press, 1991], 45.)

9. See Rémy Lestienne (1998) for a broad discussion of the power and centrality of the concept of chance in both physical and life sciences.

10. "Central to [Darwin's] theory was the idea that variations become creative by orienting the destiny of evolution. Just as, in artificial selection, breeders continuously modify their criteria for selection in view of any fortuitous results from the preceding stage of variation, some natural variations make new selections possible." (Lestienne, 49).

11. The convergence of biology and physics in the late twentieth century seems to be lateral rather than the more conventional model, subsumption (a model that has tended to privilege physics as the most notable and pure of the sciences). In fact a number of issues seem to make possible the drawing together of these two disparate domains:

1. Physics had to relax its hopes for strict determinism, which had seemed to rule out the possibility of biological novelty, contrary to the facts of biological evolution and diversity.
2. Both physics and biology had to strengthen their understanding of evolutionary, historical, irreversible processes. The macroscopic (including macromolecular) dynam-

ics are not time symmetric, and small factors or fluctuations may have amplified effects, especially at bifurcation points where symmetry can easily be broken down.
3. The uses of terms and concepts cast in the mold of information-communication metaphors that now dominate biological explanations have to be justified by accounting for information as a by-product or side effect of dynamics. . . . The dichotomies of structure and function, form and process, genotype and phenotype, biology and physics are seen to be variation on that of information and dynamics (Yates, 1987), 625.

12. Eugene Minkowski, *Lived Time: Phenomenological and Psychopathological Studies,* trans. Nancy Metzel (Evanston, Ill.: Northwestern University Press, 1970), 7.

13. It must be hastily added that while Bergson is commonly taken as the last full-blown vitalist, much in his work mitigates against such an understanding. Where he affirms vitalism in the face of the mathematization of nature, at the same time he seems to undermine it by asserting the interchangeability of mind and matter, their difference of degree: " . . . from mind to matter there is but a fundamental difference of degree, which depends on the capacity to gather and conserve. Mind is matter which remembers its interactions, its immanence. But there is a continuum from the instantaneous mind of matter to the very gathered matter of minds" (Lyotard, 1991), 40.

14. Spafford argues that, as regards the properties "a-life" scientists want to associate with the definition of life, a computer virus could qualify as life. Yet he concludes that this indicates a problem with the definition of life on which computer programs have relied. He cites the following criteria, which he believes the computer virus satisfies:

1. Life is a pattern in space-time rather than a specific material object.
2. Self-reproduction, in itself or in a related organism.
3. Information storage of a self-representation.
4. A metabolism that converts matter / energy.
5. Functional interactions with the environment.
6. Interdependence of parts.
7. Stability under perturbations of the environment.
8. The ability to evolve.
9. Growth or expansion. (Eugene H Spafford, "Computer Viruses—A Form of Artificial Life?" in *Artificial Life II.* ed. C. Langton, C. Taylor, J. D. Farmer, and S. Ramussen, [Redwood City, Calif.: Addison-Wesley, 1992], 741.)

While noting, indeed arguing in favor of the analogy, Spafford is clearly disturbed at the implication that a hard and fast line may not be able to be drawn dividing life from its simulation, and at the very end of his paper he reasserts in somewhat dogmatic form exactly that which the paper has helped problematize. He argues that "we must never lose sight of the fact that 'real life' is of much more importance than 'artificial life,' and we should not allow our experiments to threaten our experimenters" (744), when in fact his own arguments make it increasingly difficult to divide the experimenter from the experiment. For more on the links between biological and computer viruses, see Andrés Moya, Esteban Domingo, and John J. Holland, "RNA Viruses: A Bridge Between Life and Artificial Life," in *Advances in Artificial Life,* ed. F. Morán, A. Moreno, J. J. Mereko, and O. Chacón (Berlin: Springer-Verlag, 1995); Richard Dawkins, *The Blind Watchmaker* (New York: Norton, 1986); and Andrew Ross, *Strange Weather, Culture, Science, and Technology in the Age of Limits* (London: Verso, 1991), 77.

15. Langton makes explicit the relative indifference of biological concepts of life to the specific modes of materiality to which it has up to now been confined:

> Certainly life, as a dynamic physical process, could haunt other physical material: the material just needs to be organized in the right way. Just as certainly, the dynamic processes that constitute life—in whatever material bases they might occur—must share certain universal features—features that allow us to recognize life by its dynamic *form* alone, without reference to its *matter*. This *general* phenomenon of life—life writ large across all possible material substrates—is the true subject matter of biology. (Chris Langton, "Artificial Life," in *Artificial Life,* vol. IV [Redwood City, Calif.: Addison-Wesley, 1989], 2.

Whenever the specificities of matter are regarded merely as "substrate," "ground," or "support" of a program, form, or idea, it seems that we return to the reign of Platonism and the profound somatophobia to which it gave rise. It is significant that Langton's concept of matter as substrate has been challenged, not entirely surprisingly, from the point of view of molecular biology, "according to which 'form' and 'matter' do not represent separate realms." (Claus Emmeche, "Life as an Abstract Phenomenon: Is Artificial Life Possible?" in *Toward a Practice of Autonomous Systems,* ed. Francisco J. Varela and Paul Bourgine [Cambridge: MIT Press, 1992], 466.)

16. For a current overview of the role of computer simulation and what have been called "artificial societies," see Nigel Gilbert and Rosaria Conte, eds., *Artificial Societies: The Computer Simulation of Social Life* (London: University College of London Press, 1995).

17. Gilles Deleuze, *Bergsonism* (New York: Zone, 1988).

18. These are clearly abiding concerns in Deleuze's writings, from his work on Hume through his analysis of Proust and his understanding of the time-movement in his studies of cinema to his more recent writings on thinking and philosophy. Outlining this trajectory would no doubt warrant a book-length study (maybe in another lifetime!).

19. As Bergson says,

> There is in matter something more than, but not something different from, that which is actually given. Undoubtedly, conscious perception does not encompass the whole of matter, since it consists, in as far as it is conscious, in the separation or "discernment," of that which, in matter, interests our various needs. But between this perception of matter and matter itself, there is but a difference of degree and not of kind, pure perception standing toward matter in the relation of the part to the whole. This amounts to saying that matter cannot exercise powers of any kind other than those which we perceive. It has no mysterious virtue; it can conceal none. (Henri Bergson, *Matter and Memory,* trans. N. M. Paul and W. S. Palmer [New York: Zone, 1988], 71.)

20. Henri Bergson, *The Creative Mind: An Introduction to Metaphysics,* trans. Mabelle L. Andison (New York: Citadel Press, 1992), 93.

21. "The past and the present do not denote two successive moments, but two elements which coexist: One is the present, which does not cease to pass, and the other is the past, which does not cease to be but through which all presents pass. . . . The past does not follow the present, but on the contrary, is presupposed by it as the pure condition without which it would not pass. In other words, each present goes back to itself as past." (Deleuze, 1988, 59.)

22. "Everything is already *completely given:* all of the real in the image, the pseudo-actuality of the possible. Then the sleight of hand becomes obvious: If the real is said to resemble the possible, is this not in fact because the real was expected to come about by its own means, to 'project backwards' a fictitious image of it, and to claim that it was possible at any time before it happened? In fact it is not the real that resembles the possible, it is the possible that resembles the real, because it has been abstracted from the real once made, arbitrarily extracted from the real like a sterile double." (Deleuze, 1988, 98).

23. Cf. Bergson:

One might as well claim that the man in flesh and blood comes from the materialization of his image seen in the mirror, because in that real is everything to be found in this virtual image with, in addition, the solidity which makes it possible to touch it. But the truth is that more is needed here to obtain the virtual than is necessary for the real, more of the image of the man than for the man himself, for the image of the man will not be portrayed if the man is not first produced, and in addition one has to have the mirror. (Henri Bergson, *The Creative Mind: An Introduction to Metaphysics,* trans. Mabelle L. Andison [New York: Citadel Press, 1992], 102.)

24. The processes of resemblance and limitation constituting realization, Bergson argues, are subject to the philosophical illusion that there is *less* in the idea of the empty rather than the full; and less in the concept of disorder than order, where in fact the ideas of nothing and disorder are *more* complicated than of existence and order:

Underlying the doctrines which disregard the radical novelty of each moment of evolution there are many misunderstandings, many errors. But there is especially the idea that the possible is *less* than the real, and that, for this reason, the possibility of things precedes their existence. They would thus be capable of representation beforehand; they could be thought of before being realized. But it is the reverse that is true. . . . [W]e find that there is more and not less in the possibility of each of the successive states than in their reality. For the possible is only the real with the addition of an act of mind which throws its image back into the past, once it has been enacted. But that is what our intellectual habits prevent us from seeing (Bergson, 1992, 99–100.)

25. "As reality is created as something unforeseeable and new, its image is reflected behind it into the indefinite past; thus it finds that it has from all time been possible, but it is at this precise moment that it begins to have been always possible, and that is why I said that its possibility, which does not precede its reality, will have to precede it once the reality has appeared. The possible is therefore the mirage of the present in the past; and as we know the future will finally constitute a present and the mirage effect is continually being produced, we are convinced that the image of tomorrow is already contained in our actual present, which will be the past of tomorrow, although we do not manage to grasp it." (Bergson, 1992, 101.)

26. Existence is supposed to occur in space and time, but these are understood as indifferent milieux instead of the production of existence occurring in a characteristic space and time. Difference can no longer be anything but the negative determined by the concept; either the limitation imposed by possibles of each other in order to be realized, or the opposition of the possible to the reality of the real. (Gilles Deleuze, *Difference and Repetition* trans. P. Patton [New York: Columbia University Press, 1994], 211.)

27. "Actualization breaks with resemblance as a process no less than it does with identity as a principle. Actual terms never resemble the singularities they incarnate. In this sense, actualization or differenciation is always a genuine creation. It does not result from any limitation of a preexisting possibility. . . . For a potential or virtual object, to be actualised is to create divergent lines which correspond to—without resembling—a virtual multiplicity. The virtual possesses the reality of a task to be performed or a problem to be solved: it is the problem which orientates, conditions, and engenders solutions, but these do not resemble the conditions of the problem." (Gilles Deleuze and Félix Guattari, *What Is Philosophy?* trans. Hugh Tomlinson and Graham Burchell [New York: Columbia University Press, 1994], 212.)

28. While the real is in the image and likeness of the possible that it realizes, the actual, on the other hand, does *not* resemble the virtual from which we begin and the actuals at which we arrive, and also the difference between the complementary lines according to which actualization takes place. In short, the characteristic of virtuality is to exist

in such a way that it is actualized by being differentiated and is forced to differentiate itself, to create its lines of differentiation in order to be actualized (Deleuze, 1988, 97).

29. This notion of individuation is articulated by Gilbert Simondon, who has been so influential in much of Deleuze's writings, especially in *A Thousand Plateaus,* regarding the processes of individuation. Individuation is seen in terms of a series of states of metastable equilibrium; it is thus necessarily regarded in terms of becoming. Simondon may have succeeded in going a step further than Bergson in seeing the implications of movement as the internal condition of individuation or being itself:

> The concept of being that I put forward, then, is the following: a being does not possess a unity in its identity, which is that of the stable state within which no transformation is possible; rather, a being has a *transductive unity,* that is, it can pass out of phase with itself, it can—in any arena—break its own bounds in relation to its *center.* What one assumes to be a *relation* or a *duality of principles* is in fact the unfolding of the being, which is more than a unity and more than an identity; becoming is a dimension of the being, not something that happens to it following a succession of events that affect a being already and originally given and substantial. Individuation must be grasped as the becoming of the being and not as a model of the being which would exhaust his signification. . . . Instead of presupposing the existence of substances in order to account for individuation, I intend, on the contrary, to take the different regimes of individuation as providing the foundation for different domains such as matter, life, mind and society. (Gilbert Simondon, "The Genesis of the Individual," trans. Mark Cohen and Sanford Kwinter, in *Incorporations,* ed. Jonathan Crary and Sanford Kwinter [New York: Zone, 1992], 311–312.)

30. "[T]ime is something. Therefore it acts. [T]ime is what hinders everything from being given at once. It retards, or rather it is retardation. It must, therefore, be elaboration. Would it not then be a vehicle of creation and of choice? Would not the existence of time prove that there is indetermination in things? Would not time be that indetermination itself?" (Bergson, 1992, 93.)

Chapter 2. De Landa / Deleuze and the Open-Ended Becoming of the World

1. Gilles Deleuze, *Difference and Repetition* (New York: Columbia University Press, 1994), 222.

2. Gregoire Nicolis and Ilya Prigogine, *Exploring Complexity* (New York: Freeman, 1989).

3. Deleuze, *Difference and Reptition,* 214.

4. Ibid., 212.

5. Gilles Deleuze and Felix Guattari, *A Thousand Plateaus* (Minneapolis: University of Minnesota Press, 1987), 336.

6. Ian Stewart, *Does God Play Dice?: The Mathematics of Chaos* (Oxford: Basil Blackwell, 1989), chap. 6.

7. Deleuze and Guattari, *Thousand Plateaus,* 330.

8. Ibid., 336.

9. Ibid., 411.

10. Ibid., 329.

11. Stuart Kauffman, *The Origins of Order: Self-Organization and Selection in Evolution* (New York: Oxford University Press, 1993), chap. 3.

12. George Kampis, *Self-Modifying Systems in Biology and Cognitive Science: A New Framework for Dynamics, Information, and Complexity* (Oxford, Eng.: Pergamon, 1991), 235.

13. Deleuze, and Guattari, "Thousand Plateaus," 239.
14. Deleuze, *Difference and Repetition*, 189.
15. Ibid., 169.
16. Ibid., 192.

Chapter 3. Rajchman / Diagram and Diagnosis

1. Etienne Balibar, *Les frontières de la démocracie* (Paris: La Decouverte, 1992), refers to geographic or social limits where democracy stops, and yet where it must take the chance of discovering new spaces. Putting democracy back into play at such points constitutes "the very definition of a politics of the left" (16).
2. Gilles Deleuze and Claire Parnet, *Dialogues*, (New York: Columbia University Press, 1987). 124–25). The term *individuation* is developed from Gilbert Simondon, where it is distinguished from *individualization* of given species or genres. *Individuation* thus implies that a society never reduces to the strata or classes that compose it, that always something the escapes it, so that one can say, "Society is always leaking" (*en fuite*). (*Dialogues,* 135).
3. Gilles Deleuze, *Cinema 2: The Time Image* (Minneapolis: University of Minnesota Press, 1998): I discuss the related theme of seeing in Foucault in "Foucault's Art of Seeing," in *Philosophical Events* (New York: Columbia University Press, 1990).
4. See "Societies of Control," in *Critique et clinique* as well as the appendix on "Man" in *Foucault*. I think we might read Foucault's analysis of the "welfare-warfare" state along the same "diagnostic" lines as a political form questioned or transformed through "globalizaing" forces. One might, in particular, look at the theme of cities discussed by Foucault in relation to the "politics of health."
5. See "Bartleby" in *Essays Critical and Clinical* trans. Daniel Smith and Michael Grec (Minneapolis: University of Minnesota Press, 1997), 68–90. For a related view of William James, see David Lapoujade, *William James: Empiricisme et Pragmatisme* (Paris: Puf, 1997).
6. In a sort of companion-piece, I develop the question of pragmatism further: "A New Pragmatism?" in *Anyhow* (Cambridge: M.I.T. Press, 1998).
7. Quoted in Gilles Deleuze, "What Is a Dispositif?" in *Michel Foucault, Philosopher,* trans. Timothy J. Armstrong (New York: Routledge, 1992), 165.
8. Deleuze and Parnet, *Dialogues* (New York: Columbia Univesity Press, 1987), p. 146.
9. What Is Philosophy? (New York: Columbia Univesity Press, 1994) 106ff.
10. "Bartleby." See also "What Is Philosophy?"
11. *What is Philosophy?* (New York: Columbia Univesity Press, 1994), 75.
12. See "Philosophy and the Future," in *Rorty and Pragmatism: The Philosopher Responds to His Critics,* ed. Herman J. Soatkamp, Jr. (Nashville: Vanderbilt University Press, 1995), 197ff. Rorty's "Clear Image" of the Future (p. 203) is in fact an old idea; in Deleuze's pragmatism there is another art of seeing.

Chapter 4. Alcoff / Becoming an Epistemologist

1. Catherine Elgin, *Between the Absolute and the Arbitrary* (Ithaca: Cornell University Press, 1997), 1.
2. Ibid.
3. Michael Devitt, *Realism and Truth*, 2d ed. (Cambridge, Mass.: Blackwell, 1991), 29.
4. Even the phrase "ontologies of becoming" will seem anathema to some readers,

who take ontology as an enterprise to be wedded to a metaphysics of presence, or the belief in a transparent, unmediated reality. However, the latter is only *one* version of an ontological or metaphysical account, and although it is currently dominant, it has faced important rivals throughout the history of western philosophy. It is not helpful, in my view, to erase the heterogeneity of this history in reductive accounts that read the metaphysics of presence into every philosophical era, whether this is done on the continental or the analytic side. Rather, we should define these terms more generally and should understand every proposal about the ultimate nature of the "real," even those accounts that see this ultimate nature as a construct, an ideological effect, or an ineffable force in flux, as entering a debate that is most usefully and broadly named metaphysics. Thus, the differences between accounts of the "real" are usefully characterized not as between those who do metaphysics and those who don't, but as between approaches to metaphysical questions, which of course includes an account of which questions, under what formulation, can be asked. If one says that a metaphysics of presence is false, one thereby commits oneself to some beliefs about reality or lived experience (or whatever terms one chooses) such that *that* view does not obtain.

5. This claim is made by John Skorupski, "The Intelligibility of Scepticism," in *The Analytic Tradition*, ed. David Bell and Neil Cooper (Oxford: Blackwell, 1990), 1–29. The problem of skepticism alluded to here is global skepticism, or the fear that we may have no knowledge at all.

6. Barry Allen, *Truth in Philosophy* (Cambridge, Mass: Harvard University Press, 1993), 149.

7. Ibid., 163.

8. Ibid., 164.

9. Ibid., 163.

10. Ibid.

11. Alternatively, if one held that all there is is passing for true, but that this does not amount to truth itself, one could launch a political critique by posing one set of historically conditioned norms over another. The operative criteria might be political or aesthetic but would be understood as extraepistemic. But this is not Allen's position, given that he wants to legitimate what passes for true as the truth itself. It is closer to Rorty's position. In any case, the move to criticize truth claims on purely political grounds rather than on epistemic grounds (and the very belief that one can do so) is a serious mistake, as I shall be arguing further on.

12. Jürgen Habermas, *The Philosophical Discourse of Modernity*, trans. Frederick Lawrence (Cambridge, Mass.: MIT Press, 1987), 279.

13. In my *Real Knowing: New Versions of the Coherence Theory* (Ithaca, N.Y.: Cornell University Press, 1996), chaps. 4 and 5.

14. See Michel Foucault, "Two Lectures," in *Power/Knowledge: Selected Interviews and Other Writings, 1972–1977*, ed. Colin Gordon, trans. Colin Gordon et al. (New York: Pantheon, 1980), 117–119, and 131–133.

15. Foucault, *Discipline and Punish: The Birth of the Prison*, trans. Alan Sheridan (New York: Random House, 1979), 28.

16. Foucault, "Two Lectures," 81.

17. Ibid., 85.

18. Foucault, "The Concern for Truth" in *Michel Foucault: Politics, Philosophy, Culture*, ed. Lawrence Kritzman (New York: Routledge, 1988), 257.

19. Foucault, "Truth and Power," in *Power/Knowledge*, 133.

20. Brian Massumi, *A User's Guide to Capitalism and Schizophrenia* (Cambridge, Mass.: MIT Press, 1992), 22.

21. Wendy Brown, *States of Injury: Power and Freedom in Late Modernity* (Princeton, N.J.: Princeton University Press, 1995), xii.

22. Ibid., 36, 37.

23. Ibid., 41.

24. Ibid., 40.

25. Ibid., 42.

26. Ibid., 44.

27. Ibid., 48.

28. Ibid., 45.

29. Ibid., 49.

30. Ibid., 49.

31. Ibid., 48.

32. Ibid., 43.

33. Foucault, "Two Lectures," 86.

34. Hilary Putnam, *Reason, Truth, and History* (Cambridge: Cambridge University Press, 1981), 122–124.

35. Ibid., 123.

36. Ibid., 123.

37. Ibid., 49.

38. Putnam, *Renewing Philosophy* (Cambridge, Mass.: Harvard University Press, 1992), 123.

Chapter 5. Casey / The Time of the Glance

1. See James Elkins, "Everything Can Only Be Seen in a Glance," unpublished text (Spring 1998). Elkins argues in this paper that even the chiton, the "sea cradle" that lives on seaside rocks, is able to glance into its environment.

2. Jacques Derrida, *Speech and Phenomena*, trans. David Allison (Evanston, Ill.: Northwestern University Press, 1973), 65. Derrida italicizes "the blink of the instant," whose bodily analogue is the blink of the eye.

3. Heidegger discusses the "hint" or "sign"(*der Wink*, not the equivalent of the English "wink" despite the homography) in a comparable way: "A hint can give its hint so simply . . . that we release ourselves in its direction without equivocation. But it can also give its hint in such a manner that it refers us . . . back to the dubiousness against which it warns us." ("The Nature of Language," in *On the Way to Language*, trans. P. D. Hertz [New York: Harper, 1971], 96.)

4. T. S. Eliot, "Burnt Norton," *Four Quartets*, stanzas I and V.

5. Bergson argues that duration dissolves the rigidity of the B series: duration is "a memory interior to change itself, a memory that prolongs the before in the after and prevents them from being pure snapshots (*instantanés*) that appear and disappear in a present that would be incessantly reborn."(*Duration et simultanéité: à propos de la théorie d'Einstein* [Paris: Alcan, 1922], 55.)

6. J. M. McTaggart, "Time," chap. 33 of Book V of *The Nature of Existence*, Vol. 2 (Cambridge: Cambridge University Press, 1927); reprinted in R. M. Gale, *The Philosophy of Time* (New York: Humanities, 1978), 87–88.

7. Henri Bergson, *Creative Evolution*, trans. A. Mitchell (Lanham, Md.: University Press of America, 1983), 308; translation modified. More succinctly stated: "Our duration is not merely an instant that replaces another instant: for then there would never be anything but the present" (ibid., 4). For the arrow to exist in a point of time, that is to say, an

instant that is the present, is for it to coincide with a fixed position in such a way as to be inextricably tied to it: tied to its actuality, which is distinct from the actuality of every other point-instant. But, as Bergson asserts, "The arrow *is not* ever in any point of its trajectory" (ibid., 308; translation modified). Bergson is here remarking that the arrow is motionless if the arrow can *ever* be located at a determinate point of its trajectory.

8. Where an instant is an "immobile section (*coupe*)" of time that requires the abstract idea of succession to string together otherwise utterly disparate points—and thus to produce a travesty of time, its punctiform homogenization—the moment of the glance is a "mobile section of duration." Each not merely reflects or mirrors duration but *is* an aspect of duration in its very movement: a cut *into* duration rather than something cut out of it. (I borrow the phrase "mobile section of duration" from Deleuze, *Cinema 2: The Time-Image*, trans. H. Tomlinson and R. Galeta [Minneapolis: University of Minnesota Press, 1989], 98.)

9. Bergson, *Creative Evolution*, 5. Bergson adds: "Doubtless we think with only a small part of our past; but it is with our entire past, including our original bent of soul, that we desire, will, act. Our past thus manifests itself integrally to us by its thrust and in the form of tendencies, even though only one weak part of it is represented." (ibid.; translation modified.)

10. Deleuze, *Cinema 2*, 82 (his italics).

11. Deleuze speaks of "the hidden ground of time, that is, its differentiation into two flows, that of presents which pass and that of pasts which are preserved. Time simultaneously makes the present pass and preserves the past in itself." (ibid., 98.)

12. On the "memory of the world," see Maurice Merleau-Ponty, *The Visible and the Invisible*, trans. A. Lingis (Evanston, Ill.: Northwestern University Press, 1968), 194. Earlier, Merleau-Ponty spoke of "the world's vast Memory" (*Phenomenology of Perception*, trans. C. Smith [New York: Humanities Press, 1962], 70). Note that Deleuze, influenced explicitly by Bergson and tacitly by Merleau-Ponty, states that "memory is not in us; it is we who move in a Being-memory, a world-memory" (*Cinema 2*, 98).

13. "It is we who are internal to time, not the other way around. . . . Time is not the interior in us, but just the opposite, the interiority in which we are, in which we move, live, and change" (Deleuze, *Cinema 2*, 82). But if this is not true of the arrow—whose time is internal to its own specific motion—it is true of every experience of time in which subjectivity is at stake, to the point where Deleuze can claim that "the only subjectivity is time, nonchronological time grasped in its foundation" (ibid.).

14. On ecstatico-horizonal temporality, see Martin Heidegger, *Being and Time,* trans. J. Macquarrie & E. Robinson (New York: Harper, 1962), pp. 377ff.

15. The fact that they are *mobile* sections, i.e., themselves moving and not merely the image of movement, may distinguish them from the Zenonian impasse that is occasioned by immobile sections, but it does not free them from the implicit hegemony of what Bergson can only call "the Whole": the whole of duration, of temporality, of time itself. There are two relevant wholes at stake here: the "whole" formed by virtual images that exists at the edges of the world: "memories, dreams, even worlds are only apparent relative circuits which depend on the variations of this Whole"(Deleuze, *Cinema 2*, 81); and the whole constituted by duration:"through relations, the whole is transformed or changes qualitatively. We can say of duration itself or of time, that it is the whole of relations"(Deleuze, *Cinema 1: The Movement Image*, trans. H. Tomlinson and B. Habberjam [Minneapolis: University of Minnesota Press, 1986], 10). For Bergson's own original use of "Whole," see *Creative Evolution*, 10–12 et seq.

16. Deleuze, *Cinema 1*, 10. On the "Open," a term he shares with Heidegger, Deleuze has this to say, by way of Bergson: "If the living being is a whole and, therefore, compa-

rable to the whole of the universe, this is not because it is a microcosm as closed as the whole is assumed to be, but, on the contrary, because it is open upon a world, and the world, the universe, is itself the Open" (ibid.).

17. Moreover, as I glance I take myself outside my self-contained self into a mirror world that has its own spatiality and temporality. I hover in this world, no longer simply in myself nor utterly beyond myself either. There, in this spectral space, I am suspended on my own glance, the victim of the movement-images I have myself generated in time. The longer I glance, the more unreal the situation seems to become. If there is another mirror present, my glancing image will be multiplied in disconcertingly complex ways, either by engendering what Hegel might call a bad infinity of such images (if the mirrors are aligned with each other *en face*) or by promulgating ghostly self-spectators who glance at myself glancing at myself (if the extra mirrors are set at an oblique angle to the main mirror). Even with these complications, however, my glance—both the first glance I cast and any subsequent glance—folds back upon myself as its progenitor: in fact, I cannot escape the return look if I see my own look at all: to see myself seeing is to see myself seen. The return is built into the scene of glancing itself, every bit as much as the outgoing motion by which it begins.

18. At least "pure recollection" (*souvenir pur*) is virtual in status; whenever an item from this virtual stronghold is in fact recalled, it occurs as a concrete *souvenir-image*, which is an actuality, a psychological fact. As Bergson says, the *souvenir-image* "participates in *souvenir pur*, which it begins by materializing, and in perception, where it tends to be incarnated." (*Matière et Mémoire* [Paris: Alcan, 1921], 143.)

19. Bergson, *L'énergie spirituelle* (Paris: Bibliothèque de Philosophie contemporaine, 1919), 136; his italics for "virtual" and "actual." Deleuze argues, more incisively than Bergson himself, that without this virtual doubling of the present in pure memory, inactual and unconscious as it is, recollection of the past itself would never be possible: "The past would never be constituted if it *had not been* constituted first of all, at the same time that it was present. There is here, as it were, a fundamental position of time and also the most profound paradox of memory: The past is "contemporaneous" with the present that it *has been*. . . . The past would never be constituted if it did not coexist with the present whose past it is" (Gilles Deleuze, *Bergsonism*, trans. H. Tomlinson and B. Habberjam [New York: Zone, 1991], 58–59. His italics.) Merleau-Ponty converges on this line of thought by saying that "past and present are *Ineinander*, each enveloping-enveloped" (*The Visible and the Invisible*, 268). More specifically still, Merleau-Ponty suggests "the idea that every perception is doubled with a counter-perception" and speaks of "chiasm my body—the things, realized by the doubling up of my body into inside and outside—and the doubling up of the things (their inside and their outside)" (both citations ibid., 264). But the doubling in question is not of perception with memory but of the body with itself in terms of inside / outside dimensions. Deleuze repeats the Bergsonian gesture by alluding to the mirror in this very context: "The present is the actual image, and *its* contemporaneous past is the virtual image, the image in a mirror." (*Cinema 2*, 79, his italics.)

20. Bergson, *L'énergie spirituelle*, 136 (my italics).

21. The phrase *un souvenir du présent* (in italics in the text) is found ibid., 137. As Bergson further specifies, "C'est, dans le moment actuel, un souvenir de ce moment" (ibid.). "Moment" here rightly replaces "instant."

22. On the "unconscious" aspect of virtual memory, see Deleuze, *Bergsonism*, 55–56, 71–72; and Bergson himself in *Creative Mind*, trans. M. L. Andison (Greenwood: Westport, Conn., 1946), 88–89; and *Matière et Mémoire*, 152–163.

23. Deleuze, *Cinema 2*, 80: "The more or less broad, always relative, circuits, between the present and the past, refer back, on the one hand, to a small internal circuit between a

present and *its own* past, between an actual image and *its* virtual image; on the other hand, they refer to deeper and deeper circuits which are themselves virtual, which each time mobilize the whole of the past." The latter circuits are none other than the durational wholes to which reference has already been made. They designate the upper and more capacious parts of the celebrated cone of time whose diagram is found in *Matière et Mémoire*, chap. 3, 177.

24. Deleuze, *Bergsonism*, 59.

25. Merleau-Ponty, *The Visible and the Invisible*, 139. My italics. Variants on this include "the things touch me as I touch them and touch myself"(261) and "it is through the world first that I am seen or thought"(274). It is worth noting that by taking this late step in his thought Merleau-Ponty is in fact drawing close to Bergson, for whom animation, visibility, etc., belong as much to the things at which we look as to ourselves. This emphasis is contrary to Husserl's stress on the unidirectionality of intentionality, which sends its visual ray outward (i.e., being "consciousness *of* X") but does not receive it back. On this comparison, see Deleuze, *Cinema 1*, 60: "[for phenomenology] the intentionality of consciousness was the ray of an electric lamp. . . . For Bergson, it is completely the opposite. Things are luminous by themselves without anything illuminating them." Deleuze significantly omits Merleau-Ponty's affinity with Bergson on this very issue, including Merleau-Ponty's notion of "rays of the world." (see *The Visible and the Invisible*, 218, 240ff, 265.)

26. Deleuze, *Cinema 2*, p. 81.

27. Deleuze remarks that recollecting the past "we place ourselves *at once* (*d'emblée*) in the past; we leap into the past as into a proper element" (*Bergsonism*, 56; his italics), with specific reference to Bergson's emphatic use of "d'emblée" in *Matière et Mémoire*, chaps. 2 and 3).

28. On the structure of the "all-at-once," see *The Phenomenology of Internal Time-Consciousness*, part 3. The time line appears as the horizontal line in Husserl's celebrated diagram of time in part 1. On the ray of the ego, see *Ideas I*, secs. 35, 37, 67.

29. Bergson, *Creative Evolution*, 3.

30. Ibid., 2.

31. Ibid., 5.

32. The existential eternity of the body is related to the rays of the world: "Describe the world of the 'rays of the world' beyond every serial-eternitarian or ideal alternative—Posit the existential eternity—the eternal body" (Merleau-Ponty, *The Visible and the Invisible*, 265).

33. Bergson, *L'énergie spirituelle*, 6: "sur ce passé nous sommes appuyés, sur cet avenir nous sommes penchés."

34. *Creative Evolution*, 7.

35. Ibid., 11.

36. Ibid., 6.

37. Ibid.

38. "The sense organs . . . consist essentially of apparatuses for the reception of certain specific effects of stimulation [as well as] protection against excessive amounts of stimulation. . . . They may be compared with feelers which are all the time making tentative advances towards the external world and then drawing back from it." (S. Freud, *Beyond the Pleasure Principle*, *The Standard Edition of the Complete Psychological Works of Sigmund Freud*, vol. 18 [London: Hogarth, 1955], 28).

39. *L'énergie spirituelle*, 5.

40. *The Visible and the Invisible*, 265; with reference to the *Phenomenology of Perception*, trans. C. Smith (New York: Humanities, 1962), 189, where Merleau-Ponty refers to

"forms of behavior [that] deviate from their preordained direction, through a sort of *leakage* and a genius for ambiguity that might serve to define man" (his italics).

41. Other perforators would include certain "nomadic" concepts, avant-garde works of art, disruptive social movements, etc. But the very inconspicuousness of the glance, its closeness to our everyday bodily behavior, renders it all the more effective in its perforative power.

42. Bergson, *Creative Evolution*, 4.

43. *Ideas I*, sect. 122. Derrida discusses this sentence in *Speech and Phenomena*, 104: "Contrary to the assurance that Husserl gives us a little further on, 'the look' cannot 'abide'."

44. Bergson, *Duration et simultanéité*, 56.

45. "A man is so much the more a 'man of action' as he can embrace in a glance a greater number of events: he who perceives successive events one by one will allow himself to be led by them; he who grasps them as a whole will dominate them"(*Creative Evolution*, 301–302). Just before, Bergson had said that "from our first glance at the world, before we even made out *bodies* in it, we distinguish *qualities*"(300; his italics). The man of action is someone who tries to stabilize the inherently unstable qualities of matter by his imperious glance. Bergson adds this further sentence immediately after that concerning the man of action: "In short, the qualities of matter are so many stable views that we take of its instability"(302). When Deleuze states that "each movement will have its own qualitative duration"(*Cinema 1*, 1), he surely would include the glance as a "movement" and would argue that its "own qualitative duration," however distinctive it may be, is only part of an indivisible duration—of which the glance's momentary duration would be only a part or aspect.

46. For the assertion of one duration of the universe, see *Duration et simultanéité*, 56 (I have underlined the word "one"); for the hypothesis of one universal Time, see *ibid.*, 58.

47. For the claim about duration as "the Absolute," see *Creative Evolution*, 298: "Then the Absolute is revealed very near us and, in a certain measure, in us. It is of psychological and not of mathematical nor logical essence. It lives with us. Like us, but in certain aspects infinitely more concentrated and more gathered up in itself, it *endures*" (his italics).

48. *Creative Evolution*, 299 (my italics).

49. Even form, previously held sacrosanct by philosophers as the preserve of nonchange, is subject to change: "What is real is the continual change of form: form is only a snapshot view of a transition"(ibid., 302; partly in italics).

50. "[In *A Thousand Plateaus*] we tried to make the ritornello one of our main concepts, relating it to territory and the Earth, the little and the great ritornello" (interview with R. Bellour and F. Ewald in September 1988; incorporated in *Negotiations: 1972–1990*, trans. M. Joughin [New York: Columbia University Press, 1995], 137; cf. the translator's n. 1, *ibid.*, 200). For the original discussion, see Gilles Deleuze & Felix Guattari, *A Thousand Plateaus*, trans. B. Massumi (Minneapolis: University of Minnesota Press, 1987), 299–302, 310–350.

51. *Creative Evolution*, 308 (my italics).

52. Bergson writes: "As the shrapnel, bursting before it falls to the ground, covers the explosive zone with an indivisible danger, so the arrow which goes from A to B displays with a single stroke, although over a certain extent of duration, its indivisible mobility" (ibid., 309).

53. Ibid., 305.

54. Ibid., 306: "We take snapshots, as it were, of the passing reality, and, as these are characteristic of the reality, we have only to string them on a becoming, abstract, uniform and invisible, situated at the back of the apparatus of knowledge, in order to imitate what there is that is characteristic in this becoming itself."

55. Ibid., 306 (his italics).

56. William James, "Bergson and His Critique of Intellectualism," in *A Pluralistic Universe* (New York: Longmans, Green, 1909), 238 and 232 respectively. The previous statement reads in full: "Sensibly, motion comes in drops, waves, or pulses; either some actual amount of it, or none, being apprehended." Concerning the droplike nature of time, James adds: "The times directly *felt* in the experiences of living subjects have originally no common measure"(ibid., 232; his italics).

57. Bergson, *Creative Evolution*, 307.

Chapter 6. Olkowski / Flows of Desire and the Body-Becoming

1. Gilles Deleuze, *Nietzsche et la philosophie*, (Paris: Presses Universitaires de France, 1962); trans. Hugh Tomilinson, *Nietzsche and Philosophy* (New York: Columbia University Press, 1983). Henceforth cited as *Nietzsche*.

2. Gilles Deleuze, *Difference and Repetition*, trans. Paul Patton (New York: Columbia University Press, 1994); originally published in French as *Différence et répétition* (Paris: Presses Universitaires de France, 1968).

3. The early appearance of the term *regime* here is interesting, but it becomes significant in *Capitalism and Schizophrenia*, vol. 2, where "regimes of signs" are formulated as the organization of desiring and social-machines in various power arrangements. The word also retains its more conventional French meaning: a set of rules or laws, but also a rate of flow, or a rate of speed. Not only do different regimes have different laws or rules, but they occur at different speeds.

4. See Gilles Deleuze and Félix Guattari, trans. Robert Hurley, Mark Seem, and Helen R. Lane as *Anti-Oedipus: Capitalism and Schizophrenia* vol. 1 (Minneapolis: University of Minnesota Press, 1983). Originally published in French as *L'Anti-Oedipe: Capitalisme et schizophrenie*, (Paris: Les Éditions de Minuit, 1972); cited henceforth as *L'Anti-Oedipus*.

5. See Alice Jardine, *Gynesis: Configurations of Woman and Modernity* (Ithaca, N.Y.: Cornell University Press, 1984), 209. Cited henceforth as *Gynesis*.

6. Jacques Donzelot, "An Antisociology," trans. Mark Seem, Semiotext(e) 2, no. 2 (1977): 27–44. Originally published in French as "Une anti-sociologie," *Esprit* (December 1972): 835–855.

7. George Büchner, *Lenz*, trans. Michael Hamburger, (Chicago: University of Chicago Press, 1972), 44. Henceforth cited as *Lenz*.

8. Gilles Deleuze and Félix Guattari, *A Thousand Plateaus: Capitalism and Schizophrenia* (Minneapolis: University of Minnesota Press, 1987). Originally published as *Mille plateaux: Capitalisme et schizophrenie* (Paris: Éditions de Minuit, 1980). Henceforth cited as *Plateaus*.

9. See, for example, Karl Marx, *Grundrisse*, trans. Martin Nicolaus (New York: Vintage, 1973), 85—100, where Marx makes it clear that production is preceded by some kind of social organization, and identifies production with both distribution and consumption. Cited henceforth as *Grundrisse*.

10. Deleuze argues that it is Hume who substituted the external and changing relation A *and* B for the internal and essential relation A *is* B, thereby inaugurating the moving series "and, and, and," which makes way for the concept of open systems, unities, or wholes, as opposed to unities that transcend the parts. See *Empiricism and Subjectivity: An Essay on Hume's Theory of Human Nature*, trans. Constantin V. Boundas (New York: Columbia University Press, 1991). Originally published as *Empirisme et subjectivité: Essai sur la nature humaine selon Hume* (Paris: Presses Universitaires de France, 1953).

11. The notion of "partial objects" is borrowed from Melanie Klein's analysis of the infantile basis of schizophrenia. Klein writes: "In this very early phase . . . the ego's power of identifying itself with its objects is as yet small, partly because it is itself still uncoordinated and partly because the introjected objects are still mainly partial objects." See "A Contribution to the Psychogenesis of Manic-Depressive States" (1935), in *Love, Guilt and Reparation* (New York: Delacorte, 1975), 363. Presumably this is of use to Deleuze and Guattari because it allows them to talk about bodies or body connections in terms of flows as opposed to complete egos and complete objects, which are already totalized and structured in accordance with the Oedipal signifier.

12. In a crucial respect this reading differs from Brian Massumi's lucid and creative account in *A User's Guide to Capitalism and Schizophrenia: Deviations from Deleuze and Guattari* (Cambridge: MIT Press, 1992); that is, this reading emphasizes the creative aspects of desiring-production and the breakdown in desiring-production as opposed to the process of overcoding and capitalist becoming-consumer—even though capital is the point of view of their analysis of history.

13. Eugene Holland, "Schizoanalysis: The Postmodern Contextualization of Psychoanalysis," in *Marxism and the Interpretation of Culture*, ed. Cary Nelson and Lawrence Grossberg (Urbana: University of Illinois Press, 1988), 410. Henceforth cited as *Schizoanalysis*.

14. This is one of several critical respects in which Deleuze and Guattari differ from Wilhelm Reich, who, in *The Mass Psychology of Fascism,* trans. Vincent R. Carfagno (New York: Noonday, 1970), maintains that fascist governments make use of the Oedipal family structure when the head of state takes on the role of Oedipal father.

15. Gilles Deleuze, *Proust and Signs*, trans. Richard Howard (New York: Braziller, 1972), 120. Henceforth cited as *Proust.*

16. Barbara Kruger, *Remote Control: Powers, Cultures, and the World of Appearances* (Cambridge, Mass.: MIT Press, 1993), 5.

17. Such a reading has been suggested by Judith Butler in *Subjects of Desire: Hegelian Reflections in Twentieth-Century France* (New York: Columbia University Press, 1987) and Manfred Frank in "The World as Will and Representation: Deleuze and Guattari's Critique of Capitalism as Schizoanalysis and Schizo-Discourse," trans. David Berger, *Telos* 57 (Fall 1983): 166–76.

18. Gilles Deleuze, *The Logic of Sense,* Constantin V. Boundas, ed. (New York: Columbia University Press), 89–90. Originally published in French as *Logique du sens* (Paris: Éditions de Minuit, 1969), 110. Hereafter cited as *Logic.*

19. Alphonso Lingis beautifully articulates the socius of "savage" social production in his essay, "The Society of Dismembered Body-Parts"; and Jean-Clet Martin articulates that of the despotic social formation in "Cartography of the Year 1000"; both appear in *Gilles Deleuze and the Theatre of Philosophy*, ed. C. V. Boundas and D. Olkowski, (New York: Routledge, 1994).

20. Alphonso Lingis, *Abuses* (Berkeley: University of California Press, 1994), 11–12. Henceforth cited as *Abuses.*

21. See Maurice Dobb, *Studies in the Development of Capitalism* (London: Routledge and Keegan Paul, 1959), 177–186. Cited in *Anti-Oedipus*, 226 / 267–268.

22. Deleuze and Guattari here quote Marx, *Capital*, vol. III. (New York: International Publications, 1967), 827.

23. Katherine Q. Seelye for *The New York Times*, in the *Denver Post*, "Dole Throws Down the Gauntlet in Republican Response" (Wednesday, January 24, 1996), 12A.

24. The processes of repetition that produce (and are produced by) stable, habitual orders as well as the deepening of these processes through reflection are the subject of my

book *Gilles Deleuze and The Ruin of Representation* (Berkeley: University of California Press, 1999).

Chapter 7. Colebrook / A Grammar of Becoming

1. Friedrich Nietzsche, *On the Genealogy of Morals and Ecce Homo,* trans. Walter Kaufmann and R. J. Hollingdale, ed. Walter Kaufmann (New York: Vintage, 1967). Hereafter cited as *Genealogy.*

2. "Heidegger's reading of Nietzsche, in which will to power is read as the culmination of subjectivism, suggests the continual risk of Nietzsche's overman. As long as humanist reactivism is criticized by a force defined *as will,* then active becoming-human might be seen as still human all too human" (Martin Heidegger, *Nietzsche,* vol. 3: *The Will to Power as Knowledge and Metaphysics,* trans. Joan Stambaugh, David Farrell Krell, and Frank A. Capuzzi; ed. David Farrell Krell [San Francisco: Harper and Row, 1987], 3–4); hereafter cited as Heidegger, *Nietzsche.* This is perhaps why Deleuze and Guattari argue that there can be no becoming-man (*A Thousand Plateaus: Capitalism and Schizophrenia,* trans. Brian Massumi [Minneapolis: University of Minnesota Press, 1987], 291).

3. In Alexander Nehamas's terms, life is not represented by literature but is lived *as literary style* (*Nietzsche: Life as Literature* [Cambridge: Harvard University Press, 1985]).

4. Michel Foucault, *The Order of Things* (London: Tavistock, 1970), xxii. Hereafter cited as *Order.*

5. Heidegger traces the etymology of the Cartesian subject back to this function of an underlying ground. The Latin *subjectum* translates the Greek *hypokeimenon,* the "ground" of a statement or what is spoken about. With Descartes this grounding function of the statement, what is spoken about, coincides with the speaker and so becomes the modern "subject" (Martin Heidegger, *What Is a Thing?* trans. W. B. Barton, Jr., and Vera Deutsch (Lanham: University Press of America, 1967), 104–105).

6. Michel Foucault, *The History of Sexuality,* vol. 1: *An Introduction, trans.* Robert Hurley (Harmondsworth: Penguin, 1981), 144; hereafter cited as *History* 1. Foucault's criticism of the ground of life, which he associates with reactive subjectivism, might be contrasted with Deleuze's affirmation of life. This difference can be explained through Deleuze's description of differing ontologies. Deleuze refers favorably to the history of monism in his book on Foucault and contrasts this with Foucault's residual Kantian dualism. For Deleuze there is a single univocal field—of life—which it is the task of philosophy to affirm and think (Gilles Deleuze, *Spinoza: Practical Philosophy,* trans. Robert Hurley [San Francisco: City Lights, 1988], 26); hereafter cited as *Spinoza.* But Foucault's thought is also concerned with the "outside"—and this is what distinguishes him from monism and suggests a residual Kantianism. For Foucault, an exterior is produced by distribution, but the *outside* is the force of distribution itself (Gilles Deleuze, *Foucault,* trans. Sean Hand [Minneapolis: University of Minnesota Press, 1988], 86). Rather than affirm a single and self-differentiating field of life, Foucault critically separates the force of distribution from that which is distributed. This opens the way for thinking about the different strategies of Deleuze and Foucault: for Deleuze, what is called for is a way of writing adequate to life; for Foucault, we must recall the separation between any writing event and the silence of things.

7. Michel Foucault, *The History of Sexuality,* vol. 1, *The Use of Pleasure,* trans. Robert Hurley (Harmondsworth: Penguin, 1988), 7. Hereafter cited as *History* 2.

8. Michel Foucault, "What Is Enlightenment?" *The Foucault Reader,* ed. Paul Rabinow (Harmondsworth: Penguin, 1986), 32–50.

9. Marion Tapper, "Ressentiment and Power," in *Nietzsche, Feminism and Political Theory,* ed. Paul Patton (Sydney: Allen and Unwin, 1993).

10. Identifying these two movements— who speaks, and the space generated through speaking—are the first two moments in Foucault's archaeological method.

> First question: who is speaking? Who, among the totality of speaking individuals, is accorded the right to use this sort of language (*langage*)? . . .
> We must also describe the institutional *sites* from which the doctor makes his discourse, and from which this discourse derives its legitimate source and point of application (its specific objects and instruments of verification) (*Archaeology,* 51).

11. Michel Foucault, "Afterword: The Subject and Power," in *Michel Foucault: Beyond Structuralism and Hermeneutics,* ed. Hubert L. Dreyfus and Paul Rabinow (Sussex: Harvester, 1982), 208–226. 225–226. Hereafter cited as "Afterword."

12. "If philosophy is memory or a return of the origin, what I am doing cannot, in any way, be regarded as philosophy" (Foucault, *Archaeology,* 206).

13. Gilles Deleuze, *Difference and Repetition,* trans. Paul Patton (New York: Columbia University Press, 1994), 41, 136. Hereafter cited as *Difference.*

14. Gilles Deleuze and Félix Guattari, *A Thousand Plateaus: Capitalism and Schizophrenia,* trans. Brian Massumi (Minneapolis: University of Minnesota Press, 1987), 372. Hereafter cited as *Plateaus.*

15. Gilles Deleuze and Félix Guattari, *What Is Philosophy?* trans. Hugh Tomlinson and Graham Burchill (London: Verso, 1994), 47. Hereafter cited as *What Is Philosophy?*

16. Gilles Deleuze, *Empiricism and Subjectivity: An Essay on Hume's Theory of Human Nature,* trans. Constantin V. Boundas (New York: Columbia University Press, 1991), 31. Hereafter cited as *Empiricism.*

17. Gilles Deleuze and Félix Guattari. *Anti-Oedipus: Capitalism and Schizophrenia,* trans. Robert Hurley, Mark Seem, and Helen R. Lane (London: Athlone, 1984), 17. Hereafter cited as *Anti-Oedipus.*

18. James Joyce, *The Essential James Joyce,* intro. Harry Levin (London: Granada, 1977), 138.

19. Deleuze and Guattari's frequent invocation of Joyce and Virginia Woolf—both high modernist exponents of stream of consciousness in which language, rather than subjects, speaks—might be contrasted with Foucault's cited authors. Both Joyce and Woolf adopt a style that distributes sentences, effects, thought, perception, and quotation on a single plane. Consciousness is seen as a multiplicity of series and might therefore be seen as thought without a pre-given image or location, thus rendering the question of who speaks strictly unanswerable (*Plateaus,* 6, 252). Foucault's cited authors, in particular Blanchot, Robbe-Grillet, and Roussel, are, on the other hand, typical of an *intensification* of point of view, and the irreducibly constitutive character of the site of enunciation. By *retracing* language, these writers show that point of view is an *effect* of style and writing. By beginning from a writing subject, these texts show subjectivity as a textual effect. On Roussel, Foucault writes, "In order for all this machinery to become intelligible, it was not a code that was needed but a stepping back which opened the field of vision, removed these mute figures to a horizon, and presented them in space" (*Death and the Labyrinth: The Work of Raymond Roussel,* trans. Charles Ruas, intro. John Ashbery [London: Athlone, 1986], 65). On Blanchot:

> If the only site for language is indeed the solitary sovereignty of "I speak" then in principle nothing can limit it—not the one to whom it is addressed, not the truth of what it says, not the values or systems of representation it utilizes. In short, it is no longer dis-

course and the communication of meaning, but a spreading forth of language in its raw state, an unfolding of pure exteriority. ("Maurice Blanchot: The Thought from Outside," in *Foucault / Blanchot*, trans. Jeffrey Mehlman and Brian Massumi [New York: Zone, 1987], 11.)

20. Luce Irigaray, *Speculum of the Other Woman*, trans. Gillian C. Gill (Ithaca N.Y.: Cornell University Press, 1985).

21. In the Renaissance there is, Foucault argues, a sense of the continuity between the visible and articulable on "a single, unbroken surface" (39). *The Order of Things* is an archaeology of the disruption of this surface and the new questions of knowledge as proper observation (classical period) and then as located perspective (modernity). But *The Order of Things* also traces the visible as a different series with which language intersects. In this sense, thought is a sustained encounter with the revealing of the visible. At the same time language has its own "luminosity" and "shining"; it is not a mirror but a space in which the visible is reconfigured. But the luminosity of language is at the limit of thought: "We are so ill-equipped to conceive of the shining but crude being of language" (339). The relation between knowledge and the visible is a folding: knowledge is at once a revealing and a doubling of the visible, as well as being a series in its own right. Because speaking is *not* seeing, language is not representation. But the visible is not just a pure presence that precedes articulation; the visible is itself looped with the invisible.

22. "This also proves that it is vain to seek, beyond structural, formal, or interpretive analyses of language, a domain that is at last freed from all positivity, in which the freedom of the subject, the labour of the human being, or the opening up of a transcendental destiny could be fulfilled" (*Archaeology*, 112).

23. Consider the third paragraph of *History 1*, where the narrating voice is not Foucault's but the inflated tone of modern, enlightened sexual liberation:

> But twilight soon fell upon this bright day, followed by the monotonous nights of the Victorian bourgeoisie. Sexuality was carefully confined; it moved into the home. The conjugal family took custody of it and absorbed it into the serious function of reproduction. On the subject of sex, silence became the rule. (3)

24. Donald Davidson, *Inquiries into Truth and Interpretation* (Oxford: Clarendon, 1984), 184.

25. Richard Rorty, *Consequences of Pragmatism: Essays: 1972–1980* (Minneapolis: University of Minnesota Press, 1982), 103.

26. Richard Rorty, *Contingency, Irony, and Solidarity* (Cambridge: Cambridge University Press, 1989), 79.

Chapter 8. Kaufman / Klossowski or Thoughts-Becoming

1. Michel Foucault, "Theatrum Philosophicum," in *Language, Counter-Memory, Practice*, trans. Donald F. Bouchard and Sherry Simon (Ithaca, N.Y.: Cornell University Press, 1977), 196.

2. Pierre Klossowski, "Digressions à partir d'un portrait apocryphe," *L'Arc* 49 (1972): 11–14 (11). All translations are mine unless otherwise indicated.

3. Pierre Klossowski, *Les Lois de l'hospitalité* (*The Laws of Hospitality*) (Paris: Gallimard, 1965).

4. Pierre Klossowski, *Roberte Ce Soir* and *The Revocation of the Edict of Nantes*, trans. Austryn Wainhouse (New York: Marion Boyars, 1989), 148.

5. Klossowski, *Roberte Ce Soir*, 12–13.

6. Ibid., 53.

7. The depiction of women is of signal importance with regard to another of Klossowski's works, *La Monnaie vivante* (Paris: Eric Losfeld, 1970), photographs by Pierre Zucca. This book, which is part treatise on economics and part pseudopornographic photography, has encountered resistance not only due to its unorthodox treatment of economics but also due to the nature of the photographs, which depict Klossowski's wife, Denise Morin-Sinclaire, in a series of "tableaux vivants," or staged stills, often wearing elaborate costumes. A recent edition of *La Monnaie vivante*, is printed without the photographs (Paris: Joelle Losfeld, 1993).

8. Gayle Rubin, "The Traffic in Women: Notes Toward a Political Economy of Sex," in *Toward an Anthropology of Women*, ed. Rayna Reiter (New York: Monthly Review, 1975), 174. For a different formulation of the woman as a catalyst or enabler of male homosocial relations, see Eve Kosofsky Sedgwick, *Between Men: English Literature and Male Homosocial Desire* (New York: Columbia University Press, 1985), especially pp. 1–27.

9. Not surprisingly, very little explicitly feminist work has been done on Klossowski, with the exception of Anne-Marie Lugan-Dardigna's *Klossowski: L'homme aux simulacres* (Paris: Navarin, 1986).

10. Gayle S. Rubin, "Thinking Sex: Notes for a Radical Theory of the Politics of Sexuality" in *The Lesbian and Gay Studies Reader*, ed. Henry Abelove, Michèle Anna Barale, David M. Halperin (New York: Routledge, 1993), 13–14. For an interview with Rubin in which she compares the two essays, see Gayle Rubin with Judith Butler, "Sexual Traffic," *Differences* 6 (Summer–Fall 1994), 62–99.

11. Since about 1970, Klossowski has devoted himself exclusively to painting; he continues to paint to this day in his Paris studio. There have been numerous exhibitions of his work. For a complete listing, see the bibliography in Alain Arnaud, *Pierre Klossowski* (Paris: Seuil, 1990), 209. Klossowski comes from a notably literary and artistic family. His younger brother Balthazar is the celebrated artist Balthus. For an brief overview of Balthus's life and work, see Ted Morgan, "Balthus," *Observer Magazine* (January 30, 1994): 36–41. As a young man, Klossowski was well acquainted with Ranier Maria Rilke and served for a time as André Gide's secretary.

12. Lynn Hunt, "Pornography and the French Revolution," in *The Invention of Pornography: Obscentiy and the Origins of Modernity, 1500–1800* (New York: Zone, 1993), 301–307. Hunt notes that "in the early years of the Revolution, politically motivated pornography accounted for about half of the obscene literature produced, and it portrayed aristocrats as impotent, riddled with venereal disease, and given over to debauchery. . . . The central figure in such attacks was Queen Marie Antoinette herself" (307).

13. Ibid., 330.

14. Kathryn Norberg, "The Libertine Whore: Prostitution in French Pornography from Margot to Juliette," ibid., 227.

15. Klossowski, *The Revocation of the Edict of Nantes*, 125–126.

16. Ibid., 133–134.

17. Jane Gallop, *Intersections: A Reading of Sade with Bataille, Blanchot, and Klossowski* (Lincoln: University of Nebraska Press, 1981), 105–106.

18. For an essay that explicitly takes up convalescence in Klossowski, see Ann Smock, "Far from the Old Folks at Home: Klossowski's *Les Lois de l'hospitalité*," in *Double Dealing* (Lincoln: University of Nebraska Press, 1985). Smock briefly considers the question of "revocation" (75–76), and her footnotes give considerable attention to Deleuze's writings on Klossowski (see especially notes 4–9, pp. 131–134). I have treated sickness in Klossowski's reading of Nietzsche and its relation to mind-body dualism in "Towards a Feminist Philosophy of Mind," in *Deleuze and Feminist Theory*, ed. Ian Buchanan and Claire Colebrook (Edinburgh: Edinburgh University Press, 1998).

19. Klossowski, *Nietzsche and the Vicious Circle*, trans. Daniel W. Smith (Chicago: University of Chicago Press and London: Athlone, 1997), 16.

20. See Daniel W. Smith, "Translator's Preface," in *Nietzsche and the Vicious Circle*, ix.

21. It is interesting to consider another analysis where pain is integrally related to mental states: Elaine Scarry's account of pain and its relation to imagining in *The Body in Pain: The Making and Unmaking of the World* (New York: Oxford University Press, 1985). Scarry focuses primarily on pain resulting from war or torture, which arguably has a very different attendant psychic structure than pain induced by sickness. Nonetheless, what I find striking about Scarry's account is the way pain and imagining operate according to the same logic, albeit in a somewhat different fashion. She writes, for example, that "pain and imagining are the 'framing events' within whose boundaries all other perceptual, somatic, and emotional events occur; thus, between the two extremes can be mapped the whole terrain of the human psyche" (165). Here, the relation of pain and imagining might be compared to the body-soul relation in Klossowski.

22. Quoted in Klossowski, *Nietzsche and the Vicious Circle*, 20.

23. Ibid., 23.

24. Ibid., 24–25.

25. Ibid., 30.

26. For more on Deleuze's concept of becoming, see especially Gilles Deleuze and Félix Guattari, *Anti-Oedipus: Capitalism and Schizophrenia*, trans. Robert Hurley, Mark Seem, and Helen R. Lane (Minneapolis: University of Minnesota Press, 1983).

27. Gilles Deleuze, *Nietzsche and Philosophy*, trans. Hugh Tomlinson (New York: Columbia University Press, 1983). Although there is considerable overlap at the level of the actual argument, especially if Deleuze's "forces" are replaced by a more Klossowskian system of pulsional energetics, the two studies of Nietzsche are based in very different contexts. Whereas Klossowski devotes much of his study to an analysis of Nietzsche's personal letters (albeit in such an impersonal fashion that it does not even approximate the domain of biography), Deleuze's study has a much more philosophical grounding, insofar as Nietzsche is discussed through the lens of Kant and, to a lesser degree, Hegel. For a detailed analysis of Deleuze's relation to his philosophical predecessors, see Michael Hardt, *Gilles Deleuze: An Apprenticeship in Philosophy* (Minneapolis: University of Minnesota Press, 1993), 26–55.

28. Klossowski, *Nietzsche and the Vicious Circle*, 49–50.

29. Deleuze, *Nietzsche and Philosophy*, 66. trans. Hugh Tomlinson Minneapolis: U of Minnesota Press, 1983

30. Gilles Deleuze, "Klossowski or Bodies-Language" in *The Logic of Sense*, trans. Mark Lester (New York: Columbia University Press, 1990), 291.

31. It is interesting to compare the term *revocation* with Klossowski's use of *vocation* in his early novel *La vocation suspendue* (Paris: Gallimard, 1950), which describes a man who falls away from his calling as a priest (an event that parallels Klossowski's own life). In my reading, "revocation" and "suspended vocation" are virtually identical and include both hailing and revoking.

32. Deleuze, "Klossowski or Bodies-Language," 289.

33. In his discussion of the disjunctive synthesis, Deleuze writes that "a disjunction that remains disjunctive and that still affirms the disjointed terms, that affirms them throughout their entire distance, *without restricting one by the other or excluding the other from the one*, is perhaps the greatest paradox," Deleuze and Guattari, *Anti-Oedipus: Capitalism and Schizophrenia*, 76.

Chapter 9. Weiss / The Durée of the Techno-Body

1. Interestingly, when I went back to confirm this reference in our library archives, I found that this sensationalist heading did not appear in the local edition of the *New York Times*; it appeared only in the out-of-town edition.

2. The issues raised by animal cloning did not die down in the year that elapsed after "Dolly" was born. On January 21, 1998, the *New York Times* reported that American scientists had successfully cloned two calves from fetal cells using a more efficient procedure than the one Scottish scientists had used to produce Dolly. Not only was the cloning procedure itself different (showing that successful cloning can occur through more than one method), but the American scientists also inserted a "dummy" gene into the twin calves' makeup which will pave the way for further genetic manipulation of the dairy livestock population in the future. This "accomplishment," aptly termed "pharming," holds out the promise of producing cows who can be neural cell donors for human beings suffering from hemophilia, Parkinson's disease, and diabetes. Some scientists are also working with pharmaceutical companies to generate proposals for genetically engineered cattle that will produce human serum albumin, a protein currently given to people who have suffered severe blood loss. See Gina Kolata, "Scientist Reports First Cloning Ever of Adult Mammal," *New York Times* (February 23, 1997): A1, A22; Carey Goldberg and Gina Kolata, "Scientists Announce Births of Cows Cloned in New Way," *New York Times* (January 21, 1998): A14.

The article of January 21, 1998, discussing the successful cloning of the twin calves, "George" and "Charlie," in contrast to the article of February 23, 1997, announcing the birth of "Dolly" the sheep, did not even merit the front page (with the exception, in the out-of-town paper, of a color photo of the two calves huddled together with a subtitle that informed the reader where the story was to be found). This reveals the extent to which the media (and perhaps the public) no longer view animal cloning as a very worrisome issue. Nonetheless, concerns about human cloning remain, and these concerns were amplified a few weeks before the birth of "George" and "Charlie" by one midwestern doctor's announcement to the media that he was planning to open a "cloning clinic" for infertile couples (his name is Richard Seed). Now the issue seems to involve determining which governmental agency, if any, has the authority to regulate and prohibit the use of cloning technology on a human population. The fact that the issue has changed in one year from horrified denials that humans could ever be next to whether the U.S. Food and Drug Administration has the authority to prohibit their being next makes it seem quite plausible that the move to prohibit human cloning will itself be transformed, in time, to the development of policies designed to regulate how, where, when, and to or for whom it will happen.

Indeed, it is striking that the *New York Times* article (published less than a year after the "miracle" of "Dolly's" birth) announcing the birth of "George" and "Charlie" doesn't even focus on the ethical ramifications of the procedures—cloning and genetic alteration—undertaken to produce them. Instead, the article emphasizes the possibilities for improving human health through genetic alteration of future herds of cattle and seems to assume that such genetic manipulation of the livestock population is ethically permissible. Indeed, in this last year several cows pregnant with similar offspring have given birth all over the country.

3. See Gina Kolata, "Scientist Reports First Cloning Ever of Adult Mammal," *New York Times* (February 23, 1997): 22.

4. Rosi Braidotti, *Nomadic Subjects: Embodiment and Sexual Difference in Contemporary Feminist Theory* (New York: Columbia University Press, 1994), 55. Hereafter cited as *Nomadic Subjects*.

5. See Rosi Braidotti, "Signs of Wonder and Traces of Doubt: On Teratology and Embodied Differences," in *Between Monsters, Goddesses, and Cyborgs: Feminist Confrontations with Science, Medicine, and Cyberspace*. ed. Nina Lykke and Rosi Braidotti (London: Zed, 1996), 135–152. Hereafter cited as *Between Monsters*.)

6. See Mary Douglas, *Purity and Danger: An Analysis of the Concepts of Pollution and Taboo* (New York: Routledge, Chapman, and Hall, 1992); and Julia Kristeva, *Powers of Horror: An Essay on Abjection*, trans. Leon S. Roudiez (New York: Columbia University Press, 1982). Both Douglas and Kristeva provide detailed descriptions of the culturally nuanced ways in which human beings designate certain bodily zones and fluids as abject. In doing so, they argue, we psychically detach these zones and fluids from our own corporeal experience only to reincarnate them in others' bodies, thereby upholding our own "purity" in contrast to these "disgusting" others. Braidotti's invocation of the "monster within," who is projected onto the other as the "true" monster, is part and parcel of this process.

7. Henri Bergson, *An Introduction to Metaphysics*, trans. T. E. Hulme (New York: Macmillan, 1903, 1955). Hereafter cited as *Metaphysics*. Bergson also discusses this distinction extensively elsewhere in his works. What is striking about *An Introduction to Metaphysics*, in particular, is Bergson's claim that essentially different philosophical methodologies (i.e., analytical versus intuitive approaches) are necessary to study time and temporality respectively. While I am not completely in agreement with him on this issue, insofar as I do not view time and temporality to be as separable as he does, I do find his insight that different phenomena have their own forms of temporalization and therefore require different methodological approaches to be helpful and illuminating with regard to new (and as yet unimagined) biotechnologies.

8. How contemporary biotechnologies alter our sense of time, in both its "inner" and its "outer" dimensions, is an issue that does need to be taken up, but this project is not only beyond the scope of the present study but also beyond the scope of traditional philosophical inquiry. This means, not that the issue cannot be interrogated, but that to do so requires multiple interdisciplinary approaches and an enormous amount of experimental data not usually made use of by philosophers. It is crucial that philosophers make themselves better acquainted with such data however, if they are to speculate, as Braidotti does, on how our new biotechnologies will alter our experience of time.

9. Donna Haraway, "A Cyborg Manifesto: Science, Technology, and Socialist-Feminism in the Late Twentieth Century," *Simians, Cyborgs, and Women: The Reinvention of Nature* (New York: Routledge, 1991), 149–181. Hereafter cited as *Reinvention*.

10. Although whether there is any matter that is truly devoid of organic properties is itself a debatable question for some contemporary scientists.

11. Paul Ricoeur, "Word, Polysemy, Metaphor: Creativity in Language," in *A Ricoeur Reader: Reflection and Imagination*, ed. Mario J. Valdés (Toronto: University of Toronto Press, 1991), 65–85. Hereafter cited as *Ricoeur*.

12. Nina Lykke, "Between Monsters, Goddesses and Cyborgs: Feminist Confrontations with Science," in *Between Monsters, Goddesses and Cyborgs*, 13–29.

13. Patricia Bayer Richard, "The Tailor-Made Child: Implications for Women and the State," in *Expecting Trouble: Surrogacy, Fetal Abuse, and New Reproductive Technologies*, ed. Patricia Bolling (Boulder, Colo.: Westview, 1995), 9–24.

14. Anne Balsamo, *Technologies of the Gendered Body: Reading Cyborg Women* (Durham, N.C.: Duke University Press, 1996), 130–131. Hereafter cited as *Technologies*.

15. Lykke, "Between Monsters, Goddesses and Cyborgs," 27.

16. Simone de Beauvoir, *The Second Sex*, trans. by H. M. Parshley (1949; New York: Vintage, 1989).

17. Gilles Deleuze, *Bergsonism*, trans. Hugh Tomlinson and Barbara Habberjam (1966; New York: Zone, 1988), 80.

Chapter 10. Cheah / Spectral Nationality

1. For philosophical arguments about how the nation-people and the ideal state embody the transcendence of human finitude, see respectively, Johann Gottlieb Fichte, *Addresses to the German Nation*, trans. R. F. Jones and G. H. Turnbull, ed. George Armstrong Kelly (New York: Harper and Row, 1968); and G. W. F. Hegel, *Philosophy of Right*, trans. T. M. Knox (Oxford: Oxford University Press, 1967), §§ 325–328. Ernst H. Kantorowicz makes a similar historical argument about the ontotheological character of the European state by linking both patriotism and the absolutist idea of the mysteries of the state to the *corpus mysticum* in medieval theology. See his *"Pro Patria Mori* in Medieval Political Thought," *Selected Studies* (New York: Augustin, 1965), 320–321: "Once the *corpus mysticum* has been identified with the *corpus morale et politicum* of the people and has become synonymous with nation and 'fatherland,' death *pro patria*, that is for a mystical body corporate, regains its former nobility. Death for the fatherland now is viewed in a truly religious perspective; it appears as a sacrifice for the *corpus mysticum* of the state which is no less a reality than the *corpus mysticum* of the church. . . . [T]he quasi-religious aspects of death for the fatherland clearly derived from the Christian faith, the forces of which now were activated in the service of the secular *corpus mysticum* of the state." See also "Mysteries of the State: An Absolutist Concept and Its Late Mediaeval Origins," ibid., 381–398.

2. Frantz Fanon, *The Wretched of the Earth*, trans. Constance Farrington (New York: Grove Weidenfeld, 1963), 131–132. Hereafter cited as *Wretched*.

3. The religious tone is unmistakable: "In undertaking this onward march, the people legislates, finds itself, and wills itself to sovereignty. In every corner that is thus awakened from colonial slumber, life is lived at an impossibly high temperature. There is a permanent outpouring in all the villages of spectacular generosity, of disarming kindness, and willingness . . . to die for the 'cause.' All this is evocative of a confraternity, a church, and a mystical body of belief at one and the same time. No native can remain unmoved by this new rhythm which leads the nation on." (*Wretched*, 132.)

4. "In the colonial situation, culture, which is doubly deprived of the support of the nation and of the state, falls away and dies. The condition for its existence is therefore national liberation and the renaissance of the state." (*Wretched*, 132.) Note that there are three terms; *culture, nation,* and *state.* The nation is consciousness, culture is the expression of that consciousness in the form of spirit, and the state is its institutional embodiment.

5. Cf. "This party has sadly disintegrated; nothing is left but the shell of a party, a name, the emblem, and the motto. The living party, which ought to make possible the free exchange of ideas which have been elaborated according to the real needs of the mass of the people, has been transformed into a trade union of individual interests. . . . [T]he party has made itself into a screen between the masses and the leaders." (*Wretched*, 169–170.)

6. A more careful reading of the figures of the automaton, the marionette, and the turnspit that Kant uses in his discussion of the mechanism of nature as opposed to the spontaneity of pure practical reason in the Analytic of the Second Critique would be productive. See Immanuel Kant, *Critique of Practical Reason*, trans. Lewis White Beck (New York: Macmillan, 1989), 97–105, Ak. 94–102.

7. See Immanuel Kant, *Critique of Judgment*, trans. Werner Pluhar (Indianapolis:

Hackett, 1987) 65, 253–254, Ak. 374–375. Kant also describes constitutional monarchy as "an animate body" and absolutist monarchy as a "mere machine" (*Critique of Judgment*, 227, Ak. 352). See Fichte, *Addresses to the German Nation*, 120.

8. G. W. F. Hegel, *Lectures on the Philosophy of World History. Introduction: Reason in History*, trans. H. B. Nisbet (Cambridge: Cambridge University Press, 1980), 48.

9. Edward Said, *Culture and Imperialism* (London: Chatto and Windus, 1993), 277.

10. Partha Chatterjee, *Nationalist Thought and the Colonial World—A Derivative Discourse?* (London: Zed, 1986). Hereafter cited as *Nationalist*.

11. See Partha Chatterjee, *The Nation and Its Fragments—Colonial and Postcolonial Histories* (Princeton, N.J.: Princeton University Press, 1993), 235–236: "What Marx did not see too well was the ability of capitalist society to ideologically reunite capital and labor at the level of the political community of the nation, borrowing from another narrative the rhetoric of love, duty, welfare, and the like. . . . It is not so much the state / civil society opposition but rather the capital / community opposition that seems to me to be the great unsurpassed contradiction in Western social philosophy. Both state and civil society institutions have assigned places within the narrative of capital."

12. Benedict Anderson, *Imagined Communities—Reflections on the Origin and Spread of Nationalism*, rev. ed. (London: Verso, 1991), 86. Hereafter cited as *Imagined*.

13. See, for instance, Marnia Lazreg, *The Eloquence of Silence—Algerian Women in Question* (New York: Routledge, 1994); Marie-Aimée Hélie-Lucas, "Women, Nationalism, and Religion in the Algerian Liberation Struggle," *Opening the Gates—A Century of Arab Feminist Writing*, ed. Margot Badran and Miriam Cooke (Bloomington: Indiana University Press, 1990), 104–114; Cherifa Bouatta, "Feminine Militancy: *Moujahidates* during and after the Algerian War," and Doria Cherifati-Merabtine, "Algeria at a Crossroads: National Liberation, Islamization, and Women," both in *Gender and National Identity: Women and Politics in Muslim Societies*, ed. Valentine Moghadam (London: Zed, 1994), 18–39 and 40–62 respectively.

14. I have argued this at length in "Given Culture: Rethinking Cosmopolitical Freedom in Transnationalism," *Boundary 2*, 24, 2 (Summer 1997): 157–197; and in "The Cosmopolitical—Today," in *Cosmopolitics—Thinking and Feeling Beyond the Nation*, ed. Pheng Cheah and Bruce Robbins (Minneapolis: University of Minnesota Press, 1998), 20–41.

15. Jacques Derrida, *Aporias: Dying—Awaiting (One Another at) "the Limits of Truth,"* trans. Thomas Dutoit (Palo Alto, Calif.: Stanford University Press, 1993), 3. Hereafter cited as *Aporias*.

16. Jacques Derrida, *Specters of Marx: The State of the Debt, the Work of Mourning, and the New International*, trans. Peggy Kamuf (New York: Routledge, 1994), 125–126. Hereafter cited as *Specters*.

17. For a fuller elaboration of living on, see Derrida's essay, "Living On / Border Lines," trans. James Hulbert, in *Deconstruction and Criticism*, ed. Geoffrey Hartman (New York: Continuum, 1979), 75–176. This essay, which was written fifteen years before *Specters of Marx* but which clearly anticipates the direction of the later book, is ostensibly a reading of Blanchot but also Shelley's *The Triumph of Life,* and it links living on to the condition of possibility of narrative.

18. Our death is always possible, but it is a possibility that is impossible for us because we can never experience it. By the time we can "experience" "our" death, it will be too late. Derrida's extended argument is that as the possibility of the impossible, the experience of radical finitude is the radical contamination of the proper (including what is proper to man): "If death, the most proper possibility of *Dasein*, is the possibility of its impossibility, death becomes the most improper possibility and the most ex-propriating, the most

inauthenticating one. From the most originary inside of its possibility, the proper of *Dasein* becomes from then on contaminated, parasited, and divided by the most improper" (*Aporias*, 77).

19. In a footnote, Derrida stresses that he is not opposing a philosophy of death to a philosophy of life: "We are attempting something else. To try to accede to the possibility of this very alternative (life and / or death), we are directing our attention to the effects or the petitions of a survival or of a return of the dead (neither life nor death) on the sole basis of which one is able to speak of 'living subjectivity' (in opposition to its death)." (*Specters*, 187, n. 7.)

20. For Derrida's formulation of why the constitution of the publicness of the public sphere by technomediation requires a hauntology that is prior to and makes possible ontology and any discourse on life and death, see *Specters*, 50–51. Cf. Derrida, "Call It a Day for Democracy," in *The Other Heading—Reflections on Today's Europe*, trans. Pascale-Anne Brault and Michael B. Naas (Bloomington: Indiana University Press, 1992), 94–95, where he suggests that the spectrality of the public sphere requires categories of analysis that take us beyond the basic alternative of manipulation and unorganized spontaneity. My argument has been that even sophisticated theories of nationalism, which take into account the complexity of organization, still rely on an ontology of life.

21. Derrida's understanding of globalization through the figure of transnational migrancy becomes even clearer in the list of ten injunctions in *The Other Heading*, 77–79. Cf. Gayatri Chakravorty Spivak, "Limits and Openings of Marx in Derrida," in *Outside in the Teaching Machine* (New York: Routledge, 1993), 111–115.

22. The analytical distinction Amin makes is between Marx's theory of the capitalist mode of production on a world scale (presupposing a truly generalized world market that integrates commodities, capital, and labor and results in global homogenization) and capitalism as an existing world system (leaving labor unintegrated and leading to polarization). Samir Amin, *Re-Reading the Postwar Period: An Intellectual Itinerary*, trans. Michael Wolfers (New York: Monthly Review, 1994), 74. Hereafter cited as *Re-Reading*.

23. See, for instance, Howard Stein (ed.), *Asian Industrialization and Africa: Studies in Policy Alternatives to Structural Adjustment* (New York: St. Martin's, 1995).

24. "Dr. M: We Don't Need 'Hot Money,'" *The Star*, (Kunla Lumpar, Malaysia: Sunday, June 14, 1998). Emphasis added.

25. Martin Khor, "IMF 'Cure' Pushes Indonesia to Crisis," *The Star* (Kuala Lumpur, Malaysia: Monday, May 11, 1998).

BIOGRAPHICAL NOTES

Linda Martín Alcoff is an associate professor of philosophy, political science, and women's studies at Syracuse University. She is the author of *Real Knowing: New Versions of the Coherence Theory* (Ithaca, N.Y.: Cornell University Press, 1996), has coedited *Feminist Epistemologies* (New York: Routledge, 1993), and edited *Epistemology: The Big Questions* (London: Blackwell, forthcoming).

Edward S. Casey, professor of philosophy at SUNY, Stony Brook, is also department chair there. He is the author of a number of books, among them *Imagining and Remembering* and, most recently, *Getting Back into Place* (Bloomington: Indiana University Press, 1993) and *The Fate of Place* (Berkeley: University of California Press, 1997). His new book, *Representing Landscape*, is forthcoming.

Pheng Cheah received his Ph.D. from Cornell University and is currently associate professor of English at Northwestern University. He is coeditor of *Thinking Through the Body of the Law* (New York: New York University Press, 1996), and (with Bruce Robbins) *Cosmopolitics: Thinking and Feeling Beyond the Nation* (Minneapolis: University of Minnesota Press, 1998), and author of articles on legal philosophy, neocolonial globalization, feminist theory, and contemporary critical theory. He is also a lawyer.

Claire Colebrook teaches at the Centre for Comparative Literature and Cultural Studies at Monash University in Melbourne. She has published articles on William Blake, feminist ethics, Heidegger, Foucault, Derrida, Irigaray, and philosophy and literature. Her book *New Literary Histories* (Manchester: University of Manchester Press, 1997) examines the relationship between poststructuralism and new historicism. *Representation and Ethics* (Edinburgh: University of Edinburgh Press, 1998) concerns the relationship between political representation and representation in language. She is currently completing a third book on irony.

Manuel De Landa is the author of two books on philosophy, *War in the Age of Intelligent Machines* (1991) and *A Thousand Years of Nonlinear History* (1997), and of many philosophical essays published in various journals. He teaches a seminar at Columbia University on "Theories of Self-Organization and Urban History" and lectures around the world on the philosophy of science and technology.

Elizabeth Grosz is professor of comparative literature at SUNY Buffalo. She is the author of *Space, Time and Perversion* (New York: Routledge, 1995), and *Jacques Lacan: A Feminist Introduction* (London: Routledge, 1990) and has edited and coedited many anthologies on feminist theory.

Eleanor Kaufman is a fellow of the Society for the Humanities at Cornell University. She is coeditor, with Kevin Jon Heller, of *Deleuze and Guattari: New Mappings in Politics, Philosophy, and Culture* (Minneapolis: University of Minnesota Press, 1998).

Alphonso Lingis is a professor of philosophy at Pennsylvannia State University. His many publications include *Excesses: Eros and Culture* (New York: SUNY Press, 1984), *Deathbound Subjectivity* (New York: SUNY Press, 1989), *The Community of Those Who Have Nothing in Common* (Bloomington, Indiana Univeristy Press, 1994), and *Foreign Bodies* (New York: Routledge, 1994).

Dorothea Olkowski is professor of philosophy at the University of Colorado, Colorado Springs, and founder and former director of the program in Women's Studies there. She is the author of *Gilles Deleuze and the Ruin of Representation* (Berkeley: University of California Press, 1999) and the editor of *Feminist Enactments of French Philosophy* (Ithaca, N.Y.: Cornell University Press, forthcoming).

John Rajchman teaches philosophy in New York and Paris. His most recent book is *Constructions* (Cambridge, Mass.: MIT Press, 1998), and he is the author of *Deleuze* (Cambridge, Eng.: Cambridge University Press, forthcoming) and *Brain-City* (Cambridge, Mass.: MIT Press, forthcoming).

Gail Weiss is an associate professor of philosophy in the graduate program in the human sciences at the George Washington University. She is the author of *Body-Images: Embodiment as Intercororeality* (New York: Routledge, 1998) and the coeditor of *Perspectives on Embodiment: The Intersections of Nature and Culture* (New York: Routledge, 1999).

INDEX